Effective Leadership, Management and Supervision in Health and Social Care

Post-Qualifying Social Work Practice – titles in the series

To order, please contact our distributor: BEBC Distribution, Albion Close, Parkstone, Poole BH12 3LL. Telephone: 0845 230 9000, email: **learningmatters@bebc.co.uk**.

You can also find more information on each of these titles and our other learning resources at **www.learningmatters.co.uk**.

Effective Leadership, Management and Supervision in Health and Social Care

IVAN GRAY

RICHARD FIELD

KEITH BROWN

Series Editor: Keith Brown

LearningMatters

First published in 2010 by Learning Matters Ltd

British Library Cataloguing in Publication Data
A CIP record for this book is available from the British Library

ISBN: 978 1 84445 181 4

Cover and text design by Code 5 Design Associates Ltd
Project management by Swales & Willis Ltd, Exeter, Devon
Typeset by Swales & Willis Ltd, Exeter, Devon
Printed and bound by TJ International Ltd, Padstow, Cornwall

Learning Matters Ltd
33 Southernhay East
Exeter EX1 1NX
Tel: 01392 215560
info@learningmatters.co.uk
www.learningmatters.co.uk

FSC
Mixed Sources
Product group from well-managed
forests and other controlled sources
Cert no. SGS-COC-2482
www.fsc.org
© 1996 Forest Stewardship Council

Contents

About the authors

Dr Ivan Gray holds academic and professional qualifications in social work and management. He has specialised in management development for the past 16 years and he has also lectured in social work. He is programme leader for the BA and MA in Leadership and Management at Bournemouth University.

Richard Field is Senior Fellow, Leadership and Organisation Development, at the Office for Public Management (OPM). Prior to joining the OPM Richard was director of a learning consultancy specialising in management and leadership development in the public and voluntary sectors. Previous experience includes working as a local authority accountant and as a university programme manager.

Keith Brown holds academic and professional qualifications in social work, nursing, teaching and management. He has worked in the education and training field for over 20 years, in both universities and local authorities, and is currently Director of the Centre for Post-Qualifying Social Work at Bournemouth University.

Foreword

This new text has been written by the three of us as a direct result of our desire to put in to print our thoughts, aspirations and desires to support and facilitate high quality leadership, management and supervision in Health and Social Care.

It is our view that much of the current material supporting leadership, management and supervision is not specific enough to deal with the unique challenges of operating in the Health and Social Care field. This is the reason why we wanted to write this text to help and support all those professionals who aspire to or intend to lead, manage and supervise staff within the Health and Social Care sector.

Of particular note is that one of the key recommendations of the recently published report – *Building a Safe, Confident Future: The Final Report of the Social Work Task Force* – is that the new Supervision Standards for employers should be supported by clear national requirements for the supervision of social workers and that there is the creation of dedicated programmes of training and support for frontline social work managers.

This new text explores both the issues of supervision and also effective leadership and management and is written to support the attainment of these and other management standards as identified by the General Social Care Council, Skills for Care, and the Children's Workforce Development Council.

It is our sincere desire that the text meets these needs and helps to promote and support the most effective leadership, management and supervision of our vital Health and Social Care Services.

Keith Brown
Director of the Centre for Post-Qualifying Social Work

Acknowledgements

Grateful thanks to Dr Steven Keen for his support, encouragement and advice. His guidance means that this book can be used as the companion to the recently published *Newly Qualified Social Workers: A Handbook for Practice* (Keen *et al*., 2009, Learning Matters), and will help develop in team and unit leaders the perspectives and practices that will provide newly qualified social workers with a more supported experience in their first post. Thanks also to Angela Warren for her advice and guidance on involving people who use services in service developments.

Introduction

Ivan Gray, Richard Field and Keith Brown

This book seeks to offer you a practical introduction to effective leadership, management and supervision in health and social care. It is designed for team and unit leaders, and senior practitioners, and attempts to capture as concisely as possible the key dimensions, issues, models and skills needed to lead and manage a team. It will be of interest to those on post-qualifying courses as part of the Leadership and Management pathway or those on other post-qualifying pathways. It may also be used to support in-house induction and introductory programmes for managers.

We have taken a very particular approach that has a number of dimensions:

- We have placed supervision at the heart of this book and at the heart of effective leadership and management in health and social care. We see it as a core management function in health and social care and a fundamental leadership activity.

- We have taken a project approach, that is, we have identified the key areas of activity you need to manage to lead a team efficiently and effectively and focused on each of these.

- We have adopted a problem-solving approach that encourages you to critically analyse performance and plan for improvement.

- We have provided reflection points for each key activity area and developed audit tools to help you make judgements about your leadership and current team performance and to plan improvements.

- We believe that our health and social care value base means that leaders must be participative, so engaging your team in the management of services is a common theme throughout.

- At the start of each chapter we have identified the National Occupational Standards for Management and Leadership and the Principles of Social Care Management that the chapter will help you address. These are essential benchmarks for your practice and the General Social Care Council's (GSCC) Post-Qualifying Leadership and Management pathway.

- Chapter 10 offers you further guidance on benchmarking, the GSCC requirements and developing your leadership and management practice. It also introduces the Leadership Qualities Framework, which is the basis for enhancing leadership skills and behaviours across the NHS.

The diagram below summarises the activity areas we will address in the following chapters. Supervision is at centre of all of them as the key integrating activity, in particular

Key activity areas in leadership and management

Chapters 4, 5 and 6. Chapter 4 looks at the role and importance of supervision. Chapters 5 and 6 are based on the Skills for Care (SfC) and Children's Workforce Development Council's (CWDC) Effective Supervision Unit.

Given the very practical focus of these chapters we have also provided a final chapter that offers an overview of some further key theoretical perspectives underpinning the management of people in health and social care that you may come across and invite you to reflect on their implications for your practice. We hope that this book will help you and your team in supervision and while working as a team to solve problems and improve services.

Chapter 1

A problem-solving approach

Ivan Gray

CHAPTER OBJECTIVES

This chapter will help you address the following National Occupational Standards for Management and Leadership.

- F6 Monitor and solve customer service problems.

This chapter will also help you address the following Principles of Social Care Management.

- Promote and meet service aims, objectives and goals.

- Provide an environment and time in which to develop reflective practice, professional skills and the ability to make judgements in complex situations.

Introduction

Charles Handy (Handy, 1985) has described managers as being organisational GPs. They diagnose and then develop treatment plans that treat organisational disorders. So rather than itemising a manager's roles and responsibilities, it is possible to characterise managers as primarily problem solvers. They investigate problems with service quality and formulate and implement solutions. Some writers, however, have suggested that a lot of management is actually about performing routine tasks – in which case classifying managers as problem solvers is aspirational. Nevertheless, the problem-solving process can lead to effective and efficient service delivery, as outlined in Figure 1.1.

This cycle of activities could be described as the heart of management – a logical and rational approach that brings order and control to any process. So, for instance, it is the heart of scientific management. Taylor, a classical management theorist, analysed work processes, setting objectives and developing plans that would maximise output and ensure the best use of resources (Taylor, 1911).

The problem-solving process appears in many guises and can be applied to the management of any task. It is sometimes called the decision-making process or the planning process – in fact, there are many variants. In social care it might be re-badged as the case

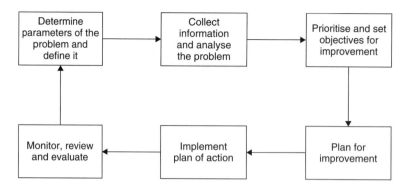

Figure 1.1 The problem-solving process

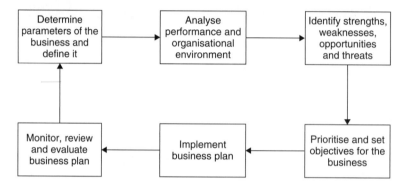

Figure 1.2 The business planning process

planning or assessment process, while in other professions it appears as the teaching or the nursing process. In management, it is applied to just about any activity area. For instance, slightly re-framed it becomes 'the business planning process' (Figure 1.2).

The process can also be used more proactively. For instance, it can become the basis for project management (Figure 1.3). Rather than identifying a problem with the delivery of an existing service, it can be used to project manage a new service development.

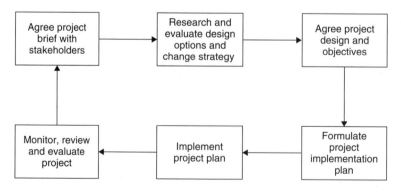

Figure 1.3 The project management process

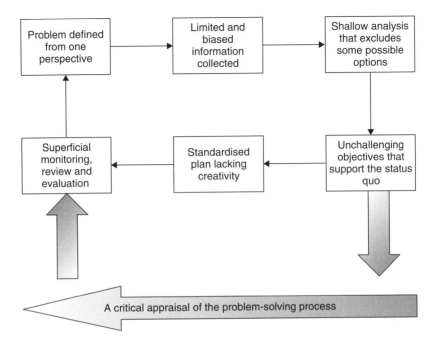

Figure 1.4 A double feedback loop

Argyris and Schon (1978) suggest the need for a double feedback loop to achieve critical problem solving (Figure 1.4). The culture of an organisation influences the problem-solving process so that everyday identification of problems and responses to problems are standardised and based on hidden assumptions that define 'the way we do things around here'. A double feedback loop challenges these value assumptions and power relationships e.g. who defines the problem, how it is defined and whether people who use services, patients and carers have been consulted and involved and so on. To give examples, environmental analysis is often underemphasised in social care assessments and limited resources can restrict options considered in any plan of action. The double feedback loop can be used to challenge the efficacy of the process itself by asking:

- Was the definition of the problem clear enough?

- Were enough sources of information used?

- Was the analysis critical?

Presented in these ways, the process is 'iterative'. Put another way, there is a feedback loop that allows progress to be reviewed and changes to be made to problem definition and analysis. However, the process can also be presented in a linear format (Figure 1.5). While the lack of a feedback loop in this representation is a disadvantage, this linear representation does have its uses, for example, it offers a logical structure to a written report.

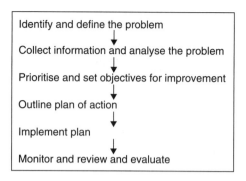

Figure 1.5 A linear representation of the problem-solving process

Levels of problem solving

Problem solving has different levels of complexity. You may well become involved in its application at all levels, though much of your work is likely to be in the top four.

Table 1.1 Levels of problem solving (based on Hamm, 1988)

Individual judgement	You apply the problem-solving process to a case, situation or activity using your professional knowledge and expertise to analyse a situation and set objectives.
Peer-aided judgement	You analyse a case, situation or activity in supervision or with a team – or analyse a situation and agree a care plan as the result of a multi-disciplinary planning meeting.
Systems-aided judgement	A process determined by experts and organisational/ professional experience that helps you solve a problem with e.g. child protection, risk assessments and flow charts used by advisors at a single access point.
Quasi-experimental	Pilot projects, action learning groups or organisational audits where a group methodically analyses a service issue and adjusts activity on the basis of findings.
Scientific research	Problem solving where there is a clear systematic research methodology, structured information collection, verifiable analysis, and the presentation and dissemination of findings and/or outcomes.

This book is designed to help you apply the problem-solving process to the key activity areas you have responsibility for. You could see these activity areas as the key projects that you must manage. Each chapter provides you with a discussion of the key issues that need to be taken into account in exploring each activity area and includes audit tools and reflection points that can be used to help analyse current practice and identify objectives for improvement.

We have given supervision extra special attention in Chapters 4 and 5 because it is so central to effective health and social care management. In fact, supervision can be seen as the most crucial arena in which problem solving takes place as it is where you and your team problem solve cases as well as making decisions together about developments you have responsibility for.

However, like most models, the problem-solving process is necessarily a simplification. Reality and application can be more complex and more problematic. Let's explore briefly each stage in turn before we discuss some wider issues such as the three Es – efficiency, economy and effectiveness.

Problem identification and definition

Applying the problem-solving process can take up a lot of resources. Therefore, you will want to direct activity towards priorities. A useful rule for thinking about this is Pareto's 80:20 rule (Haughey, 2009). This suggests that 80 per cent of breakdowns in service quality lie with 20 per cent, i.e. one fifth of the problems. It is important to try and identify these key problems and direct your time and energy towards these problems rather than those that will actually have little impact on overall quality. Quality assurance systems can help identify and quantify service quality problems; business plans can generate priorities for improvement and the analysis of risk can also be used to determine priority problems.

The clearer the problem definition the greater the focus can be given to problem analysis, objective setting and planning. Clarity can come from being able to quantify a problem; performance measures are often designed to help you do this.

Collecting information

It has been suggested that in war and in management the easier information is to come by the less useful it is. So you may need to research a problem thoroughly, including identifying evidenced-based practice and sometimes collecting data or interviewing stakeholders. In fact, information collection and exploration can be as complicated as full blown social research and just as time consuming and expensive.

However, the reality for managers is that we usually operate with insufficient information, sometimes having to make judgements on the basis of what is available at the time. This can prove costly in the long run, but in a crisis we sometimes have little choice. In general though, planned and methodical information collection can impact positively and directly on the effectiveness of problem solving.

Analysis

Problems vary in their nature and demand different, often complex approaches to the analysis of information. It may be possible to accurately measure and identify the causes of some problems, but many problems faced by health and social care managers cannot be analysed in this way and demand qualitative analysis. Qualitative and quantitative methods can be used in tandem – but much depends on the question you want to answer. For instance, if you want to improve the percentage of assessments completed within a timescale set by a performance measure, you may wish to interview staff to identify possible causes for delays. Then you could carry out a survey to try and quantify this so that you can target any dominant causes.

Many approaches to analysis exist.

- Applied social science – social science provides us with a range of different explanations for human behaviour. Each can cast a different light on an issue and also suggest a different response.

- Applying health and social care methodologies – the different perspectives of social science have generated different health and social care methodologies and interventions. These are based on theories of human behaviour and can readily be mobilised to help you analyse management problems and interventions.

- Applying management theory – just as there are different health and social care methodologies there is also a range of management theories that offer different explanations for management problems and different responses.

- Applying models of good practice – sometimes there are models of good practice that can be used to compare current practices against.

- Using standards and benchmarks – it is increasingly the case that desirable behaviour is defined by the production of detailed standards e.g. the National Management Standards (MSC, 2008). These can be used to judge not just an individual's performance but the general performance of a particular activity. So, for instance, the Effective Supervision Unit (SfC, 2007) could be used to set development objectives for an individual manager or audit performance across a service (see Chapters 5 and 6).

- Analysing the change environment – analysis needs not only to address the problem but the capacity of individuals, teams and organisations to implement change and how any change might be managed effectively and successfully (see Chapter 7).

- Systems analysis – if organisations or services are viewed as interacting social systems then analysis should approach problems as multi-dimensional and caused by the interaction of several systems, all of which may need to be addressed. Analyses should also explore the impact of an intervention in one part of the total system on the system as a whole. Otherwise a solution in one area could create a problem elsewhere.

- Critical reflection – we can as readily critically reflect on our management interventions to bring improvement as well as on social care interventions. This can mobilise all the above but also relies upon self-awareness and self–examination.

- Action learning – it is possible to work with a team helping them to analyse a problem and identify possible causes.

Setting objectives

A common approach to objective setting is that they should be SMART:

- S-specific
- M-measurable

- A-achievable

- R-realistic

- T-timely.

This is a popular formulation which was and still is contrasted with a tendency in health and social care to be inexact. It has value, but should not be used slavishly as 'process', as well as 'outcome' objectives matter, particularly in a value orientated activity like social care. An objective such as 'To ensure that stakeholders are committed and motivated in implementing the change', is not 'SMART' but it might be crucial in determining the success of a service improvement. One could argue that it could be made measurable, but this might be an unnecessary effort that doesn't do justice to the qualitative nature of the objective. It certainly will not be hard to reach for evidence that stakeholders are engaged and motivated.

It is important to remember that objectives serve two crucial purposes. They structure planning *and* evaluation i.e. each objective should have a plan of action that identifies the detailed steps that are necessary to achieve the objective. Monitoring may well focus on the implementation of this plan of action, but evaluation should involve a review of each objective.

Objectives can have different priorities. Some may need to be identified as 'success criteria' and can be separated out as such, to provide the crucial measures against which a problem-solving activity or project can be evaluated.

Plan of action

As already noted it should be possible to link each element of an action plan to an objective or objectives. A simple plan identifies what will be done, when and who will do it. There are more complicated planning methods such as bar and Gantt charts that can assist with planning more complex implementations and facilitate monitoring (Net MBA, 2009).

There are also opportunities here to identify creative ways of achieving objectives rather than relying on standardised responses. Involving your team in planning can often generate creative options.

Risk analysis can be used to identify and gauge the possible causes of breakdown in an improvement plan. Sometimes when a risk is judged to be considerable, a contingency plan can be developed that can be quickly put in place when a problem is identified.

When broad, alternative options for achieving objectives are identified, techniques such as a decision-making matrix can be used to try and make an informed judgement about the best way forward.

It is good practice to include an objective that encompasses the monitoring and evaluation of any implementation. This should be planned for in advance to avoid the tendency to leave evaluation to the last minute and do it badly.

Monitoring and evaluation

It is all too common not to monitor evaluation. This can have a number of unfortunate outcomes, including the implementation stalling. It is essential to determine who will monitor and how. Early identification of difficulties in implementation can often lead to timely resolution, as it can be unusual for plans to go smoothly. Rather disruption or re-thinking should be planned and allowed for.

Monitoring can be aided by establishing milestones. These are key dates along the 'journey' of implementation that pinpoint when crucial activities will have been completed. This gives a welcome structure to monitoring, and a project or development team can use these 'way marks' to meet and consider progress and respond to problems.

Evaluation is a review of the project's effectiveness. It should explore each of the objectives in turn, as well as asking whether the problem as a whole has been responded to or whether the aim of the project has been achieved. Insights can arise that can then inform other developments. As implementation or work on the problem or project is likely to be ongoing it can allow a re-analysis and the setting of new objectives and a new plan. In effect it allows us to learn from experience and continuously improve services.

Effective evaluations:

- are planned;
- are evidenced;
- explore the overall aim of the intervention, each objective and any success criteria;
- involve key stakeholders;
- are the basis for personal and organisational learning and development.

Some wider issues arising from the problem-solving process

Oversimplification

It can be argued that the problem-solving process oversimplifies reality and that actual problem solving is very different. For instance, things don't happen stage by stage. Information is coming in all the time leading to changes in analysis, plans and objectives in altogether a much more fluid process.

One can argue that a representation of the actual process would be confusing. The important thing, perhaps, is to have a simple model that we can use to help order our thinking and actions. Accepting, for instance, that the actual process of assessment is more complicated, with a practitioner moving flexibly around the cycle, does not mean that a formal analysis, objectives and agreed plans are not necessary.

The problem-solving approach can also be seen as too positivistic i.e. it assumes a knowable objective reality that can be analysed and changed rationally. An alternative interpretation would be that meaning is created by people, so that the process of defining the problem, agreeing objectives and a plan of action are more important than 'scientific' analysis. This might be the case in public services where there could be several stakeholders with different problem definitions, analyses and objectives that have to be recognised and reconciled. However, the importance of mobilising groups and communities as problem solvers could be seen as the pathway to effectiveness in any organisation. Senge's (1990) formulation of a learning organisation emphasises the importance of group problem solving as does Total Quality Management (Oakland, 1996) and theories of Communities of Practice (Wenger, 1998, 2006). Case planning meetings, reviews and case conferences can all be seen as exercises in group problem solving. For instance, a good chairperson is likely to consciously try and follow the problem-solving process, encouraging people to share information and analyse it rather than jumping straight to a possible plan of action.

Participation and problem solving

In today's environment we can argue that all managers must be problem solvers as they proactively seek to improve services where they can, using the resources they have at their disposal.

We would argue the same applies to health and social work staff and everyone – users, carers, your team and the network of service providers – must be involved in organisational problem solving to improve services. This adds a new dimension in that following the process in Figure 1.1 will make an individual manager's practice more methodical, but they could end up being very controlling in their approach.

A participative approach means that managers must lead the problem-solving team, involving people in the process according to their ability. In fact, some activities can and should be delegated to team members. As a team or unit manager your job is to organise the team to deliver and improve services. You don't need to do it all yourself and nor should you attempt to do so.

A further crucial dimension to problem solving is involving people who use services and carers in problem solving, not only in relation to their own care plan but also in service improvements (see Chapter 5).

---

*REFLECTION POINT **1.1***

- *Do you methodically apply the problem-solving process in Figure 1.1 to your work?*
- *What are the strengths and weaknesses of your application at each stage?*
- *Are you better at particular stages rather than others?*
- *Do you apply a double feedback loop? (See Figure 1.4.)*
- *How effective are you at involving your immediate team, the multi-disciplinary team, people who use services and carers in problem solving?*

Effectiveness

This book is designed to help you be effective as a manager. Effectiveness can be defined as *producing the intended result* (Dictionary.com, 2009), so the essence of effectiveness is determining objectives with your team, people who use services and carers and achieving them. This means effectiveness is achieving service outcomes and is dependent on the application of the problem-solving process to our activities. The problem-solving process can sometimes be referred to as the 'management control loop'. This could be seen negatively, implying that it is about managers exercising their power. However, more positively, it can be seen as the means by which teams take control of activities and processes to ensure that they meet needs, or how people who use services and patients take control of their own care or treatment. In other words, it is how human beings manage and control their activities to achieve the outcomes they desire. That is not to say that the potential for managers to dominate the process is not an important issue. Who actually has 'control' matters a great deal. Control can lie with people who use services and patients as well as with managers. Crucially, the problem-solving process provides method; the method through which objectives are determined, plans are developed, progress is monitored and evaluated and services are improved. People who use services will need to be supported in applying this method to managing their own care as much as managers and professionals need it in their practice. Broadly it can be applied at three levels, all of which need to be addressed if a team is to deliver a service effectively (Table 1.2).

Table 1.2 Application of problem solving and the components of effectiveness

Business or unit planning	Determining the objectives and the direction of the team or unit as a whole.
Service and process improvement	Analysing the effectiveness of processes and activities, setting objectives and determining plans for improvement.
Case management	Assessing need, agreeing objectives, care and treatment plans for individuals and families.

Chapter 8 addresses business planning and Chapters 4, 5 and 6 address case management. Other chapters explore different processes providing the basis for service improvement e.g. Chapter 7, managing change and developing the organisation and Chapter 9, managing training and development. However, if the problem-solving process or management control loop provides the method that allows us to be effective, there is another crucial dimension to effectiveness we must also consider – leadership. One way of looking at effectiveness is to see it as having two dimensions (Table 1.3):

Table 1.3 Two dimensions of personal effectiveness

Managing the task	Application of the problem-solving process or the 'management control loop' to provide method.
Leading people	Mobilising and engaging teams and stakeholders so that their energy and expertise drives the application of the problem-solving process and thereby service delivery and improvements.

One could readily envisage a situation where a manager is effective in managing the task, so for instance there is a methodical approach to assessment and case planning and progress is carefully monitored and reviewed, but their personal skills are poor. Their team could be alienated and demoralised as leadership is over-controlling and the team are unable to take the initiative and contribute their expertise.

On the other hand, it is possible to envisage a manager being personable, committed, inspiring, participative and supportive, but without method and unable to manage tasks to achieve outcomes. The team, therefore, has no sense of direction; work is not planned, progress cannot be monitored and services cannot improve. Effectiveness demands a marrying of method with means or, in other words, managing both tasks *and* people. Therefore, the next two chapters address self-awareness and your leadership style as they provide the foundation for good practice.

A final dimension of effectiveness to consider

Our view is that the government is beginning to get it right by emphasising the importance of investing in management and leadership development in recent health and social care initiatives. The effectiveness of first line managers has a crucial impact on service quality in health and social care, hence our investment in this book. However, the theories, models and perspectives we offer are only vehicles that are dependent upon your drive and motivation if they are to impact on practice and service quality. This is the final crucial dimension of effectiveness, a hidden one that is too easily lost when leadership and management development initiatives are centrally driven. Essentially, the all-important crucial dimension is 'you' – your energy and motivation.

Leading and managing in health and social care is a tough job, but it does offer many rewards, not least the opportunity to have a greater impact on service quality and improvement. Another big motivator is the pleasure that comes from leading and developing our teams and witnessing their increasing motivation and effectiveness. Enabling and empowering our colleagues is as essential to our value base as enabling and empowering people who use services. If a hidden dimension of effectiveness is your motivation and energy as a leader, your personal value base – and the extent to which you are able to express it in your leadership and management – is a crucial factor in determining your motivation.

The leadership and management strategy for the NHS outlined in *Inspiring Leaders: Leadership for Quality* (DH, 2009b) puts more emphasis on succession planning and career development than any of the social care strategy documents (SfC, 2004). Succession planning is nevertheless a crucial part of the social care good practice model (SfC, 2004, pp22–23) and constitutes another key factor in ensuring that you are able to develop your practice and ensure it has the maximum possible impact on service quality. In Chapter 10 we explore in some detail the management of your own training and development, including career planning. Right from the outset, however, you are invited to take control of your own practice as a manager and leader, to relate it to your value base – to seek to enjoy the experience of leading your team or unit and to build and develop a productive and rewarding career.

If effectiveness is marrying task management with people management it is necessarily associated with economy and efficiency. In fact, since the early 1980s the 'three Es' – economy, efficiency and effectiveness – have been seen in public services as essential to

---

ACTIVITY **1.1**

Jot down your responses to the following questions.

- *What motivates you to lead and manage?*
- *What do you hope to achieve as a leader and manager?*
- *Looking at the dimensions of effectiveness discussed above, where do your strengths lie?*
- *What would you like to improve on?*

---

achieving 'value for money' (Bovaird and Nuttley,1989). Efficiency involves achieving the maximum level of output with the least possible expenditure of resources and economy, purchasing inputs at the lowest possible cost, while maintaining the required quality. Achieving effectiveness and meeting your objectives if you have unlimited resources is obviously much easier than if you have limited resources. In health and social care if we meet the needs of one family or improve one aspect of the service, but in doing so have not been efficient and economic, resources will not be available to meet the needs of others or for other service developments. Constantly, the choices we make in determining objectives and planning interventions must take into account the resources available and seek to achieve service outcomes at minimum cost, including staff and manager time. The relationship between planning and budgeting will be properly explored in Chapter 7. Suffice to write at this point that one of the biggest challenges for leaders and managers in health and social care is the efficient and economic achievement of service outcomes, i.e. with efficiency, economy and effectiveness.

REFLECTION POINT **1.2**

- *How important is economy and efficiency to you and your team?*
- *What might you do to increase awareness?*
- *Can you identify activities that are not economic and efficient where resources might be freed up to meet other needs?*

Chapter summary

- Problem solving is at the heart of effective management.
- It is important to follow the problem-solving process in both managing individual care plans and developing services and to critically reflect on how well you do this.
- The problem-solving process can be applied in most of your work e.g. business planning, project management.
- It is important to manage tasks methodically using the problem-solving process, but it is crucial to involve your teams, the multi-disciplinary team, people who use services and carers within the process.

- Effectiveness is, therefore, dependent upon leadership.

- Your motivation is also crucial to effectiveness as is developing your own practice and career.

- You need to achieve your and your organisation's objectives, i.e. be effective, while also achieving economy and efficiency.

FURTHER READING

Handy, C. (1985) *Understanding Organisations.* London: Penguin Business.

A much-valued introductory text used on many courses and which introduces the idea of the manager as 'Organisational GP'.

For an excellent range of problem-solving tools, visit the Institute for Innovation and Improvements website at **www.institute.nhs.uk/quality_and_service_improvement_tools/quality_and_service_improvement_tools/project_management_guide.html**

Their project management guide provides a problem solving/project management process broken down into stages with tools and techniques to support each stage. The process and tools are used to scope, analyse, plan, implement, evaluate and disseminate service improvements.

Chapter 2

Self-awareness and leadership

Richard Field

CHAPTER OBJECTIVES

This chapter will help you address the following National Occupational Standards for Management and Leadership.

- B6 Provide leadership in your area of responsibility.
- D1 Develop productive working relationships with colleagues.

This chapter will also help you address the following Principles of Social Care Management.

- Value people, recognise and actively develop potential.
- Develop and maintain awareness and keep in touch with service users and staff.

Introduction

Forming and sustaining productive relationships with those we work with irrespective of role and status is at the heart of effective leadership. As leaders we need to be able to relate to a range of people, recognising and valuing their individuality in terms of personality, interests, needs and preferences. The ability to relate requires both awareness of self and of others. Within this chapter you will find a number of reflection points and activities, each of which is intended to prompt self-audit and reflection.

By the end of this chapter you should:

- understand the importance of self-awareness and the centrality of this to effective leadership;
- have further developed your awareness of self;
- have further developed your capacity to understand and value difference;
- have identified ways in which you might adapt your behaviour in order to relate to those around you.

This chapter is informed by a number of assumptions.

1. In order to be effective we need to be able to relate to a diverse range of people from within and outside our organisation.

2. As individuals we share certain similarities but at the same time differ and are unique.

3. We all have natural preferences – just as we are left or right handed we have ways of seeing, interpreting and responding to the world around us.

4. Our natural preferences are reflected in our behaviours.

5. While our natural preferences serve us well in many circumstances there are times when we need to behave 'unnaturally'.

6. Many of us can and do behave 'unnaturally' when required.

7. We are more likely to be successful when our natural preferences fit the situation we face, and less so when they do not.

8. We can all learn to be effective in a wider range of situations by developing our range of behaviours.

9. We all have a choice about *what* we do and *how* we behave.

10. We need to take individual responsibility for our behaviour and associated outcomes.

Relating to individuals

At the heart of effective leadership is an ability to work effectively with others. This is not optional; it is essential.

In the course of a single day most of us have 360 degree interactions with our managers, those who report to us, colleagues and people outside of the organisation. One of the challenges we each face therefore is how to work with a wide range of people, some of whom we experience as being different, which can be a potential source of benefit and joy but is all too often puzzling, frustrating and difficult.

Transactions form the basis of most management activity i.e. 'in return for this I want that', enforced largely through reward and sanction. However, if these are the only sources of power used by a leader or manager they will soon encounter situations where their ability to influence is much diminished. Management and leadership increasingly occur in situations where reward and sanction are inappropriate or inadequate; other forms of influence need to be deployed. The effective leader understands that each person they seek to influence is different and the approach adopted needs to reflect this individuality.

---

*REFLECTION POINT **2.1***

Take a few moments to think of someone who at some point in a working relationship you experienced as being different from you. At what point did you first notice this difference and did you view this positively or negatively? What specifically did you notice about them as being different? Have you noticed this with other people?

Did the point at which you noticed a difference occur early in your relationship or emerge later? Often, difference is most keenly felt when a relationship has not yet properly formed or where there is a problem or stressful situation.

Points of difference can negatively or positively affect a relationship. Negative effects can occur where a difference is noticed but neither understood nor valued. When difference is understood, valued and contributes to a relationship the outcome can be very positive.

CASE STUDY *2.1*

John and Jane

When John is given a task he likes to be clear about what is required, when it has to be completed by and what the output should look like. John is reluctant to start working on a task until he has what he considers to be sufficient guidance. John has a preference for procedures, seeking these when given a task and in turn giving them when he asks a subordinate to complete a task.

Jane who is John's line manager prefers to give staff as much freedom as she can, tends not to interfere in how a task is done and provides little guidance unless asked. Jane has a preference for options and likes working for someone who lets her 'get on with it', in turn granting the same freedom to her subordinates.

John and Jane mismatch in terms of whether they prefer procedures or options; a difference that is quite common and can be a source of frustration and impatience between two people. Figure 2.1 shows the typical responses of people mismatching in this way.

	Manager provides considerable direction	**Manager provides very little direction**
Report requires considerable direction	*Match* Manager's style coincides with the direct report's requirements	*Mismatch* 'Why doesn't my manager tell me exactly what they want me to do?' (Report) 'Why can't my member of staff use their initiative? – I am fed up with spoon-feeding them.' (Manager)
Report requires considerable freedom	*Mismatch* 'Why can't my manager just let me get on with it? I don't like being micro-managed.' (Report) 'Why does my member of staff question why something has to be done or how I want it done?' (Manager)	*Match* Manager's style coincides with direct report's requirements

Figure 2.1 Mismatch example

Where a person has a strong preference, like Jane has for freedom regarding how she undertakes tasks, they are likely to encounter lots of people who they experience as having the opposite preference, which in Jane's case is procedural. It follows that some of the problems we have with those we experience as different is not so much due to their behaviour but to our own preference.

In mismatch situations, rather than continuing to think of other people as being different from you, try asking yourself 'how do I differ from them?' This can significantly affect how we perceive difference.

If you know your natural tendency is to offer minimal instruction and find that some staff have difficulty with this, you can choose to behave differently by providing greater detail when you allocate a task. This should minimise anxiety for staff with a procedural prefer- ence and avoid the need for you to provide additional guidance later. At the same time it might be helpful to continue giving less guidance to those people who need more free- dom. This ability to flex behaviour according to task, context and personality is highly desirable.

Awareness of difference often leads to recognising that this adds something to, rather than detracts from, a relationship. It is a mark of emotional intelligence that we can progress from recognising difference, to valuing it and finally to harnessing it. Understanding, valuing and working effectively with those we experience as being differ- ent is vital to personal and organisational success.

Developing this understanding is a lifetime's work. Consciously or not you will have already started this work and this section should help you consolidate this and prompt new insights and learning.

Dee Hock, former Chief Executive of Visa International, captures this perfectly:

> *The first and paramount responsibility of anyone who purports to manage is to manage self: one's own integrity, character, ethics, knowledge, wisdom, temperament, words and acts. It is a complex, unending, incredibly difficult, oft-shunned task. We spend little time and rarely excel at management of self, precisely because it is so much more difficult than prescribing and controlling the behaviour of others. However, without management of self no-one is fit for authority, no matter how much they acquire, for the more they acquire, the more dangerous they become. It is the management of self that should occupy 50% of our time and the best of our ability.*

> (Hock, D., 2000, paragraph 15)

Leaders achieve their ends through those they work with and as a consequence their abil- ity to build and sustain relationships is of paramount importance. Daniel Goleman (1998) advances the view that the primordial task of leaders is to drive the collective emotions of the organisation, thus requiring emotional intelligence.

The ability to work effectively with diverse colleagues is becoming increasingly important and requires us to sense how others might be, understand how we might be affecting the situation and diagnose how we might modify our actions should we so choose. At the heart of this is a need for self-awareness.

Relating in groups and teams

At work we belong to work, project and management teams or groups comprising colleagues within the same service, organisation or sector. Increasingly we work alongside people who use our services and their representatives, politicians, staff of other agencies, etc.

Leaders and managers need to be able to:

- move in and out of teams with ease;
- collaborate with those from other professions, agencies or sectors;
- work in novel, complex and uncertain contexts;
- deal with diverse problems.

When working as a team we need access to a range of experience, knowledge and skills appropriate to the context and challenges faced. Increasingly the operating environment demands a high level of team diversity as reflected in different personalities, professional backgrounds, varying attitudes to risk, etc. Such diversity increases the range of problems that the team will be able to tackle and raises the likelihood of innovation. The greater the complexity and the rate of change in the environment in which the team operates, the greater the desirable level of diversity within the team.

However, a high level of team member diversity is accompanied by the significant challenge of learning how to work effectively together. The potential for misunderstanding, disagreement and plain 'not getting along' are high in these circumstances. Teams with relatively low levels of diversity can be expected to form more quickly, reach agreement more readily and be easier to manage. As levels of diversity increase, relationships between members are likely to become more difficult to the point where, without emotional intelligence, the effectiveness of the team is likely to fall.

When working in groups and teams there are therefore two major challenges; how to achieve the task and how to work with each other. Frequently, team members make the mistake of focusing only on task, an approach which may work while the task is progressing well and in a way that meets the needs, interests and preferences of every member. However, life is rarely this easy and at some point difficulty is likely to be experienced either with the task and/or how we relate to each other. With luck the team will include someone with natural facilitation skills, or be led by a charismatic leader who is able to resolve such issues. Without this luck it will be up to team members to resolve any problems at the point at which they occur, something which is difficult if earlier attention has not been paid to process and how team members work with each other.

Team members can therefore choose either to consciously work on process and relationships from the outset of team formation or react to relationship problems as and when they occur.

Whatever the choice, team members need to work productively with those they experience as different, which involves them:

- understanding themselves and what they bring to a team;
- appreciating how others might be and valuing what they bring;

- developing a range of behaviours that will help team members work effectively with each other.

To an extent this range of behaviours has to be learnt; some are not natural and require a certain effort. While it might be possible for a person working with others to make all the adjustments necessary for the relationship to work this can be both demanding and unfair. Where three or more people are working together it is highly unlikely that all the required adjustments can be made by one person. Ideally, everyone involved in a team should be able to flex their behaviour. The degree of adjustment made by each person is consequently lower and less demanding. Individual team members can also develop an ability to intervene when two people are in unproductive conflict. This ability is possessed by many people, however, the knowledge of this is often largely unconscious and could nearly always be developed further.

This sub-section ends with an opportunity to reflect on your experience of flexing your behaviour.

ACTIVITY **2.1**

Identify a time when you have modified your approach to a situation as it unfolds.

- *What was the situation?*
- *Who was involved?*
- *What were you trying to achieve?*
- *How did your approach change?*
- *What prompted you to change your approach and why?*
- *Was the change of approach successful?*
- *What have you learnt as a result?*

Flexibility, outcome clarity, awareness and motivation (FOAM)

For many people leading appears to be a largely unconscious process at which they are quite successful. It is highly unlikely that you could have got this far in your career without being able to read situations and change the way you behave in response. At the heart of this ability is emotional intelligence, defined by Daniel Goleman as *how leaders handle themselves and their relationships* (Goleman, 1998, p6).

An effective leader prepares for each situation they face, selecting an approach they believe will deliver the intended outcomes while being prepared to adjust their behaviour as the situation unfolds. Selection and adjustment are related skills that require flexibility, outcome clarity, awareness and motivation (FOAM), each aspect of which is explored below.

Flexibility – an ability to select and deploy a range of approaches in a situation

A person who can only behave one way will occasionally be successful but more often will experience difficulty and perhaps failure. A one-size-fits-all approach to dealing with situations is limiting and effective leaders are able to select an approach from a range available to them and deploy this with skill. Deciding how to approach a particular situation is an important skill, as is an ability to change or flex the chosen approach as the situation unfolds.

CASE STUDY 2.2

Susan's situation

Susan has to give difficult feedback to a colleague who she knows quite well and expects will be upset and possibly angry. Accordingly she has decided on an approach and prepared thoroughly.

However, a little way into the conversation it appears to Susan that her colleague is not taking the feedback seriously, in which case the intended outcome of the conversation will not be realised. Susan's approach so far has been calm and gentle; her judgment however is that she is failing to convey the seriousness of the situation. Susan is aware that she is beginning to lose control of the situation and is becoming irritated and tense, which based on previous experience can lead to her becoming aggressive. Thankfully Susan has access to a range of approaches to giving this feedback and switches to one which is more appropriate to her colleague's reaction.

Access to a range of approaches to situations can be developed through formal education, training, coaching, observation, reading, etc. The rest of this book will help you understand different approaches to many aspects of management and leadership; however, this represents just a start, for personal development should continue for the rest of your career if not the remainder of your life.

Outcomes – an ability to developed well formed outcomes

For any situation there are a set of outcomes that can be pursued and which drive how we behave and the energy we will commit to a line of action. In many situations there is an immediate and obvious outcome that can become the sole focus of our attention, perhaps to the detriment of other less obvious ones.

CASE STUDY 2.3

Susan's situation (. . . continued)

Returning to Susan's situation, her initial concern is that the 'Person receiving the feedback understands it and commits to acting in the way Susan wants in future'.

This immediate and obvious outcome comprises a number of smaller outcomes, which it is useful to specify. In addition there are other outcomes regarding how Susan wants to experience the conversation and the impact she would like this to have on the longer-term relationship. Susan actually wants:

CASE STUDY **2.3** *(CONT.)*

- *the person receiving feedback to:*
  - *accept it;*
  - *understand what they need to do in future;*
  - *feel they can change their behaviour;*
  - *want to change their behaviour;*
- *to be seen to be fair and developmental;*
- *the conversation to be positive, to be heard and respected;*
- *the future relationship to be enhanced rather than damaged as a result of how the feedback conversation progresses.*

Having a full range of outcomes in mind helps Susan plan and monitor the feedback conversation.

Awareness – of self and others

Understanding ourselves is the first step in developing our ability to work effectively with others.

There are a considerable number of frameworks or theories that can help us understand how we and others behave; enable us to anticipate how we are likely to react and behave in certain circumstances; and offer insights as to productive ways of behaving in certain situations.

These theories vary from relatively simple ideas such as whether someone prefers procedures or seeks options through to the more complex theories of personality such as the Myers Briggs Type Indicator (MBTI). Four such frameworks that are explored later in this chapter are:

- metaprograms, habits or filters;
- timelines;
- MBTI;
- maps of the world.

Motivation – to achieve the desired outcomes

While the ability to be aware, flexible and understand desired outcomes is extremely important, this is only of value if the person is motivated to act. It is possible for someone to be involved in a situation where they sense what is happening, understand this is unlikely to lead to their desired outcomes and know how to correct the situation and yet fail to act. Motivation to act is highly important to leadership.

Figure 2.2 indicates the impact of any missing or weak part of FOAM.

The remainder of this chapter focuses on awareness of self and others.

Flexibility	Outcome clarity	Awareness	Motivation	Implication
X	✓	✓	✓	Inability to act when you know what is wrong.
✓	X	✓	✓	Uneasiness about how a situation is developing without knowing why.
✓	✓	X	✓	Carrying on regardless, unaware that intended outcomes are at risk.
✓	✓	✓	X	Knowing what you want to achieve, seeing that it is going wrong, and knowing what needs to be done to correct it but failing to act.

Figure 2.2 FOAM

Awareness of self and others

Metaprograms, habits or filters

Neurolinguistic programming (NLP) identifies a considerable number of metaprograms or habits that are thought to affect how we behave (O'Connor and Seymour, 2003). The earlier example of procedures and options is a metaprogram and a further four are offered below. When looking at these it is helpful to identify:

• which of these best describes your preferred habit; and

• someone you know who appears to have the opposite habit.

It is important to recognise that all of these habits are potentially valuable and each of us need to consider how best to respond to people who exhibit the opposite habit.

Towards and away
Some people are motivated by an outcome they value and want and are more likely to embrace change if they understand the benefits and can see the attractiveness of what is being proposed. Other people tend to be motivated more to avoid what they do not like and for them change is more likely to be embraced when they understand why the current state is considered undesirable and are assured that risks associated with the change have been identified and will be managed.

General and specific
Whenever we communicate we make a series of choices about what we include and how we express it; one aspect of that which is particularly apparent when problem solving concerns the level at which something is described. A manager calling a meeting may state

that they are concerned by something that they have chosen to label 'staff sickness'. When discussing this issue the manager may find some colleagues offer contributions such as 'I think the real issue here is staff morale not sickness' or perhaps 'I think this is a wider problem with society', both of which are examples of thinking more generally or 'chunking up' an issue. Other individuals tend to the opposite habit, which is to be more specific with typical contributions being along the lines of 'I think the real problem is actually long-term sickness' or perhaps '. . . long- term sickness in 'A' team'. These individuals tend to see things in more specific terms and 'chunk down' issues.

Difference and similarity

Some people develop their understanding of an issue or problem by spotting and removing apparent inconsistencies or contradictions in what they are being told. These apparent inconsistencies may be within a conversation, between two or more speakers or by comparison with what they understood previously. Contributions such as 'I thought this morning you said that there were no circumstances when you would . . . but you just said that . . .' is a typical contribution of someone who tends to understand by eliminating 'difference'. People with a 'difference' habit can appear a little critical and their questions interpreted as challenging. Other people have a tendency to learn by spotting similarity between comments made by different people and/or by the same person over time. Contributions such as 'Is this another example of the poor leadership behaviour that you were talking about this morning?' are typical of someone who has a similarity habit. People with this habit tend to appear positive both in terms of what they say and their body language.

Internal and external

Ask a person 'how do you know if you have done a good piece of work?' and you will tend to get one of two typical responses. With the first response people indicate that they will know they have done a good job when someone tells them, for example during their annual appraisal, via customer feedback or more generally comments made by other people. This type of response suggests the person may be externally referenced, getting their standards from other people and for them it is likely to be important that they receive feedback, recognition and praise without which they may be uncertain of how well they are performing. A second type of response is 'I just know when I have done a good job' and is typical of someone who has a strong sense of their own internal set of

---

REFLECTION POINT *2.2*

Taking one of these metaprograms, identify a situation when you are aware of both habits being involved. (e.g. where you exhibited a 'towards' habit and another person an 'away' habit).

- *What impact did these different habits have?*
- *How did you feel?*
- *To what extent did your habit cause you to behave in a way that was unhelpful?*
- *Would it have been possible to behave in a way that better matched the habit of the other person?*

standards. Such internally referenced people tend to have less need for feedback and may reject the comments of others if they do not accept their standards.

Timelines

It is suggested that each of us has one of two attitudes to time, either being time conscious and concerned about timekeeping, an attitude often referred to as being *through time*; or, relatively unaware of time and less concerned about timekeeping, an attitude often referred to as being *in time.*

These attitudes to time can be quite marked and are often a source of irritation between individuals. Those with a 'through time' disposition tend to be punctual, if not early for meetings and can get irritated by someone who is late, perhaps viewing them as being disorganised, inconsiderate or downright rude. People with an 'in time' orientation may view those that do not share this preference as being time obsessed and sometimes rude as their need to avoid being late for their next meeting means they inappropriately curtail their current conversation.

Those of us with a 'through time' preference would do well to consider the behaviour of 'in time' people differently. A more positive view is that 'in time' people are 'in the moment' giving their full attention to what they are currently doing; if as a consequence they are slightly late for their next appointment or commitment does it really matter?

Others of us with a preference for being 'in time' would do well to question whether the behaviour of 'through time' people helps ensure that planned actions occur when desired and that best use is made of the time of everyone concerned. While the natural habits of 'through time' and 'in time' people may be a strong influence on our managerial or

---

CASE STUDY 2.4

Suzi's time problem

Suzi is a trainer with a through time preference and a tendency to get irritated by participants who turn up after the planned start time for a session. Suzi likes to start her sessions promptly as this is what she has planned and because there are a number of like preferenced people who turn up early or at least on time. When Suzi started as a trainer, if a participant was late she used to interpret this as rudeness, an inability to plan their life, etc. to which she used to respond by either:

  i) ignoring them when they did arrive;

  ii) acknowledging their presence but not bringing them up to date.

After one or two difficult incidents Suzi realised that the reason for arriving after the start time might be outside of the person's control and, in any case, pursuing either of her usual responses is unlikely to facilitate the learning of latecomers and may mean that they are not able to contribute fully to the learning of others.

A third option which is less natural to Suzi, but more appropriate, is to greet participants who arrive after the start time warmly, ensure they are comfortable and bring them up to date as soon as practicable.

leadership style it is possible to learn how to behave differently thereby improving personal performance.

Myers Briggs Type Indicator (MBTI)

There are more sophisticated models that help us explain how we differ and which form the basis of psychometric instruments used for personal development; one such example is the Myers Briggs Type Indicator (Reinhold, 2010).

The MBTI is a well established instrument that helps individuals understand their own and others' personality preferences. MBTI helps individuals realise the benefits of diversity and develop effective ways of working with those they experience as different. Used with teams MBTI stimulates awareness of overall team type and enables strengths and potential development needs to be identified. In particular MBTI helps participants develop effective approaches to communication, problem solving, change and conflict management.

At the heart of MBTI are four dimensions, presented below as questions.

- *Where do you prefer to focus your attention? How are you energised? (Extroversion or Introversion)*
- *What kind of information do you prefer to pay attention to? How do you acquire information? (Sensing or Intuition)*
- *How do you prefer to make decisions? (Thinking or Feeling)*
- *Which lifestyle do you prefer? (Judging or Perceiving)*

(MBTI, 2007, Step 1)

In respect of each dimension a person has a preference, for example extroversion (E) or introversion (I), and the instrument reports the preference along with the clarity with which this is reported.

With four dimensions there are 16 possible combinations, each of which has typical characteristics associated with the preference reported for each dimension and the interaction between them. MBTI can be completed in two levels or steps. Step 1 results in the identification of a four-letter type such as ENTJ (Extroverted, Intuitive, Thinking and Judging). MBTI Step 2 results in more detailed feedback in respect of 20 facets that make up the four dimensions. Step 2 provides a much richer picture of preference and therefore can make a more significant contribution to developing self-awareness.

Maps of the world

The fourth framework or idea is that each one of us carries with us a 'map of the world' through which we make sense of what is going on around us, use to reach decisions and guides our behaviour. This map covers all aspects of our lives including at work, our understanding of patient/user needs, how our organisation works, how we should behave, etc.

Our maps constantly evolve and include material derived from family life, schooling, friends, our first and subsequent jobs, particular events, training and general experience, etc. Frequently the development or revision of our maps is largely unconscious and our use of these tends to be unquestioning.

As a simple illustration of a map identify seven ways a manager can motivate their staff. Look at your responses and sift them into those that are a form of reward and those that involve punishment.

Typically, managers working in a public service organisation tend to offer ideas involving reward rather than punishment. Now taking the reward responses divide these into two further categories, those that:

- *involve monetary incentives, cars, perks and any other extrinsic rewards; and those that*

- *concern the nature of the work, e.g. interesting tasks, empowerment, support, praise, training and other intrinsic rewards.*

Managers with a public service background are more likely to offer reward responses and within this intrinsic examples, as this tends to be their experience of being managed and seeing others managed, possibly reinforced through internal training programmes. Equipped with this map of the world a manager faced with a member of staff who they consider needs motivating is likely to automatically turn to intrinsic rewards.

Individual maps can significantly affect our behaviour and the likelihood of personal and organisational success as illustrated by David's tale.

David's tale

David is a middle manager aged 47 who is frustrated at his inability to progress within his organisation. David consistently receives positive feedback and his annual appraisals indicate no areas where his performance could be improved. David's line manager encourages him to go for promotion on a regular basis. David is considered to be a hard worker and prides himself on his flexibility, punctuality and excellent sickness record. With regard to promotion David believes that experience and proven competence should determine promotion decisions.

In the last three years David has applied for three promotions, each time being shortlisted and interviewed yet failing to get the post. On two occasions posts were awarded to external applicants and on the third occasion the post was given to a much younger internal candidate; none of these managers possessed the same experience as David.

The only feedback David has received regarding his recent applications is that his CV could be updated and that when being interviewed he should offer more detailed examples of how he would approach particular situations. He has been told that on each occasion the successful applicant did a better interview on the day.

Early in his career David had considerable success when going for promotion and considers himself to be good at job interviews.

CASE STUDY 2.5 (CONT.)

David's map	New material – not yet assimilated in David's map	Implications
Employees should be honest, punctual, work hard, volunteer for new duties and seek development. Success comes to those who are experienced, have shown they can perform and deserve it. Interviews are an opportunity to show that you have performed in the past and will be able to in the future. Recently David has come to the view that his face does not fit and that the organisation wants younger and preferably external appointments. He considers there to be no point in making any further application.	Recruitment/promotion decisions are based on interview performance on the day, not prior job performance. The application form is the basis for short-listing and the interview alone is the basis for appointment decisions. There is a need for the panel to tick all the boxes – so candidates should prepare carefully and 'play the game'.	If David is to be successful he needs to: i) let go of the belief that 'interview success should be based on experience and proven competence' and replace this with 'success goes to those that interview well'; ii) challenge his view that he is being discriminated against; iii) confront his inability to perform at interview and learn how to 'play the new game'.

Significant influences on David's map are:

- his father who had very strong views about how people should behave at work and be rewarded;

- a line manager whose views were broadly consistent with the views of David's father;

- early recruitment/promotion experiences over the first 15 years of working life – David was first time successful in four job applications early in his career;

- the interpretation of recent interview experiences arising from conversations with peer colleagues of a similar age and similar interview experiences.

Recognising the required change in his map is painful to David, causing him to wonder about the relevance of his values, challenging him as to whether he should change his behaviour and surfacing a need to develop interview competence. David has a number of choices including:

- continuing with his existing map, applying for jobs as now in the hope that sooner or later he will be part of a group of applicants where everyone else is worse at interviewing;

- continuing with his existing map, cease applying for promotion and accept his career is over;

- changing his map, developing interviewing skills and continuing to apply for jobs.

While maps are personal to the individual concerned the maps of team members are likely to share common features. A team of accountants, for example working for a public service organisation, will typically find that the professional territory of their individual maps is similar. The part of their maps that covers how their organisation works is also likely to be shared and similar in certain respects to other groups.

Working on an inter-professional, inter-organisational or inter-sectoral basis poses many challenges including coping with the diversity of maps held by those involved. Working with this diversity is easier where the different maps are recognised and shared early in the relationship.

However well developed our maps are there will be occasions when these fail to help us understand a situation we face. Such map 'failure' arises for a number of reasons, including:

- changes in the external environment that are novel and not covered by our map;
- the age of our maps, which for many senior managers contain material that that is over 30 years old;
- content within our maps that has never been challenged until a particular point in our lives is reached.

Change is often a time when our map of the world is tested and some of the difficulty experienced with major change is the need for maps to be re-drawn. If we are unaware of the importance and content of our maps this re-drawing can be quite a slow and painful process.

As individuals we have a simple choice.

- Seek to understand our maps, recognising that while these are potentially invaluable they are probably not the only way of thinking about an issue and might need to change. Just as maps shape our thinking they also limit it. Proactive map-making can be a real spur to creativity as it affords an opportunity to play with different ways of looking at a situation.

- Fail to engage with our maps, allowing these to unconsciously influence our actions until a point is reached when they no longer seem appropriate and we experience having them re-drawn for us. This approach tends to make us more reactive to change and we are likely to find the process more painful.

Chapter summary

- Arguably it does not matter which of the ways of looking at difference you use. What is important is to develop awareness of self and an ability to anticipate how others might be, using this understanding to inform your behaviour.

- For some people metaprograms prove useful while others prefer timelines or perhaps MBTI. Remember that these are only a few of the models that are available and it may be worth extending your map of the world to include other popular models, addressing for example learning styles and team roles.

- An ability to work with a wide range of people is essential for successful leadership. Particularly in novel, complex and uncertain times, diversity is of considerable value; the difference you experience in another person may ultimately be the difference between success and failure.

- High levels of diversity demand high levels of emotional intelligence, without which there may be unproductive conflict, dysfunctional behaviour and a failure to benefit from the specific contribution of a person who differs in some respect.

FURTHER READING

Goleman, D. (2003) *The New Leaders.* London: Little Brown.

This excellent book explores the concept of 'primal leadership' and how leaders can build resonance across six leadership styles.

Keirsey, D. and Bates, M. (1984) *Please Understand Me.* 5th edition. California: Prometheus Nemesis.

For those wishing to explore difference using the Myers Briggs Type Indicator this book offers a very good foundation.

Knight, S. (2002) *NLP at Work.* 2nd edition. London: Nicholas Brealey Publishing.

This book provides a useful introduction to NLP with examples and tasks set within the work context.

Chapter 3
Developing your leadership style

Ivan Gray

CHAPTER OBJECTIVES

This chapter will help you address the following National Occupational Standards for Management and Leadership.

- B6 Provide leadership in your area of responsibility.
- F1 Manage a project.

This chapter will also help you address the following Principles of Social Care Management.

- Value people, recognise and actively develop potential.
- Develop and maintain awareness and keep in touch with service users and staff.
- Inspire staff.

Leadership as development and empowerment

Hersey and Blanchard's theory of situational leadership (Hersey and Blanchard, 1974 and 1993) offers an approach to leadership that is congruent with health and social care values. It has stood the test of time and offers practical guidance to practitioners on how they might lead effectively.

It is 'situational' in that a leader's behaviour needs to vary from situation to situation, according to the characteristics of the individual staff member. They see staff as being at different developmental levels that demand different leadership styles (see Table 3.1) and identify two key variables that make up the developmental level – motivation to do and experience in the job. So, if your staff member is very new they might not understand the purpose of the work and have a limited understanding of the values that underpin practice. They may not have the skills and knowledge to carry out tasks. Therefore, they may need to be instructed and tightly supervised if they are to function at all.

At the other end of the scale, an experienced staff member should be self-motivated and well-equipped to do the work. They will have a strong value base and the skills and knowledge of essential procedures and objectives to practise effectively. So, if your staff member is experienced you may well be able to delegate to them. They should be able to take responsibility for their work, reporting back to you on progress and significant issues – but otherwise working independently. Two further stages of staff development and corresponding leadership styles are identified in the model (Table 3.1), giving four levels of development and four levels of corresponding leadership styles.

The model appears applicable to health and social care situations for a number of reasons. It is congruent with health and social care theory (e.g. Egan, 1998, Tuckman, 1965), developmental, participative, needs-led, focuses on delegation and is dependent on good supervisory practice.

Yet, as a theory it has been criticised as being too crude, with just four developmental stages and four styles. But this structure does provide a simplified model to get our heads around given the complexity of reality. The principle is the crucial feature, not the detail, and their central idea of development as a continuum means that all staff have needs that must be met by their leader if they are to progress.

Table 3.1 Developmental level, leadership style and supervision – based on Hersey and Blanchard, 1974 and 1993

Developmental level of staff member	Leadership style	Helping them develop and move on
D1: Newly appointed and unqualified. They don't have the skills and knowledge to do the job yet and their practice won't be informed by social care values. They can be very under confident.	S1: Instruct and train – They need clear directions on what to do and need to be closely supervised to make sure it has happened. You may need to work alongside them or pair them with an experienced team member. Give them frequent supervision sessions to debrief and reflect.	With your support their confidence will grow as they complete tasks successfully. In supervision explain the reasons for approaching a task in a particular way. Discuss user's and carer's needs and relevant values. Use national occupational standards to define good practice and provide planned training and developmental activities to develop competence.
D2: Newly qualified or post induction. They will be motivated and will have some knowledge and skills and a strong value base. However there will be some areas of work that will be completely new to them and they may lack confidence in their new situation.	S2: Coach – They will need some instruction to cope with new tasks but will have other areas where they are able to determine the way forward for themselves. Use experienced team members to help with coaching and build on their baseline of skills.	They may be less confident than they seem so give positive feedback. Encourage them to transfer skills and understandings from areas where they have experience to new tasks. Be clear from the beginning that there will be gaps in their experience. Encourage them to be open about what they can or cannot do. Encourage them to evaluate their practice with you.

Table 3.1 (continued)

Developmental level of staff member	Leadership style	Helping them develop and move on
D3: Established in their post. They will generally now have the understanding, skills and experience to work effectively.	S3: Supporting – You need to only occasionally step in to facilitate or help with a decision but they will still need regular supervision.	New tasks or slightly different situations can still throw them but helping them think things through is usually enough. Encourage them to identify what they still find challenging and identify cases and situations that will create challenges.
D4: Experienced or senior practitioner. They have the required knowledge and skills and a strong value base. They may well know more than you do!	S4: Delegate – They must have space to use their expertise, lead on case management and contribute to service development.	Ensure all cases are reviewed methodically in supervision, as even the most experienced can hit problems. Help may be required to help them adjust to service changes especially if they have been in post a long time. Make it clear that you acknowledge and value their expertise. Allocate complex cases that will stretch them. Involve them in developing services and supporting and supervising others. Look to future career options.

Hersey and Blanchard's theory highlights the question, *have I got my leadership style right*? This is an important question because if people are offered leadership that meets their needs, they will develop and improve their performance. However, getting the style wrong can be very damaging. Delegating to someone who is inexperienced when you should be giving clear directions and carefully monitoring their work could mean they flounder and fail. Conversely, telling or instructing an experienced member of staff, when you should be giving them space to use their knowledge and experience could generate anger, resentment and depression.

CASE STUDY 3.1

I had worked for several years in Children's Services but an opportunity came up to take on the leadership of an established business that I couldn't say no to. At first it was a disaster. I'd go out on a sales call or do some work in the office and when I reappeared they were either waiting for me to tell them what to do next or, having finished the work they were doing some time ago, were taking a 'fag break'. Sometimes I even had to go and find them. I had got used to leading a team where people took responsibility for the work – my new business team had always been told what to do and closely supervised to ensure they did it. It took a while, and for a bit I had to accept the need be quite directive, but I worked on developing them and now they work much more independently.

CASE STUDY 3.1 (CONT.)

My move away from Children's Services also turned out to be a problem in other ways. It had taken me years to build up a liaison group with the youth and community workers and some local voluntary organisations. This resulted in some useful projects and even some funding and was an area of work I was very proud of. When I left, a colleague was asked to take over until an appointment was made to my post. I gave them the minutes of the meetings and quickly discussed the pertinent issues. A few months after I left, I met up with another former colleague, who told me the liaison group had collapsed. Either the person my manager had asked to take over didn't care or else they had no idea what they were doing. It was strange as I'd always found them to be very capable. In hindsight, I think I was in such a hurry to go and so pleased to hand things over, I perhaps didn't give the handover enough time and thought.

REFLECTION POINT 3.1

In the case study above what was the developmental level of the team and individual and what management style did the manager use?

Can you identify situations where you have used the wrong management style? What effects did this have?

Supervision and effective delegation

Delegation and supervision are at the heart of Hersey and Blanchard's model of situational leadership. As staff members develop over time and their motivation and expertise increases, they are given increasing autonomy and the manager gradually delegates responsibility to them as their ability to do the job develops. So delegation skills are essential to effective management. It is worth exploring the principles of delegation in more detail.

What is delegation?

When the Roman Empire covered most European and Mediterranean countries communication was difficult. To govern effectively the Senate appointed 'legates' that carried an ivory baton to show their authority and that they acted on behalf of the Senate and the people of Rome. Legate means 'to depute' and legates took on the power of the state but were held responsible to it. Therefore, when you delegate you in effect create legates who exercise some of your power independently. This process of delegation is crucial in a professionalised service. The essence of a professional is that they have professional autonomy, i.e. decision-making powers.

The earliest form of management theory and practice was called Scientific Management or Taylorism after its originator (Taylor, 1947). Taylor thought that a manager's role was to, through a process of observation and analysis, determine the most efficient (uses least resources) and effective way (gets best results) of carrying out a task. Taylor would observe workers shovelling coal into a cart and determine the best way of doing it requiring the minimum number of workers in the fastest possible time. Supervisors then instructed the workers and ensured the most efficient and effective method.

This 'do it by numbers' approach has its strengths. In high risk situations, such as child and adult protection, we are expected to follow procedures to minimise the risks of mismanagement. However, in not allowing discretion, a service is standardised. In health and social care people's needs vary. It is important that services recognise this and provide an individualised response. To follow the analogy, scientific management breaks down if every pile of coal is different – requiring a different response to be managed efficiently and effectively.

Yet, there is a difference between accountability and responsibility. As the manager of the service you will always be held accountable, i.e. held to account for the quality of the service and any problems in its delivery and resourcing. You are also responsible in that you make the decisions that effect service quality and delivery. If you have accountability, but not the responsibility, you are little more than a scapegoat.

In delegating you distribute responsibility and the ability to respond to problems. You give other people discretion, the ability to respond and make some decisions. You, however, remain accountable for the service. If you like, 'the buck stops here'. A number of people can be responsible for the service but as the manager only you are ultimately accountable.

Why delegate?

Delegation increases the resources available
Very valuable outcomes arise from delegation. As staff members are able to work more independently, team resources are mobilised to tackle the team task. Staff members are able to contribute their expertise, energy and time and this greatly increases the total volume of resources available to respond to the needs of users and carers.

Delegation increases responsiveness
If a manager is very controlling and does not delegate decision-making every decision has to go through them and this slows down the whole process. If the team is freed up to assess need and make decisions, provision is more likely to meet the needs of service users and carers and, as it has been negotiated with them, is more likely to be acceptable. Staff members are also more likely to come up with creative options to enhance the service.

Manager time
As the team work more independently delegation also frees up manager time, giving them more time to manage. They can give more time to integrating the team's work with the network of provision, improving the quality of support systems and procedures and developing strategy. If you have an inexperienced team and cannot delegate you may find you are a lot busier and have much less time for these wider duties.

Manager expertise and project work
Delegation allows all the resources of the team to be fully mobilised in carrying out the team task. This means that the team can be more effective than your expertise alone will allow. The expertise and creativity of the team can then be released by your effective delegation and leadership skills.

In the theory and practice of 'distributed leadership', management tasks and responsibilities are also distributed amongst the team (Watson, 2002). Team members can be given responsibility for particular tasks or else delegated development projects. There are good practical and ethical arguments for this style of leadership and it has the advantage of allowing you to grow the next generation of managers by allowing them to share your management tasks.

Staff morale

People's job satisfaction is dependent on delegation. Working independently and having discretion is motivating and the creativity it allows can be very rewarding as staff see that they have had a direct impact on service quality and are responding to peoples' needs. Delegation is also essential to personal development. We can develop our practice by being allowed to undertake more challenging tasks with appropriate support.

If there are benefits to good morale, the effects of the negative behaviours that staff can develop if they are over-controlled can be very damaging.

The negative effects of poor delegation

- Depression and withdrawal – unable to develop or practise effectively, staff can become depressed. They can end up doing just enough to be seen to do their job and will be resistant to change.

- Anxiety – being over-controlled creates anxiety. Given the complexity of cases and the need to sometimes respond quickly to a situation, staff are constantly trying to second guess their manager. This can generate fear that they have not responded 'correctly', (or rather as their manager would want them too).

- Conformity – to avoid anxiety and displeasing their manager staff stick to safe responses and avoid or ignore other possibilities. This can mean they are not making judgements about risk as well as not responding to need. They can hide things from their manager to keep themselves safe.

- Anger – their poor relationship with their manager and their frustration can generate anger. Staff can be argumentative or destructive or they express their anger elsewhere or direct it onto others, perhaps even taking it home with them.

- Sabotage – anger at their manager, who represents the organisation, can become anger at the organisation. They can deliberately sabotage operations and systems and can be more prone to complaint and industrial action. Even mischievous behaviour can be very destructive.

- Dependency – they conform to their manager's 'micro-management', never making a move without checking it out first and unable to act without instruction.

- Moving on – staff reduction is a problem in health and social care. The cost of advertising a post, making an appointment and inducting staff is considerable and vacancies can be costly to cover. Staff members who are unhappy and leave quickly also destabilise teams and services.

What are the essential skills of delegation?

The essential skills of delegation are displayed in Figure 3.1. We explore each of the dimensions in turn.

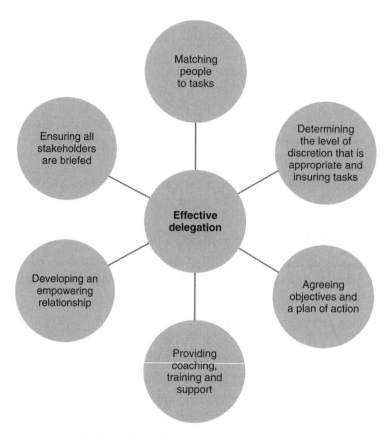

Figure 3.1 Effective delegation

Matching people to tasks

At its heart much of delegation is about risk management. Its starting point is matching people to the task and this is based on assessment. Firstly, you need to assess the task and secondly, you assess team capability. Complex, high risk tasks are allocated to skilled and experienced staff members. Simple, low risk tasks are allocated to less experienced workers. This has the effect of generally reducing the level of risk to users, carers, staff, the organisation and yourself of things going wrong. Yet, you may not know the capabilities of your staff team. Tasks can quickly become more complex than they first appear and you may be forced to allocate work to less experienced people because there is no one else to take it on. Most of these problems can be dealt with by determining the level of discretion that is appropriate and, in effect, insuring tasks.

Determining the level of discretion that is appropriate – insuring tasks

Blanchard *et al.* (1994) came up with the helpful idea of a manager issuing an insurance policy when they delegate a task. If we take the two characteristics of a working situation or activity that we identified earlier, task complexity and staff capability, there is a third variable that as a manager you have most control over, the nature of your supervision.

Figure 3.2 The three variables that determine the success of a delegated work activity

You have at your disposal a number of supervisory modes. If we take the original meaning of 'supervision', having oversight or overseeing a task, then you can vary the amount of an activity you expect to 'see'. Blanchard *et al.* (1994) suggest that this works like an insurance policy. Where you have a very experienced staff member who is dealing with work they are motivated to do and have consistently dealt with effectively, you might issue a low risk 'third party, fire and theft' policy. You will always need to review progress, but with a 'third party, fire and theft policy' staff work independently.

On the other hand, with an inexperienced member of staff and a potentially complex or high risk situation, you might issue a 'fully comprehensive' insurance policy with breakdown cover. You ask them to take certain actions, then report back to you frequently before doing anything else. You may even decide on maximum oversight and, like a driving instructor, be there beside them to make sure they are coping. This allows us to identify a number of levels of supervision that lie between a 'fully comprehensive' insurance policy and 'third party, fire and theft':

A FULLY COMPREHENSIVE POLICY

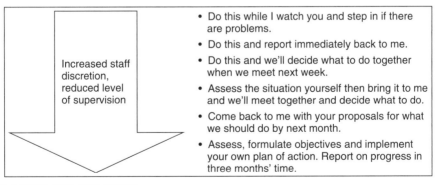

THIRD PARTY, FIRE AND THEFT

Figure 3.3 Supervisory mode and level of staff discretion (based on Blanchard et al. *(1994))*

This brings us to our next feature of effective delegation.

Agreeing objectives and a plan of action

While it is essential that you are clear about levels of responsibility and reporting mechanisms you also need to be clear about the task. You can do this by setting clear objectives or, if staff are experienced, by negotiating the objectives with them or by asking them to set their own. Objectives are statements of the broad outcomes to be achieved and the basis against which the success of the activity will be evaluated.

If you delegate a substantial project to a staff member i.e. the design and introduction of a service development or system, you shape the project by agreeing the objectives and review progress against them. A good project manager will want to agree objectives with you, their sponsor, from the start and before they start work on anything. A less experienced project manager will not see the importance of doing so.

Even so, there is still a gap between the objective and the plan of action. The staff member may know where they are headed, but can choose the most appropriate route (Figure 3.4).

PROJECT OBJECTIVES

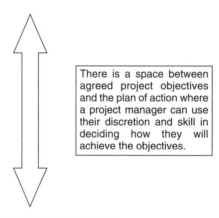

There is a space between agreed project objectives and the plan of action where a project manager can use their discretion and skill in deciding how they will achieve the objectives.

PLAN OF ACTION TO ACHIEVE THE OBJECTIVES

Figure 3.4 Objective setting and creative space

If you do not want to give discretion when delegating a task or project then you should provide the delegated person with a detailed plan of action rather than a broad objective. That is, you will tell them how things should be done. Even when dealing with an experienced project manager you will probably influence the ultimate plan of action. But if the delegated person has no discretion at all it is important to remember that they are not managing the task or project at all – you are.

Looking back to Figure 3.3 you can see that the different levels of discretion range from telling the staff member the plan of action to letting them formulate the objectives and the plan themselves. This brings us to an important point. As a manager a crucial part of your job is developing people so that you can delegate more to them. This is a process of you gradually letting go and allowing more independent action as you judge that the staff member is ready for it. This is the basis for staff development through work-based learning.

At the heart of staff development through work-based learning is you making judgements about someone's capability, the task to be undertaken and the level of risk. Just as with helping people who use services and patients develop independence and improve their quality of life, if there is no risk there is no gain. It is about giving space when you know, with support, on the basis of your knowledge about their previous performance, someone can succeed. This brings us to the next important feature of delegation – providing coaching, training and support.

Providing coaching, training and support

Effective delegation demands more from you than matching staff to tasks and agreeing reporting mechanisms and responsibilities. To begin with you will need to brief them on the history of activities they are taking over and the broader context in which they are set. It can be very helpful to share your experiences and perspectives on people, relationships and likely reactions so they do not blunder into situations. Exploring likely problems and possible options can also mean they begin a task confident and well prepared.

As you supervise a staff member and delegate to them you can also mobilise development activities to help them, e.g.:

- coaching and one-to-one discussion in supervision with you or a colleague;
- shadowing a colleague or colleagues;
- sitting in on planning meetings, reviews, conferences, etc.;
- visits and short placements;
- guided reading;
- distance learning;
- e-learning;
- taught components and programmes;
- dedicated and structured supervision sessions;
- mentoring by colleague or colleagues;
- group work and learning sets.

However, it is not uncommon for staff members to have difficulty applying these developments to practice. Reality can be more complex than the theory until it is applied. You manage the place where training becomes practice. Beyond these learning opportunities there is another crucial factor that determines the effectiveness of delegation and whether a staff member develops their practice – the nature of their relationship with you.

Developing an empowering relationship

The quality of the supervisory relationship is crucial in determining whether cases and service development projects are managed well and whether staff can develop their practice. You cannot delegate effectively if you do not have the interpersonal skills that allow you to build the empowering relationships that are necessary to support it. The skills you need are the same ones that are the basis of our professional practice, so you are already well-equipped. Rather it is about applying them to your supervision to create an empowering culture. So, what are the features of an empowering supervisory relationship?

- Shared understanding – you need some common ground to provide the basis for your relationship. It helps if both you and your staff member have an understanding of what makes effective delegation, and also building empowering relationships.

- Trust – if there is no trust between you, issues will be hidden and cannot be explored together and resolved. Trust comes from experience and is built over time. Listening carefully to people and encouraging them to share their views and experiences is crucial – you must also be willing to share what is sometimes uncomfortable to you too. Giving positive feedback is important as is being straight with staff if there are problems. Honest mistakes are inevitable in our work and most problems come from the systems and conditions in which we practise and are not for an individual to resolve.

- Openness – try to not have secrets. People pick up on them through non-verbal cues and it creates an atmosphere of mistrust and anxiety where people are trying to take into account what is not known.

- Shared control – people need to be able to influence the relationship, contributing not only to its development but to the content of the dialogue that is its purpose. Accepting that at first you may need to be more controlling, even directive, make sure that as time goes on this is reduced with the staff member making more and more of a contribution. If you are empowering your staff member it should look like Figure 3.5.

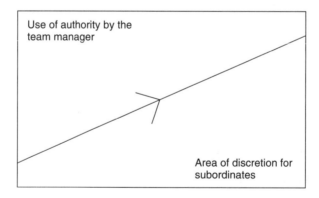

Figure 3.5 Based on Tannenbaum and Schmidt's leadership continuum taken from Mullins, 2007, p373.

- Criticality and a shared value base – the relationship should allow both of you to reflect together on practice in the context of a joint commitment to improving it for the benefit of people who use services and patients. Your shared value base should provide common ground and motivate you both to step back and challenge each other's perspectives. You should also reflect on the quality of your relationship and the effectiveness of your supervisory relationship.

Ensuring all stakeholders are informed

The final element of effective delegation is to remember that we all practise within a number of interrelated systems and groups that make up our own organisation and all the systems and groups that make up the network of provision. If you are delegating responsibility for projects or a crucial team function to a staff member it is important that everyone knows that you have done this. For instance, if someone is representing the team on a working group make sure that everyone knows this and expects them to be there and everyone is clear about what decisions they can make or not make on the team's and your behalf.

What are the blocks to delegation? – the riptide effect

A common leadership problem is the failure to delegate. If the benefits of delegation are so obvious, and impact very forcibly on managers, why do they fail to delegate? There are a number of possible reasons.

Lack of knowledge and skill
If you are not aware of the importance of delegation and do not know how to manage it, you cannot practise effectively. For instance delegation is very difficult if you do not know how to vary supervision to reduce risk. Also, many managers are not evaluating their own practice and planning for improvement, i.e. they do not really have a handle on their own Continuing Professional Development (CPD). The only real way to check out if you are delegating effectively is to check it out with the customer, those you supervise. The effectiveness of delegation must appear on the supervision agenda.

Lack of self-awareness or interactive skills
Beyond knowledge, it is important that you are self-aware (see Chapter 2). For instance, you may well have a bias towards a particular leadership style. You may well like to tell or instruct people or you may like to delegate whenever you can, almost regardless of circumstances. Effective delegation means, however, that you must vary your style according to the needs or characteristics of the staff member and the nature of the task, so no one style can work. You must be aware of any bias and seek to counteract it.

Building an empowering relationship also demands self-awareness. You will not succeed if you are curt, sarcastic, angry, blaming or play games. Listening is crucial and you will need to be aware of non-verbal as well as verbal communication, and pick up on discomfort and issues that are difficult to share.

Organisational culture and regulations
An organisation's rules and procedures and job descriptions can limit delegation. The organisation's culture or 'how we do things around here' can also limit your practice. It is also worth remembering that managers can be figureheads. It will be important that you are seen to take on certain activities to give them credibility and some situations will demand your legitimate authority if anything is to happen. Also, organisational politics can make it wise to keep certain responsibilities and activities to yourself.

Fear
Delegation demands risk taking and is anxiety provoking. Keeping hold of responsibilities gives the illusion of control but in reality it does not really work. Controlling managers are not able to cope with the volume of work and simply create new risks through making hurried or ill-informed decisions, forgetting about things or delaying decision-making and action.

Expertise

We often become managers because we are good practitioners. We often also enjoy practising and can miss the job satisfaction it gives us, especially when we are new to management and can find some management tasks unpleasant or daunting because of our lack of experience. It is too easy to find ourselves practising instead of managing, because we like it, because we can do it better than the staff member, or else because we need it to give us a sense of security and familiarity in a troubled world.

Personal beliefs and experience

We are influenced by our previous experiences, including being managed. So, if we have experienced say, a very controlling management, we can seek to copy it or, if it has proved damaging, to avoid it. Personal experiences also make a difference. In fact they can have a deeper impact and be harder to control. For instance, a very authoritarian family experience can mean people are very controlling or find it hard to control at all, even if it is necessary.

Time

Good delegation takes time. It demands careful assessment and analysis, careful monitoring and review, careful briefing and good long-term support. Under pressure delegation very often suffers.

Crises

In a crisis we often have to act quickly and this sometimes means getting involved in work we should have delegated or in making decisions ourselves. Crises mean sometimes we must step in and be more directive, when otherwise we would have seen a more enabling approach as appropriate.

These blocks to delegation are very powerful factors and they are ever present. There is a tendency to see delegation as a series of one-off acts, but these factors working together mean that delegation is an ongoing process. Good delegation is dependent on leadership, good supervisory practice, self-awareness and the constant self-evaluation of management practice by managers in the long term.

Delegation demands constant attention and the blocks could be portrayed as creating a consistent force, a riptide that a manager must fight against (Figure 3.6). It is worth thinking of it in these terms and we can imagine a good team shape like a pattern of buoys in a mooring – with the team manager a little distanced from the team by delegation so that they can support the individuals who have to carry out the work and have oversight of the team's activity. All too easily the riptide can wash the manager down into the team so they are either practising when they should be managing or else fail to delegate and become a decision-making bottleneck (Figure 3.6).

In these negative scenarios the effect on the service can be very damaging. If a manager is practising, the service gains one new practitioner but at the cost of the management supervision and support of the team as a whole. The team easily becomes dysfunctional. The short-term gain of one worker is counteracted by the long-term loss of several. If a manager becomes a decision bottleneck the team can become stuck and unable to do their work because they are waiting for the manager, who is probably overwhelmed and not coping, to decide what to do. It is almost as if the manager gets between the team

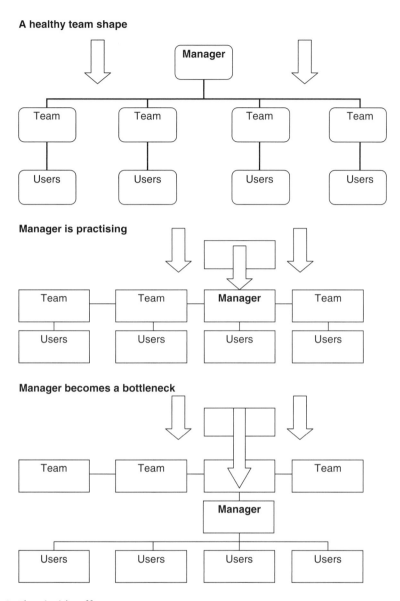

Figure 3.6 *The riptide effect*

and users of services and reduces the effectiveness of the team to the decision-making capabilities and speed of response of one person.

Given the realities of our services today, where it is easy to find yourselves short staffed, in crisis or managing an inexperienced team, it is almost inevitable that at times we will be caught by the riptide effect and washed into activities that we should be delegating. The challenge is, when the crisis is over or as the team grows, to ensure that we allocate the cases and re-establish the distance from hands-on practice our management role requires if we are to be effective.

. 1

- *Is my leadership varying to respond to the needs of individuals? Looking across my team do I have a different leadership relationship with each individual?*
- *Do I establish empowering relationships with staff?*
- *Can I see evidence of individuals taking more responsibility for supervision and increasing their contribution and exercising more control over the process?*
- *Can I see evidence of individuals as they develop taking an increasing role in enabling and developing colleagues and contributing to service developments?*

Psychological contract

Effective individual performance is as much about motivation as skill. Values and motivation are closely related but the situation can readily arise where someone has a strong value base, is skilled and knowledgeable as a practitioner, but their working conditions and relationships demotivate them so they do not perform well. Supervision is a place where motivational problems can be responded to and barriers to learning and development, as well as effective performance, overcome. The idea of the psychological contract can be very helpful in this respect (Argyris, 1960, Schein, 1965, Guest and Conway, 2002).

The idea is that beyond the formal contract of employment everyone has a 'psychological' contract that is unique to each individual and is not necessarily shared with colleagues or with managers. This contract is their expression of what they expect from the organisation and their professional career so that it is very important in determining an individual's level of motivation.

As a line manager, one of your jobs is to walk the boundary of the psychological contract for each staff member to ensure that it maintains a state of acceptable balance. So, by regular contact and discussion you stay aware of whether there is anything that is putting their psychological contract under threat or, from the employer's side, anything that they are doing which could be problematic.

The whole point about the psychological contract is that it is hidden and unique. So you cannot assume that what motivates you motivates anyone else or what motivates one person motivates another. Sometimes it is only awareness on your part that will allow you to spot non-verbal clues or pick up on hidden agendas. These can then be followed by dialogue that will clarify the problem and allow it to be expressed and responded to. Bear in mind what demotivates or motivates can seem quite trivial. Perceived unfairness about who sits where and car parking can, for some people, be crucial. Remember it's their contract; it doesn't have to make sense to you – you just need to know about it and respond. Time and patience are essential as your staff member will not volunteer the information; they may even be waiting to be asked or they may not really have worked it out yet. As you get to know individuals you will start to become more aware of 'what makes them tick' and be better able to anticipate likely problems. One-to-one supervision is an important opportunity to test out someone's psychological contract, as is what has been called 'Management by Walking Around' (Peters and Austin, 1985). In both face-to-face contacts a manager can pick up on issues that need a response.

If you identify a problem with someone's psychological contract you have a number of possible responses.

- Talk about it – just being heard and understood can make a big difference.

- Problem solve – sometimes we can actively get involved and problem solve, dealing directly with the issue.

- Negotiate – if we can't take the problem away we can balance it out with a compensatory gain somewhere else.

- Explain – sometimes clarifying the reasons for a policy or a decision can help. People sometimes do not see a policy or decision in context or understand its purpose.

- Share – a manager often has to broker team issues with senior management or other organisations. At the very least, raising the issue, even if it comes to nothing, shows you care. You may even find it is an organisational problem that affects several staff. Public recognition of an individual's unhappiness or the effort they are making can make a difference and if others share it or have come to terms with it the team can sometimes help.

- Alleviate the problem – if we can't remove a problem we might be able to limit its effects.

- Joint enquiry – often you haven't generated the problem so you are both in it together. Working with staff to determine what you could both do, can give a measure of control back.

ACTIVITY 3.2

Managing the individual's psychological contract and organisational change.

How do you check out on people's psychological contract to identify how they are feeling and what might be demotivating them?

Can you think of a situation where 'management by walking around' has helped you identify a problem that needed a response?

Do you give people a chance to air their feelings about changes and developments and do you plan together to find responses when they are unhappy?

Chapter summary

- Hersey and Blanchard's theory of situational leadership (Hersey and Blanchard, 1974 and 1993) is congruent with health and social care values and our culture of supervision.

- It requires flexibility in a leader so that they match leadership style with the needs of team members.

- Good delegation is essential to our services and to effective leadership.

- Psychological contract theory offers an individualised approach to maintaining staff motivation and also fits well with our supervisory practices.

FURTHER READING

Guest, D.E. and Conway, N. (2002) *Pressure at Work and the Psychological Contract.* London: CIPD.

Many managers have found psychological contract theory helpful in motivating and retaining staff. Guest and Conway are key proponents of the approach and for a summary and overview from the CIPD try: CIPD (2009) *The Psychological Contract.* Available at: **www.cipd.co.uk/subjects/empreltns/psycntrct/psycontr.htm**

Hersey, P. and Blanchard, K.H. (1993) *Management of Organisational Behaviour: Utilising Human Resources.* 6th edition. London: Prentice Hall.

Hersey and Blanchard's situational leadership approach has had a massive impact on leadership and supervision across the private and public sectors. This book explores their thinking in detail.

Chapter 4

The role and impo
of supervision

Ivan Gray

Supervision in a contended profession

Professional supervision is at the heart of health and social care. As the Chief Executives of Skills for Care and the Children's Workforce Development Council put it:

> *High quality supervision is one of the most important drivers in ensuring positive out-comes for people who use social care and children's services. It also has a crucial role to play in the development, retention and motivation of the workforce.*

> (SfC/CWDC, 2007, p3)

Supervision is defined as:

> *. . . an accountable process which supports, assures and develops the knowledge, skills and values of an individual, group or team. The purpose is to improve the quality of their work to achieve agreed objectives and outcomes. In social care and children's services this should optimise the capacity of people who use services to lead independent and fulfilling lives.*

> (SfC/CWDC, 2007, p4)

Supervision is a focal point where the key components of the service meet and all the key activities and relationships are co-ordinated. The centre of this crucial interface is the manager responsible for the team or unit, although supervision requires commitment, respect from all participants if it is to be of benefit to the organisation and individual. aps here that your management time is expended to greatest effect and it is here your leadership style will have the greatest influence on the working experience of ur team or unit members.

It should also be a place of conflict if it is to be a healthy place. For our services and profession are by nature contested and service provision and its management necessarily involves battling with dilemmas, ambiguity, conflicting interests, incompatible expectations and judgement calls where there are not options that can rationally be chosen as the 'best' (Healy, 2000). It is in supervision that these conflicts, that are the life and soul of social care, are identified and responded to. These conflicts begin with the very nature of supervision in social care, before even a staff member and their caseload has appeared in sight.

Supervision as a forum for dialogue

Habermas (1989), a social political philosopher of the Frankfurt School of neo-Marxist thinkers, draws attention to the tendency in modern society for public places where politics could be debated to disappear – and be replaced with 'one-way' methods of communication. In other words, debate and dialogue are being dominated by the mass media and have become 'top down'.

This is a good way of thinking about supervision in social care, as a crucial forum for dialogue where the professional and the organisation meet. It has been argued that 'managerialism' has come to dominate supervision and that professional needs and issues have been marginalised. For example, professional reflection and personal development have been replaced by performance measurement, performance management and resource management.

However, it can also be argued that supervision has never been entirely a professional domain. Its value is that it is where managerial and organisational perspectives and needs meet and are resolved. Part of the tension that is endemic to supervision is competition for the space and the agenda by the range of demands that both the social worker and social work manager must respond to.

One could argue that in the past, professional reflection and personal development dominated, at the expense of case management and performance management, to the detriment of professional practice and the service. Managers and professionals have responsibility to ensure that there is a balance between the competing but mutual needs that supervision must accommodate to be effective and it is hard to see any of these needs as expendable from anyone's perspective (Figure 4.1).

Veronica Coulshed draws attention to the uniqueness of our culture of supervision and its versatility and argues that it needs to be celebrated (Coulshed et al., 2006, p162). Our previous points attest to this. We would argue that supervision is crucial and central to effective management.

Management only conflicts with supervision and professional needs when it is crude and controlling, in other words, when it is not developmental. If supervision is managed by

Figure 4.1 Why do we need supervision?

you as a learning and development activity then it can be enabling with management and professional outcomes merging. Business and other professions could greatly benefit from a similar model and the benefit would be in business outcomes as well as in personal development and wellbeing.

Yet, professional supervision can be undermining, disempowering and an opportunity to misuse power (Hawkins and Shohet, 2000). Appraisal can be particularly damaging and needs to be approached from an ethical standpoint (Mullins, 2007). There are also good grounds for approaching supervision critically as there is reason to think that the formal model is not subject to enough critical scrutiny. If personal reflection and personal development are too easily lost from the agenda, opportunities to discuss values and the wider social and political effects of interventions are also easily mislaid (Phillipson, 2002).

Time is also undoubtedly a problem and it is this that is probably most responsible for undermining supervision, just as it is the chief culprit in explaining unhelpful leadership styles more generally. There is a danger that 'under pressure' managers will tend to dominate supervision and rather than allowing time for exploration and reflection jump straight to solutions and ways forward that are their answers or standard responses.

Supervision needs plenty of time and it needs careful planning and review. It may well be that one particular need will dominate a supervision session in which case other sessions will need a different agenda to compensate. You'll need to keep an eye on the range of needs in Figure 4.1 to ensure your supervision is balanced over time.

It is also very easy to make shortage of time an excuse for unbalanced supervision. However, there is no better use of a manager's time and it is not a good place to shortcut. You would be hard pressed to identify another single activity that is so important – in fact it could be seen as 80 per cent of your job. If you did pretty much nothing else but supervise effectively, things could go very well for the team. What often happens is what should be dealt with, and could be dealt with, efficiently in supervision ends up dealt with 'on the hop' in informal supervision. This often does not allow for proper communication and joint consideration of the issues.

Supervision is also the biggest training and development opportunity; it is more powerful than other activities not only because it co-ordinates and integrates all other options but because it is where the individual makes sense of things and actually learns. With a good enabling supervisor personal growth and development is maximised and the staff member becomes more and more confident and more able to work independently. This will relieve pressures on the manager in the long term.

As members of staff develop and are more able to take control and lead supervision, it becomes possible to meet the needs or objectives of supervision more readily. In effect, new, inexperienced staff members will at first need much more of your supervision time, but this will decrease over time. If you work a system of a set period of time per month for each person, it might be worth considering a different approach. It makes little sense to give staff whose needs vary a set menu.

Management systems and priorities can certainly divert a manager's attention. To illustrate, providing information for performance management can take a lot of a manager's time. In this sense we work in organisations that are becoming increasingly managed from the top and this can draw resources away from supporting 'frontline' staff to supporting senior managers dealing with strategy, planning, politics and resourcing. Under these circumstances a team manager or leader may need to develop a supervisory team that takes the weight of supervision with them so they can respond to the needs of middle and senior managers.

This type of supervisory team needs organising and developing. If people are supervised by different people it is all too easy for issues to be lost, the balance of supervision disturbed and the relationship at the heart of supervision not to grow and develop. It has often been pointed out that supervision is not counselling or therapy. This is a good point as supervision must also embrace the management of the task *and* service outcomes. But supervision is very similar to counselling and therapy in that it demands sharing and openness, careful listening and challenge, joint problem solving and decision making, and it also reaches for personal growth. In sum, it demands a trusting and enabling supervisory relationship. How can this be achieved if every supervision session your team find themselves working with somebody different?

If staff members work with one supervisor except in extreme circumstances, you will still need to be active in managing the supervisory team, ensuring consistency of provision and that supervisory team members develop their skills, check out problems and reflect on their practice. Sharing supervision with senior practitioners can free up firstline management time for other things, but it adds another team that needs to be led and supervised.

An endangered species in this pressured supervisory climate can be the management of emotion. Time pressures and more procedurally driven and outcome-orientated services can mean that the culture of supervision changes to downplay the importance of emotion in our work. Managerialism is often represented as undermining the amount of supervision time devoted to learning and development. What is often missed is the impact managerialism can have on supervision by undermining the management of the emotion that is essential to practice.

If the emotion of our work is not managed there can be considerable impact on our effectiveness. We don't work well if we are frightened, depressed, grieving or frozen. Distress, if not responded too, can undermine our practice and our health (Hawkins and Shohet, 2000, pp191–95). It is not just that our work involves traumatic and negative experiences, sharing other people's grief and pain. The change process itself is an emotional experience – the more fundamental the change, the more emotion. So, if our people are to respond effectively to service changes, emotion must be managed.

Expression of negative emotion is crucial in allowing people to come to terms with a situation and move on from it. Stress can result from unexpressed negative emotion and undermine our health. If we are stressed we do not have the energy to change and develop. The emotional impact of change on individuals is also significant and without expression can become a block to personal learning and development. It is perhaps ironic that just as the business world discovers 'EQ' or 'emotional intelligence' and promotes it as contributing directly to business outcomes (Goleman, 1998), in social care we might just be allowing it to be de-prioritised.

Crucially accepting and analysing the impact of emotion on our work is an essential component in managing practice. The people we work with can sometimes be frightening or they can seek to manipulate us. This can mean that we perhaps don't enquire into some things closely enough or we accept comfortable explanations. We can even become so anxious that we stop visiting them. Conversely, we can have such a good relationship with someone that we can avoid challenging them or see only the positives in a situation. Supervision must be a place where emotions can be expressed and explored.

REFLECTION POINT *4.1*

Can you identify situations in your professional practice when your emotional reaction to a situation or your relationship with a family or someone who uses services affected your judgement?

What helped or would have helped you to recognise this and change your practice?

Negative and unhelpful behaviours in supervision

Tsui (2005) takes rather a pessimistic view on the power relations in supervision and suggests that supervisors have dominant decision-making power in supervision (Tsui, 2001). However, in his concluding chapter he notes the lack of empirical research particularly into the didactic relationship between supervisor and supervisee. Drawing on work by Kadushin (1979) and Hawthorne (1975), Tsui (2001) identifies how the range of games played by supervisors and supervisees, generated by disparities in power and influence, can undermine effective supervision. Games benefit one or both parties by allowing them to avoid issues or by providing emotional rewards or feelings of superiority, so both parties often collude. They can be the basis of a pattern that shapes each supervision session, undermining effectiveness. Based on Tsui (2005 and 2001, pp96–106) and drawing on Kadushin (1979) and Hawthorne (1975), some common games played by supervisors are:

Games of abdication

It's them up there in HQ	Supervisor would like to agree with the supervisee or do things differently, but is blocked by an unsympathetic organisation and senior managers.
Poor me	Supervisor seeks sympathy of supervisee for their shortcomings and personal problems seeking the supervisee's support and protection.
I'm just one of the gang	Supervisor gives up their responsibility and distances themselves from the organisation. This can be combined with excessive socialising with the team.
So what is your professional opinion?	Supervisor never gives direction or expresses an opinion but always asks the supervisee what they think first and then agrees with their viewpoint.
Now that reminds me of the time when. . . .	Supervisor dominates supervision with stories, anecdotes and gossip so that real issues cannot be addressed.

Games of power

You take notes as I run through the action points	Supervisor uses power of their position to dominate supervision, instructing the supervisee what to do and leaving no opportunity for discussion.
I may have to report this	Supervisor threatens to report concerns to senior managers leaving supervisee in a state of constant anxiety.
Father/mother knows best	Supervisor claims to be protecting and helping the supervisee and to be working in their best interests while dominating supervision and decision making.

However, supervisees also have power and can use a supervisor's need to be liked or their insecurity to manipulate them or else they can draw a supervisor into a game where the supervisee becomes dependent on them and does not need to take responsibility. Based on Tsui (2005 and 2001, pages 96–106) and drawing on Kadushin (1979) and Hawthorne (1975), some common games played by supervisees are:

Supervisee's games

Come the revolution	Supervisee seduces supervisor into ignoring the demands of the organisation, which is painted as reactionary and part of the problem.
The mutual admiration society	Supervisee builds a supportive relationship based on flattery that boosts the supervisor's ego but undermines their authority.
If you knew the Children's Act like I know the Children's Act	Supervisee dominates the supervisor with their superior knowledge or takes the moral high ground on a value issue.
I have brought a little list	Supervisee dominates the agenda with questions so the supervisor has no time for their own agenda or to explore areas the supervisee finds more sensitive.
Heading them off at the pass or 'mea culpa'	Supervisee confesses their faults and errors before the supervisor can raise them, keeping control and mitigating the impact by their evident self-awareness.
It's all so complex and confusing	Supervisee reviews a range of different or conflicting opinions and perspectives that muddy the issue and then leaves the supervisor to try and reconcile them.

The point about games is that they have to be plausible in order to work. They are often a misuse of legitimate behaviour or a stance that is to a degree reasonable. The pay off for us can also mean we are reluctant to identify and challenge them or they can be effective in disempowering us and preventing us changing things. This makes them hard to deal with yet they can be very damaging. Keeping the quality of your supervisory relationships under review, including negative behaviours, is therefore important.

REFLECTION POINT 4.2

Review the games above; can you identify any in your practice and in your team's practice?

What can you do to engage the team in identifying negative behaviours and improving the quality of your supervisory relationships?

How can you use your own supervision to help with this?

The new supervision unit

One way to try and bring consistency to activities and increase effectiveness is the production of standards to define good practice. The Children's Workforce Development Council and Skills for Care have jointly introduced a supervision unit designed to provide a model of good practice and to assist in auditing and improving supervision (SfC/CWDC, 2007). If it is reasonable to see supervisory skills and practice as central to the management of social care then reviewing your practice against these national standards should be a crucial activity.

It is important that we take full advantage of this new unit as it has considerable potential in helping us improve supervision practices. However, we do currently practise in a management culture that is more than a bit obsessed with the production of standards or competencies. Anything that moves is likely to find itself with standards that pinpoint how precisely it should move forwards! While standards can provide an invaluable point of reference in managing an activity there are some fundamental problems as well as benefits associated with this culture.

- The phrase 'standards can provide an invaluable point of reference in managing an activity' is important. Standards only assist you in managing. They cannot replace your judgement or manage for you. There is a temptation to think that because we have standards something useful has happened. It's what you do with them that counts.

- Standards tend to be seen as somehow 'scientific' and that because a working party of experts has devised them they genuinely define an activity area. Yet the next working party will probably rewrite them to give them a slightly different slant – partly because it will be a different working party – partly because there will be new issues around influencing people's thinking. In reality they offer only one definition of good practice and there can be many significant areas they leave out completely. For instance, the Effective Supervision Unit does not cover managing service development projects or managing a supervisory team.

- Not only do standards often fail to identify all the dimensions of good practice it can also be argued that they can't succeed in defining it. Standards contain layers of definition that attempt to offer ever more detailed descriptions of an activity, but perhaps somewhere along the line they need professional understanding and judgement to be meaningful.

- This tendency to appear scientific and to offer a definition of good practice means they are illusory. Policy makers and senior managers can easily think that something useful has happened because standards have been formulated and disseminated but reality can be very different. Just because they are there doesn't mean anyone uses them. People often 'tick the boxes' and use standards very superficially.

Therefore, the introduction of standards may not necessarily improve practice and the impact of the new supervision unit could be minimal. Yet Haringey Children's Services Area Review (Ofsted, 2008) concluded that there was a need to:

establish rigorous arrangements for management of performance across all agencies, which ensure that the quality of practice is evaluated and reported regularly and reliably, and that accountability for each action is defined and monitored.

And to:

assure the competence of service and team managers in conducting rigorous and evaluative supervision and monitoring of safeguarding practice.

(Ofsted, 2008, p5)

Lord Laming's progress report on the protection of children in England recommended that:

The Department for Children, Schools and Families should revise Working Together to Safeguard Children *to set out the elements of high quality supervision focused on case planning, constructive challenge and professional development.*

(Lord Laming, 2009, p86)

There is, therefore, a need for robust analysis of the underlying quality of service provision rather than reliance on performance measures. So, we need to reach beyond the superficial picture standards and performance measures provide and use standards effectively. What does this involve?

Making standards work – people problem solve not standard solve

All that standards do is aid problem solving by offering you a description of good practice to start things off. It is the actions of managers and staff involved that will make standards meaningful and allow them to impact on practice. So, for instance, if you look at Table 4.1 and performance criterion b on page 61, 'Develop, implement and review written agreements for supervision', we can imagine two scenarios. A manager and staff member could sit down and ask themselves 'have we got a supervision contract?'. Because there is a standard one provided by their organisation that they sign, that states the agreed frequency and length of supervision, they could conclude, 'yes we have' and tick the box. In contrast, there could be a discussion about whether the contract is useful and shaping supervision to meet the needs of the manager and staff member. This might include questions about whether supervision is long enough and frequent enough but could also encompass whether the staff member has particular learning needs that should be allowed for. In the second example, the standard offers a prompt but the dialogue between the manager and the staff member gives the performance criteria depth and allows them to genuinely problem solve and bring improvements. The same applies to the situation where your manager is exploring with you your supervisory practice. You can either conclude, 'all is well; I am using the standards and auditing team practice against them' or there can be meaningful discussion about how effective the standards and subsequent audit have been, what the risks might be, what the targets for improvement are and what support you and the team might need to introduce them.

The difficulty you may be struggling with is how do you find the time for this in-depth approach, given the everyday pressures of doing the job and responding to crises? To look at it another way, what is the point of a 'quick fix' that doesn't improve anything?

Accepting limited time as a given, perhaps the best way forward is to have a long-term plan for audit and improvement that is realistic, but that gives 'quality of supervision' the priority it deserves – as perhaps the most crucial factor in improving services and meeting the needs of users and carers.

The new Effective Supervision Unit (SfC/CWDC, 2007) and an auditing framework you can use with your team have been provided below in Table 4.1. We have provided some commentary against each performance criteria to provide prompts for you and your team. You can use this audit tool in a number of ways. You could:

- complete it yourself to review your own practice;
- give it to the team to introduce them to the Effective Supervision Unit;
- work through it and discuss it in a team meeting so everyone is tuned in to the standards (this may demand time in several team meetings);
- ask people to make a judgement of how effective their supervision is and discuss it individually in supervision with each team member;
- audit the team and produce a summary of results and points people have made in the notes.

You should also refer to the guidance offered in Providing Effective Supervision (SfC /CWDC, 2007). Available from: **www.cwdcouncil.org.uk/assets/0000/2832/Providing_ Effective_Supervision_unit.pdf**

Clinical supervision

Clinical supervision in the NHS can be differentiated from supervision in social care, but they have common origins in that both have evolved from a psychodynamic model designed to support and develop psychotherapists (Rolfe *et al.*, 2001). Unlike the social care model, however, in clinical supervision management functions are separated out and ideally clinical supervision should not be imposed or used to support performance management and appraisal; its focus is developing professional practice through the support of a fellow practitioner and its content is confidential. Clinical supervision is:

> *a formal process of professional support and learning which enables individual practitioners to develop knowledge and competence, assume responsibility for their own practice and enhance consumer protection and safety of care in complex clinical situations. It is central to the process of learning and to the scope of the expansion of practice and should be seen as a means of encouraging self assessment, analytical and reflective skills.*

> (Vision for the Future, DH, 1993, p5)

However, clinical supervision needs to be set in the broader context of clinical governance:

> *Clinical governance is an umbrella term for everything that helps to maintain and improve high standards of patient care. It covers a whole range of quality improvement activities that many nurses are already doing – for example, clinical audit and practice development. It also provides a framework to draw these activities together in a more co-ordinated way.*

> (RCN, 2003b, p7)

Clinical governance, therefore, embraces clinical supervision, yet as Waskett (2009) citing Robinson (2005) notes, the practice of regular clinical supervision is more of an intention than reality – often for good reasons. Beyond problems of implementation Waskett (2009) also notes that there are no clear guidelines to promote confidence in clinical supervision among pressured managers, nor universally accepted definitions. The key issue is how to link clinical governance with clinical supervision (Waskett, 2009).

Waskett's solution to the problem of linking clinical supervision to clinical governance is not so much to link it as to leave it freestanding. While clinical supervision needs the support and intervention by managers to ensure that it happens and can play its part in clinical governance, it is separate from management supervision and clearly confidential. Rather he describes it as 'supportive' supervision and suggests that all clinicians should have regular line management and access to clinical advice from senior practitioners – different from supportive supervision (Waskett, 2009).

We therefore have dual systems that are not necessarily linked in any way. However, as McSherry *et al.* identify:

> *The challenge for implementing clinical supervision within the clinical governance framework is in breaking down the barriers in the organisation.*

> (McSherry *et al.*, 2002 p30)

The Royal College of Nursing (RCN), as one of their key principles for implementing clinical governance, propose that:

> *Clinical governance demands true partnerships between all professional groups, between clinical staff and managers, and between patients and clinical staff.*

> (RCN, 2003b, p7)

This takes us to the nub of the matter. If clinical supervision is freestanding and confidential, carrying issues that arise from it into the more general management of the service and into clinical governance is down to the individual professional. They are the only ones who can join the two up, carrying issues from clinical supervision into management supervision. If they do not do so, it can be difficult for managers to act as a broker with the wider organisation and the network of providers, picking up on service delivery and practice problems, as they will not be aware of them. Receptive managers and clinical governance systems that allow professionals to be heard will help, but the onus is on the professional.

However, in reality, clinical supervision can often be provided by managers and if it is in your contract of employment that you receive clinical supervision, records can be used in disciplinary hearings (RCN, 2003a). They can also be used in court proceedings (RCN, 2003a). Someone providing clinical supervision is also bound by professional codes of practice that expect them to intervene if they become aware of unprofessional practices, so it is perhaps the case that clinical supervision and management supervision are not so far apart in practice as they are sometimes presented.

Obviously clinical supervision is essential if a team or unit manager is not a qualified practitioner, so in multi-disciplinary teams clinical supervision becomes a necessity. Managers of integrated services can, however, find the separation of management from clinical supervision problematic, given our points above and dependency on the individual practitioner to link them together.

We have used social care's Effective Supervision Unit to explore the detail of supervision practice as it is a comprehensive model. Its dimensions are actually equally useful for clinical supervision as there is a common agenda across health and social care e.g. participation of patients and people who use services. However, Hawkins and Shohet (2000), which is recommended for further reading, offers a model and approach that encompasses all the helping professions and their audit tool may prove helpful as an alternative model as it focuses on the culture of supervision, process and the quality of the relationship (see Chapter 7, Table 7.1 in Hawkins and Shohet, 2000).

Competencies that support clinical supervision may well also be part of post outlines for NHS staff developed using the dimensions of the NHS Knowledge and Skills Framework. They are the basis for appraisal and personal development planning and so can also provide a basis for auditing supervisory practice (DH, 2004).

Reviewing your own supervision

As part of the audit, it is a good idea to review your own supervision, i.e. the supervision you receive, and set some objectives to improve it. The guidance with the unit (SfC/CWDC, 2007) states that it is applicable to all managers but particularly relevant to first line managers. This may encourage the situation where the unit is used to shape the practice of first line managers and supervisors but not the middle managers that supervise them. Given our discussions about the need to address the real quality issues in supervision and the responsibility of middle managers to make sure this happens this would seem to be very unhelpful. The Effective Supervision Unit needs to be used to audit and improve practice at every level if it is to have a lasting impact on service quality.

A later chapter (Chapter 9) looks at management development and it is part of the good practice model in the Leadership and Management National Strategy (SfC, 2004) that you receive good supervision. Try to make the Effective Supervision Unit the standards that shape your own supervision as well as your team's and apply the same evaluative processes. Reflecting on your own experience of being supervised will also help inform your practice in supervising your team.

In the next chapter we explore each performance criteria of the Effective Supervision Unit in some depth.

ACTIVITY 4.1

The audit tool below is made up of three tables and has been adapted from the Skills for Care and Children's Workforce Development Council (2007) 'Providing Effective Supervision' unit of competence. Each table has a different focus. We provide a commentary on each of the performance criteria and space for your own notes. Use the audit tool in Table 4.1 to evaluate and improve the quality of your practice as a supervisor. Rate yourself on a scale of 1–5 – 1 being a strength and 5 needing radical improvement.

Also, how could you use this tool to improve the quality of the supervision that you receive?

Table 4.1 Implement supervision systems and processes

Performance criteria	Commentary	Notes
a. Implement supervision in the context of organisational policies, performance management and workforce development.	You need to locate and familiarise yourself with the organisation's supervision, appraisal, probationary and personal development policies and procedures.	
b. Develop, implement and review written agreements for supervision.	It is usual to have a supervision contract that summarises arrangements and responsibilities. They can be rudimentary, simply stating frequency, length and who has responsibility for setting them up. More complex contracts cover cancellation procedures, preparation and so on. Others may set ground rules for the relationship and identify such things as areas of interest or for personal development.	
c. Ensure supervision records and agreed decisions are accurate and completed promptly.	You need to keep a record, at the very least, of decisions made in supervision and whoever has responsibility for recording them will need to see they are signed off. Usually it is the supervisor/s' responsibility, but you should have a signed copy for your personal file or at least access to them. Areas of disagreement should also be recorded.	
d. Enable workers to reflect on supervision issues and act on outcomes.	Your supervisor/s should encourage and give you space to reflect on your practice and identify your strengths, weaknesses and development needs and review your actions and care plans.	
e. Monitor and review own supervision practice and learning, reflecting on the	There should be opportunity for you to comment on the quality of the supervision you have	

Table 4.1 (continued)

Performance criteria	Commentary	Notes
processes and implement improvements to supervision.	received, and a chance to work together to improve it.	
f. Identify wider issues and raise them appropriately in the organisation and with other stakeholders.	Your manager or supervisor should act as a broker identifying with you practice issues that need to be picked up on in the organisation more widely, so that the quality of services can be improved.	
g. Enable access to specialist supervision, support, advice or consultation as required. Specialist supervision – can include peer, therapeutic or clinical supervision.	Specialist supervision can be an excellent way to develop your practice and can also be essential in some roles and situations which demand more support that your manager or usual supervisor/s can provide.	

Table 4.2 Develop, maintain and review effective supervision relationships

Performance criteria	Commentary	Notes
a. Create a positive environment for workers to develop and review their practice.	Supervision should challenge your practice but it should be a positive encounter that you value and where challenge is matched with encouragement and support. You should be encouraged to take responsibility and take control in reviewing and evaluating your practice.	
b. Clarify boundaries and expectations of supervision, including confidentiality.	It pays to review your previous experiences of supervision and what works or doesn't work for you. Good supervision contracts will cover these broader issues as well as clarifying confidentiality and what are (or not) suitable matters for supervision.	

Table 4.2 (continued)

Performance criteria	Commentary	Notes
c. Ensure relationships are conducted in an open and accountable way.	Both you and your supervisor/s are accountable for your practice so the relationship must be strong enough for you to share the details of your practice, including problems you are experiencing. Hidden practice can be dangerous practice.	
d. Help workers to identify and overcome blocks to performance, such as work conflicts and other pressures.	Effective practice is not just down to you. Others can influence your effectiveness in a positive fashion, as well as negatively. Your supervisor/s should also be able to help with these broader issues.	
e. Assist workers to understand the emotional impact of their work and seek appropriate specialist support if needed.	It is a tough job – one that can affect us all deeply. The emotion of your work needs to be on the agenda for the sake of your own health, but also because it can impact on your practice. Some people who use services can be manipulative or frightening – openness about their impact on you will help ensure your practice is purposeful and objective.	
f. Ensure the *duty of care* is met for the well-being of workers.	Your employer has responsibility for your health and safety including safe working arrangements outside of the office, stress and workload balance.	
g. Recognise diversity and demonstrate *anti-discriminatory practice* in the supervisory relationship.	Supervision should respond to your individual needs and actively seek not to discriminate against you.	

Table 4.2 (continued)

Performance criteria	Commentary	Notes
h. Give and receive constructive feedback on the supervisory relationship and supervision practice.	Both you and your supervisor/s need to reflect on and discuss the quality of your supervision and aim to improve it over time.	
i. Audit and develop own skills and knowledge to supervise workers, including those from other disciplines when required.	Your manager should be seeking to develop their skills as a supervisor. You can help them do this by giving them positive and constructive feedback, identifying areas where supervision can be improved. Having good supervisory practice on the agenda is also useful as the supervision of others will become one of your responsibilities as your career progresses.	

Table 4.3 Develop, maintain and review practice and performance through supervision

Performance criteria	Commentary	Notes
a. Ensure workloads are effectively allocated, managed and reviewed.	It is very difficult to come up with a definitive workload management system that determines fair workloads for all, as your work will be too complex and variable to be easily categorised and measured. Good dialogue that regularly addresses what you are being allocated, how, and whether it is manageable, is essential.	
b. Monitor and enable workers' competence to assess, plan, implement and review their work.	Your performance as a case manager should not only be evaluated, but there should be opportunities for you to develop and improve it.	

Table 4.3 (continued)

Performance criteria	Commentary	Notes
c. Ensure supervisor and workers are clear about accountability and the limits of their individual and organisational authority and duties.	Supervision is the best place to clarify any areas of confusion that can arise. Job descriptions and procedures are often not definitive – discussion works.	
d. Ensure workers understand and demonstrate *anti-discriminatory practice.*	Your qualifying course will have given a lot of attention to this topic, but do not let it drift – make it an explicit feature of your supervision agenda.	
e. Ensure work *with people who use services* is outcomes-focused and that their views are taken account of in service design and delivery.	Work with individuals needs to be achieving outcomes agreed with them. Supervision also needs to address the broader development of services and service quality and people who use services can be involved in this.	
f. Identify risks to users of services and workers and take appropriate action.	Risks need to be clearly identified, methodically assessed and actions agreed to manage them effectively. Any assessment and agreed plans should be recorded.	
g. Obtain and give timely feedback on workers' practice, including feedback from people who use services.	Both you and your supervisor have a responsibility to evaluate your practice and improve it. Actively seeking feedback on your performance (especially from people who use services and carers) and discussing and acting on it is a joint responsibility.	
h. Identify learning needs and integrate them within development plans.	It is important that you are clear about what areas of your practice you want to develop. Make sure your learning objectives and development plans are focused on these needs.	
i. Create opportunities for learning and development.	You should be offered and take opportunity to make use of a	

Table 4.3 (continued)

Performance criteria	Commentary	Notes
	range of on and off the job development opportunities. Their effectiveness in meeting your needs should be evaluated.	
j. Assess and review performance, challenge poor practice and ensure improvements in standards.	Supervision should encompass appraisal. Your performance should be evaluated jointly against agreed standards on the basis of readily identified evidence. The evaluation and agreed improvement plans should be recorded together with any differences of opinion.	
k. Enable multi-disciplinary, integrated and collaborative working as appropriate.	This is essential to service quality and demands regular review and evaluation. Chapter 6 of this book will no doubt help here as multi-disciplinary working is an essential element of practice. Many quality problems originate here and many quality improvements lie with more effective multi-agency and collaborative working.	

Chapter summary

- Good supervision is essential to service quality and provides a forum where problems and conflicts can be resolved.

- There are negative behaviours that can undermine supervision and can come from both supervisor and supervisee.

- The Effective Supervision Unit (SfC/CWDC, 2007) offers a valuable tool that can do much to improve supervision if we use it well.

- Clinical supervision is fundamentally different from managerial supervision and needs to be supported by management supervision.

- Reviewing and improving the quality of the supervision we receive as managers is essential and often neglected.

Skills for Care/CWDC (2007) *Effective Supervision*, **www.skillsforcare.org.uk/files/Effective%20 Supervision%20unit.pdf** pp13–17. London: Skills for Care.

Visit the Skills for Care or CWDC websites to explore the Effective Supervision Unit and the guidance that supports it.

Chapter 5

Implementing supervision systems and processes and developing effective supervisory relationships

Ivan Gray

C H A P T E R   O B J E C T I V E S

This chapter will help you address the following National Occupational Standards for Management and Leadership.

- B6 Provide leadership in your area of responsibility.
- D1 Develop productive working relationships with colleagues.
- SfC and CWDC Effective Supervision Unit.

This chapter will also help you address the following Principles of Social Care Management.

- Value people, recognise and actively develop potential.
- Develop and maintain awareness and keep in touch with service users and staff.
- Inspire staff.
- Provide an environment and time in which to develop reflective practice, professional skills and the ability to make judgments in complex situations.

Introduction

In the previous chapter we argued that supervision is central and pivotal to effective management in health and social care. Improving your team's understanding of supervision and your supervisory practices should always be on your agenda. In this chapter we explore each of the performance criteria of the Effective Supervision Unit that we introduced towards the end of Chapter 4 in the light of the guidance notes that support the standards. The chapter is divided into two main sections to match the first two elements that make up the unit.

- Implementing supervision systems and processes.

- Develop, maintain and review effective supervision relationships.

The final element of the unit, 'Develop, maintain and review practice and performance through supervision' will be looked at in more detail in Chapter 6. Throughout Chapters 5 and 6, we take the performance criteria for each element and discuss them. Our intention is to try and ensure that we avoid the 'tick box' approach to using standards and analyse our practice in depth in order to plan for improvement.

Take this opportunity to give depth to your practice by determining what you consider to be the essential parameters of good supervision practice. Explore each of the three elements with us and make some notes about what you think are the key issues. You may also wish to share parts of this chapter and Chapter 6 with your team to prepare or brief them as part of a team development exercise.

Implementing supervision systems and processes

Implement supervision in the context of organisational policies, performance management and workforce development

It is important to ensure that you are adhering to organisational policies on supervision. Here you also have an opportunity to be a little more searching. Supervision is where a number of policies meet and where you have opportunity with your staff members to explore how effectively they are being implemented, so try to take a broader view and ask:

- does general policy awareness and policy implementation figure in supervision?

- do the policies that directly support supervision – i.e. supervision policy *per se*, plus appraisal, and performance management, capability management and personal development planning – fit together and support your practice?

- are you using supervision to identify training and development needs and inform training audits?

- does regular supervision explore performance and developmental issues that then feed appraisal and personal development planning or are they separated out so they become separate events?

- do you take time to explore performance targets, business or unit plans and organisational strategy?

- do you identify together situations where policy is stalling or not being adhered to and intervene?

Develop, implement and review written agreements for supervision

It is too easy for a written agreement to offer little more than the required frequency and length and for this to be standardised. The example provided in the guidance notes for the

Effective Supervision Unit goes further than this and it is worth noting that the frequency and length of supervision should vary according to the needs of the individual (SfC/CWDC, 2007, p8). Frequency and length aside, the example contract covers how managers and staff members should prepare for supervision, what should be covered in it, agenda setting, value issues to be addressed, how disagreements will be dealt with, how sessions will be recorded, what will be recorded, cancellation procedures, how and when supervision will be reviewed and the policies to be followed. Other dimensions worth considering are:

- what has made supervision a positive experience for manager and staff member in the past? What has proved difficult or what negative experiences should be avoided?
- has the staff member particular learning needs and what is their learning style?
- what are the strengths and weaknesses of the individual's practice?
- what do they see as their biggest challenges?

The contract should be regularly reviewed to see that it is being complied with. When supervision is audited i.e. reviewed and evaluated, an improvement plan should be included in the contract.

Ensure supervision records and agreed decisions are accurate and completed promptly

The guidance notes (SfC/CWDC, 2007, p9) suggest that the supervisor should record the content of the sessions and that this record should be accurate and completed promptly. Actions, timescales and responsibilities should be clear. Ideally this record should be typed up on the basis of notes immediately after the session. Conversely, notes can be taken in the session and then signed off and actions agreed at the end. Records of previous sessions should be reviewed at the beginning of subsequent meetings to ensure any agreed actions have been taken. In exploring whether notes should be taken in the session the guidance suggests it is a matter for personal judgement. It can be very disruptive to have someone typing or writing during a session as their attention may not be on what others are saying. Pauses at the end of case discussion or an agenda item to write down key issues and actions can serve to offer a summary and aid the process rather than disrupt it. Be sure there is opportunity to record disagreements clearly and what will be done about them.

Enable workers to reflect on supervision issues and act on outcomes

Agreeing a contract and recording supervision are relatively tangible. This performance criteria is about the quality of the relationships and the supervisory process. So, how do you enable workers to reflect on issues raised in supervision and then act on them? Issues can be seen as case discussions, the quality of the supervision process, policy issues, developmental plans and so on – so they can be quite wide ranging. It is good practice to allow people space to reflect and listen. For some staff this will be enough – others will need help and this will mean asking them the right questions. We have included a list of questions to help encourage reflection in Appendix 1. How you enable people to act on outcomes is dependent on you both being clear what the outcomes are and expressing them as actions with timescales. Enabling people can involve you in a wide range of activities e.g. coaching, linking up with specialists or colleagues with expertise, helping them find information, identifying what might be blocking an action and trying to find a way around it. A good question to ask yourself is what evidence have you got that you are enabling people to reflect on issues and act on outcomes? Asking those you supervise is of course a good idea, but rather than quickly concluding 'yes', can you identify an aspect of your staff member's practice that you have enabled them to reflect on and where they improved their practice?

Monitor and review own supervision practice and learning, reflecting on the processes and implement improvements to supervision

There are perhaps three key dimensions to this. A crucial one is you finding time after each supervision session to reflect on the quality of supervision. This personal reflection could be targeted against particular performance criteria in the Effective Supervision Unit (SfC/CWDC, 2007) or else you may have already identified some targets for improvement that will give you a focus. We have provided some key questions in Appendix 2 to help with this. Another dimension is ensuring the quality of supervision is an important part of your own supervision. This should provide you with an objective viewpoint to aid your reflection and it should also allow you some personal support and an opportunity to problem solve if you get stuck. Finally, given that the Effective Supervision Unit (SfC/CWDC, 2007) provides you with good practice standards against which you can judge the quality of supervision it is important that any evaluation is evidenced. This brings in your team. While at the end of each session it is a good idea to check out that individuals are happy about how the session has been conducted and whether it has met their needs, there is opportunity to periodically review supervision more methodically. Activity 4.1 at the end of the previous chapter is designed to facilitate this.

It is also possible to mobilise your team to work on this performance criteria together. For instance, apart from reviewing supervision regularly with individuals against the standards you could dedicate part of a team meeting to do this. This will allow you not only to have an improvement plan for each individual, perhaps included as part of their individual contract, but also a team improvement plan. A good idea might be to involve your manager in this process. As an example of how it might work, you could leave the team alone to evaluate practice against the standards while doing the same with your manager or your supervisory team, then compare views. Don't let the 'tick box' syndrome take over here or you will be wasting your time. The real outcome you are aiming for is a team improvement plan and an improvement plan for each staff member that are both owned and which people are working on. Remember it is as much a professional responsibility as it is a manager's to ensure the quality of supervision. Their behaviours and actions can have as much impact as your's. Plans should be balanced with as many actions lying with the team as with the manager.

Identify wider issues and raise them appropriately in the organisation and with other stakeholders

You are very much a broker between your team, organisation and provider network. Team effectiveness and the quality of individual practice is dependent on the network of activities that make up the service and this reaches out beyond the organisation. It will be important for your team to see you identify and respond to problems and also identify service improvements and action them. Supervision is a crucial forum where issues that impact negatively on practice or could enhance it can be identified, so it's a good idea to build these wider issues into the recording of your sessions. Again, combining this with team activity is a good way forward. Some issues need to be dealt with on an individual basis while others can be carried into team meetings as issues that need attention from everyone or can become possible development projects. You are likely to find yourself tackling a whole range of issues from problems with, or possible enhancements to support services e.g. human resource management, training and administration, to policy and working relationships with co-providers. You may even address relationships with senior managers and service strategy and business plans.

In summary, troubleshooting and planning for service improvement are as important a part of supervision as case management. If you give it time and energy your team will become proactive and engaged. Make sure you can be seen to act on issues, although this is not just down to you – the team can raise issues as well. You don't have to succeed; in fact you might find some issues are 'stuck' or only limited improvements can be made – just be honest about these. You have a responsibility to try and 'broker' or negotiate a way forward – you do not always have the power to make things happen. The realities of practice and your organisation's and co-provider's limitations are everyone's problems, not just yours. If you build a team of problem solvers with good supervision at its heart, the barriers to improvement will sometimes irritate and depress them but they won't stop them. Formal planning systems can assist you. Quality problems and developmental possibilities identified at a team level can be fed into service planning processes and service plans. Your manager needs to be proactive and to share in this, perhaps also regularly meeting with the team.

However, some issues or practices reported to you may be so severe they must be dealt with no matter what the organisational resistance. 'Whistleblowing' has become an important issue in public services as organisations can have the effect of making people reluctant to report quality problems. Supporting whistleblowers may well be one of your organisation's policies as there is much to be gained in protecting users, carers, staff and the organisation's reputation. The Social Care Institute for Excellence (SCIE) offer guidance on 'whistleblowing' (Cass *et al.*, 2009), which can be accessed from: **www.scie.org.uk/ publications/guides/guide15/whistleblowing/index.asp**.

They suggest that staff should be encouraged to report concerns and know they will be offered protection. You may be their first port of call and should be able to alert the wider organisation or managers in other organisations if a problem is identified. If you find yourself in a position where you are not listened to, you could find yourself needing to 'whistleblow'. This is a difficult step to take, full of dilemmas. An organisation called 'Public Concern at Work' (**www.pcaw.co.uk/**) offers you and your staff guidance and support. The Code of Practice for Social Care Workers states that staff must *use estab-lished processes and procedures to challenge and report dangerous, abusive, discriminatory or exploitative behaviour and practice* (GSCC, 2004, 3.2,). However, a GSCC poll reported that nearly 50 per cent of respondents' employers had not taken action when an operational difficulty or concerns about a colleague had been reported (GSCC, 2009). A similar proportion did not think their employer would take action if they did report something. Eighty-five per cent said they would feel able to report concerns about a colleague. The most common fears cited by those who said that they would not speak out were victimisation and reprisal (GSCC, 2009).

So, accepting how difficult this area of work is, you have an important role to play in ensuring actions are taken and the responsibility to do so. You will also need to protect staff who report issues. Accepting that it is also a difficult subject to broach, it perhaps demands a full and frank discussion with your team, given our clear, personal professional responsibilities. You need to have thought through the issues and determined the situations you might face and how you will respond.

Enable access to specialist supervision, support, advice or consultation as required

Specialist supervision can include peer, therapeutic or clinical supervision. Clearly, you are not the only source of supervision and expertise. Members of your team may well be specialists who need access to professional or clinical supervision that you cannot provide or else will be more experienced than you. They may be working on service development projects that need support and supervision from outside the team. There are valuable resources out there to mobilise and help enhance your staff members' expertise. Involving experienced members of your team in supervision can not only allow them to contribute their expertise, it can assist in their personal development as well. However, the responsibility for case and project management can still lie with you, so you need to be clear on agreed actions, progress and any risks that need to be identified and managed. You may still need to provide your staff member with supervision. When staff are being supervised by others, you need to be clear about responsibilities. There will need to be clear communication between all relevant parties to ensure issues do not get muddled or missed. Your staff member also has responsibility here to ensure good communication and continuity. Confidentiality in some clinical or supportive relationships can be a problem, however – in general it is better if agendas are recorded openly and shared. If you have a supervisory team that is providing your team's supervision this will need co-ordinating as a team. You will see that we have added some criteria at the end of Chapter 6 to address this dimension.

Develop, maintain and review effective supervisory relationships

This second part of this chapter looks at developing, maintaining and reviewing effective supervisory relationships and the nine performance criteria associated with them.

Create a positive environment for workers to develop and review their practice

The culture of supervision, or the environment you create for your team, is perhaps one of the most crucial dimensions. You can have carefully drafted contracts, beautiful recordings famed for their accuracy and evaluations to die for, but culture embraces the intangibles that make all the difference. It is a product of your relationship, so both you and your supervisees have a role to play in developing it, but your leadership is of crucial significance. So what does creating 'a positive environment' demand from you?

Firstly, you need to be positive about supervision yourself. You need to value and be enthusiastic about it and you need to be prepared to invest your time and energy to develop your practice. In essence, you are a role model. Beyond this, personal effectiveness is key to creating a positive environment and you should refer to Chapter 2.

The following additional issues are worth considering.

- Prepare carefully and think back and reflect on the last session, not just the discussion and the decisions made, but also the process.

- Are you welcoming when people join you? Settle them down with coffee or tea and some small talk.

- Is the environment comfortable and free from interruptions?

- Sit with a relaxed open body posture facing the person you are supervising, preferably without a desk between you.

- Listen carefully but remember how important non-verbal communication is.

- Stay aware of your own feelings throughout. You will often pick up on discomfort just as you will feel energised and engaged if it is going well.

- Give positive feedback wherever you can.

- Don't blame people for problems. Look towards solutions.

- Don't forget how useful it can be to summarise what has been said or agreed to make sure you both understand it. This can also be a good time to write down a summary of the discussion and any action points.

- End positively with a summary of what has been achieved, evaluating the session together. Thank your supervisee and look forward to the next session by summarising what you will do in the meantime and what will be on the next agenda.

Clarify boundaries and expectations of supervision, including confidentiality

The supervision contract can do much to shape the relationship by addressing these issues. Make sure it is clear what is welcomed as well as what should not be part of supervision e.g. make it clear that any emotional reactions should be discussed; that it is okay to get things wrong as long as it is shared and resolved.

There are some big limitations to confidentiality that need to be made explicit. You are responsible for the service and the wellbeing of not just users and carers but also the supervisee. The whole point of the exercise is to ensure that you are aware of problems and issues, and agree ways forward – so there is not really anything much that can be strictly confidential. You can undertake to try and keep personal matters as confidential as possible, including personal performance issues, and wherever possible to agree with your supervisee how issues are shared and who they are shared with. However, it must be clear that if necessary you will share issues with others if they affect anyone's wellbeing, even without your supervisee's permission. If you are being supervised properly you will also be sharing the session content with your supervisor and, since they will know the cases and who they are allocated to, there is little that cannot be shared with them. The only things that are not part of supervision are personal issues that are not impacting on practice. It is important that you do not get involved in helping to resolve someone's personal problems. However, you may well end up helping them to manage the impact of their personal lives on their work.

I have heard one team manager suggest that it is important that new social workers remember that they are not 'their practice teacher'. The implication of this is that supervision should focus on case management not reflection, coaching or exploration of value issues. This is rather a debatable position. One can readily see the point that work pressures can mean that it is desirable that there is a strong focus on case management and decision making, but quality supervision can demand all the features of a practice teacher relationship especially if someone is newly qualified. However, as supervisees develop their practice over time, they will become increasingly independent.

Ensure relationships are conducted in an open and accountable way

Careful recording of discussions and agreed actions that are signed by you both do much to ensure this. Both you and your supervisee should report back on actions you have taken and people you have spoken with. The other dimensions are helped by establishing clear boundaries as above, in that by agreeing boundaries you make it clear that you are both accountable and that records are organisational records. As such, records will be shared with your manager and are therefore open to wider scrutiny. An important element of accountability is honest reporting even if things have gone badly. Openness needs to encompass personal emotions and reactions and these can be painful to recount. So, openness can demand a willingness on your part as the supervisor to role model appropriate behaviour by sharing cases that you find or have found difficult, situations that you find hard to manage or how some aspects of practice make you feel. If people are sharing things with you that are clearly difficult to be open about, acknowledge this and encourage them to continue.

Help workers to identify and overcome blocks to performance, such as work conflicts and other pressures

Part of this has been covered in the first part of this chapter in that you have a responsibility to enable workers to reflect on supervision and improve outcomes and to try and reduce the blocks to an individual's practice by influencing the wider organisation and other organisations to respond to quality problems and develop services. This can involve identifying conflicts and intervening often alongside your staff member. 'Other pressures' is a huge catch-all phrase, but it must embrace the many changes that you and your team deal with and respond to. We explore managing change in Chapter 7, but it is worth noting here that supervision is a good opportunity to review the impact of changes on individuals and to identify anything that might be preventing people from adjusting to changes. An open discussion and then some joint problem solving can do much to help people to move on. Remember too, that blocks can be psychological as well as social. Your team will all have some activities they struggle with because of lack of confidence or the associations an activity can hold. Again, an open dialogue that identifies these very personal blocks can help and can free someone from a history of avoidance or failure.

Assist workers to understand the emotional impact of their work and seek appropriate specialist support if needed

It is important that your supervisee is able to share with you the emotional impact of their job. There are perhaps two dimensions to this: ensuring that the emotional impact of case work is taken into account in understanding situations, shaping practice and making decisions; and helping them think and work through any impact on themselves. It has been suggested that the idea that a professional social worker can distance themselves from their work and be objective is a false one (Harrison and Ruch, 2007); and also that emotional involvement is essential to, and the foundation of, professional practice. Reaching for an unobtainable state of objectivity could mean that people suppress feelings. This has political, managerial and personal consequences.

For example, one can imagine a situation where a social worker has a negative reaction to a service user and makes punishing decisions that are justified by a false belief that they are professionally objective. Alternatively, an intimidating family can stop people visiting or asking the right questions and the experience of being intimidated can undermine a social worker's confidence. This is a difficult area but a crucial one, and it can be seen to demand skills of a high order from a manager and a high level of self-awareness from the social worker. Your team may benefit from specialist support to deal with some situations. They may benefit from counselling to deal with a particular issue or case they are struggling with that is having a severe emotional impact on them. Sometimes the issues we confront can be very damaging and counselling or therapy for post-traumatic stress can be advisable.

Ensure the duty of care is met for the well-being of workers

A duty of care underpins professional supervision. Staff members, managers and employer organisations all have a duty of care. You and your staff have a responsibility towards yourselves, patients, users, carers, colleagues, your organisation and public interest. Your responsibilities are determined by professional standards and codes of practice. You have responsibility to protect your staff from excessive workloads, inappropriate delegation, bullying, harassment and discrimination. You must assess risks and protect their physical and emotional health and safety and you will no doubt have organisational policies that address your health and safety responsibilities. Guidance on health and safety from the Health and Safety Executive is available from: **www.direct.gov.uk/en/Employment/ HealthAndSafetyAtWork/DG_4016686**.

Social Care workers often work alone. This often requires particular attention. There will probably be work related policies to guide you, but if not please refer to Health and Safety Executive guidance on working alone. *Working Alone. Health and Safety Guidance on the Risks of Working Alone* (HSE, 2005), available from: **www.hse.gov.uk/pubns/indg73.pdf**.

Failing in your duty of care can lead to professional de-registration. Professional standards and codes such as the GSCC Code of Practice (GSCC, 2004) for Employers and the Effective Supervision Unit (SfC/CWDC, 2007) determine your responsibilities.

Recognise diversity and demonstrate anti-discriminatory practice in the supervisory relationship

In exploring social work values, a SCIE publication advises that anti-discriminatory practice is *the major value underpinning social work* (SCIE/Marie Diggins, 2004). It uses as a benchmark for exploring communication the Central Council for Education and Training in Social Work statement of values (CCETSW, 1995). This provides a good point of reference in exploring your supervision practice.

- Identify and question values and prejudices, and the implications for practice.

- Respect and value uniqueness and diversity, and recognise and build on strengths.

- Promote people's right of choice, privacy, confidentiality and protection while recognising and addressing the complexities of competing rights and demands.

- Assist people to increase control of and improve the quality of their lives, while recognising that control of behaviour will be required at times.

- Identify, analyse and take action to counter discrimination, racism, disadvantage, inequality and injustice, using strategies appropriate to role and context.

- Practice in a manner that does not stigmatise or disadvantage either individuals, groups or communities.

Give and receive constructive feedback on the supervisory relationship and supervision practice

This is very much a two-way process in that the expectation is that you will receive feedback from your supervisees on your effectiveness as a supervisor and will also give them feedback on their effectiveness as supervisees. The Effective Supervision Unit (SfC/CWDC, 2007) provides you with a benchmark to review your joint practice but the process demands considerable skill if it is to be successful. You may like to consider the following points:

- End each supervision session by checking out what in the session was helpful or unhelpful but do build in time for a more managed review of supervisory practice.

- Don't make it an exercise in you telling them or them telling you. This is a shared responsibility and a shared practice. Review each of the performance criteria together.

- People are very sensitive to negative feedback so try and ensure you always point out the positives first before identifying areas you can both work on. Your supervisees should be as thoughtful as you are in giving you feedback. If they are not this is an important area where you may need the support of your supervisor.

- To encourage ownership prepare by both thinking through what is currently helpful and what you could each improve on.

- Your staff need to be able to challenge your power base in order to develop and take more responsibility for their own practice. It's therefore important that you can be seen to take criticism and act on it. So show that you have heard and will respond, thank people and reassure them that it is okay – don't respond defensively or aggressively. It might feel uncomfortable to you, but if they don't challenge you they might not grow.

- We are also reluctant to give people positive feedback as we find it slightly embarrassing. We tend to save it up until people leave or retire and then tell them all the things we should have said before. You have far more power and influence than you probably realise so positive feedback from you can have a big impact on morale. Aim always to increase your level of positive feedback. Just because someone is experienced don't assume they don't need it. Always give positive feedback on improvements that are implemented.

- Give clear examples of both positive practices and things that could be improved. Be clear about what you agree you will change in terms of tangible behaviours and check out that you both understand.

- Don't give too much feedback; keep it simple and targeted.

- Make sure that you review any improvement plans that you agree on and always try to have an improvement plan you are both working on. Slow, manageable, long-term improvements are often the best way forward.

Audit and develop own skills and knowledge to supervise workers, including those from other disciplines when required

Feedback from your supervisees is crucial to this performance criteria. Your own manager has a role in both auditing and in helping you develop your skills. While the Effective Supervision Unit offers a valuable basis for an audit, don't hesitate to reach beyond it to other attempts to define good practice. The National Occupational Standards for Counselling (ENTO, 2007) are worth taking a look at and writers on supervision such as Hawkins and Shohet (2000) also provide auditing tools. You can also use the reflection points in this book to assist in the process. Take a closer look at your leadership style and how you manage change, the subjects of Chapters 3 and 7. In developing your practice don't forget the range of development methods that are available for you to draw on (see Chapter 3) and try and reach beyond just attending a training course, which may or may not be available or the most effective method.

Your supervisees will need, as they develop in their career, chances to supervise others and build their own expertise as supervisors. This may well include access to supervision training but they will have gained a lot from being supervised by you and through evaluating supervision with you. Include any supervision they are undertaking on the agenda of your supervision sessions as they may need help and support to develop their own supervisory practice. Different professions can have different expectations and supervisory practices, so careful boundary setting and contracting can be important. Bear in mind the option of sharing the Effective Supervision Unit with them (SfC/CWDC, 2007) and exploring what point of reference they use.

REFLECTION POINT 5.2

- *Looking at each of the people you supervise which ones do you think you have the best relationships with and why?*

- *Who do you find difficult to supervise and why?*

- *What do you find easy or difficult in building supervisory relationships?*

- *Can you identify an aspect you could improve on?*

Chapter summary

- We need to work with our teams to develop a long-term agenda for improving supervision.

- The Effective Supervision Unit (SfC/CWDC, 2007) provides the basis for this but we need a deeper analysis of the performance criteria that make up the three elements to audit properly.

- Developing, maintaining and reviewing effective supervisory relationships is a big challenge, as it can involve changing the culture of supervision.

- Assisting workers to understand the emotional impact of their work is another crucial area of good practice.

- Giving and receiving constructive feedback on your supervision practice and developing your own skills and knowledge to supervise workers constitutes a demanding personal challenge for any line manager.

FURTHER READING

Hawkins, P. and Shohet, R. (2000) *Supervision in the Helping Professions.* Buckingham: Open University.

Hawkins and Shohet offer an established text that is useful to all professional groups and focuses on the quality of the supervisory relationship.

Tsui, M.S. (2005) *Social Work Supervision: Contexts and Concepts.* London: Sage.

Tsui focuses on power relationships in supervision and their impact on practice. If he is perhaps a little pessimistic, power awareness is crucial to effective supervision.

Chapter 6

Developing, maintaining and reviewing practice and performance through supervision

Ivan Gray with contributions from
Angela Warren

CHAPTER OBJECTIVES

This chapter will help you address the following National Occupational Standards for Management and Leadership.

- B11 Promote equality of opportunity and diversity in your area of responsibility.
- E5 Ensure your own actions reduce risks to health and safety.
- E6 Ensure health and safety requirements are met in your area of responsibility.
- D6 Allocate and monitor the progress and quality of work in your area of responsibility.
- SfC and CWDC Effective Supervision Unit.

This chapter will also help you address the following Principles of Social Care Management.

- Ensure equality for staff and service users driven from the top down.
- Promote and meet service aims, objectives and goals.
- Develop joint working/partnerships that are purposeful.
- Challenge discrimination and harassment in employment practice and service delivery.

Introduction

The final element of the Effective Supervision Unit, 'Develop, maintain and review practice and performance through supervision' is explored in this chapter. As in Chapter 5, we take each of the eleven performance criteria and discuss them.

Implementing supervision systems and processes and reviewing and developing effective supervisory relationships are essential activities, but they serve to support the crucial outcomes of developing and maintaining practice and performance. This makes this chapter an important and demanding one. In our view some of the performance criteria, each of which we explore below, are aspirational in that they are not generally a strong feature of current practice. For instance, *ensuring work with people who use services is outcomes-focused and that their views are taken account of in service design and delivery*, is the heart of the government's personalisation agenda (DH, 2008a), but is not yet established in practice.

These 'cutting edge' activities are going to be major challenges for managers and teams and will demand considerable time, energy and resources to achieve and may even be a major driver in changing organisational culture. Some activities are simply difficult and demanding *per se*. For instance, most managers find it hard to assess and review performance and challenge poor practice. Be as objective as you can in judging yourself and your team's current performance as we explore each performance criteria or activity and identify realistic possibilities for improvement.

You will notice at the end of this chapter when we have finished our exploration of the performance criteria that make up the Effective Supervision Unit (SfC/CWDC, 2007), we add further dimensions that the unit does not address. Accepting the value of standards as a point of reference, it is important that you have your own model of good practice to help you develop your leadership and management style – please add in your own dimensions.

Ensure workloads are effectively allocated, managed and reviewed

Allocation practices can vary considerably. Teams sometimes work through referrals together with the team manager or a member of the team outlining the case and then staff offering to take cases. This has the advantage of allowing staff a choice in the work they undertake, to make their own judgements about workload and to see what work is coming in and who is working on it. But this method can also lead to staff taking on cases they are not really experienced enough to handle. Group pressures can force people to take on too much work. Some of this can be balanced by a climate of open communication where the team leader can intervene and stop a case being taken by someone who is overworked or who could not readily cope with the risk and level of complexity. Team manager allocation is generally safer as it allows a choice to be made that takes into account the variables that must be allowed for in making such a decision. These include:

- features of the case e.g. complexity, risk, location, type of referral and amount of work involved;
- features of the staff member e.g. their experience and skill, interest, current workload or activities, other pressures that might be on them, their location and/or learning needs.

This does not stop open discussion with the individual about reasons for the allocation. In fact a dialogue and some agreement about the type of work to be allocated and its appropriateness is crucial. This agreement can allow a variant of the team approach to allocation where a team manager works through referrals saying who they think the case should go to on the basis of individual discussion. Allocation by the manager, therefore, is probably the best way forward, especially as it can include some initial exploration together on risks, objectives and approach.

It is worth remembering that being allocated a new case can be quite daunting to a worker. Apart from the increase in workload, some cases may prove challenging. Again, dialogue can help with this as it makes allocation personal and provides an opportunity for the team leader to express their appreciation and give feedback e.g. 'given your good work on . . . I was hoping you might take this case on'. Do not just leave a file on someone's desk or put it in their in tray like a ticking bomb. Beyond cases, much the same can be said for other types of work e.g. service development projects. These also involve matching the risks and demands of the project with the attributes of the staff member.

A caseload or workload management system can do a lot to help with allocation. Usually this involves giving a weighting to an activity that allows for complexity, risk, location and the amount of work involved. SCIE (SCIE, 2003) offer an example at: **www.scie.org.uk/ publications/guides/guide01/section3/workload.asp**. This system allows time for other activities such as team meetings, supervision, training and development, service development and project work. However, it is hard for any system to do justice to the complex variables that need to be allowed for. Rather it provides a common currency or point of reference. Individuals will vary over time in terms of their workload or activity profile. For instance, induction and initial training demands a reduced workload as does taking on a new area of work. Cases also change, so weightings and judgements about activity levels, if no weighting system is used, need to be reviewed and adjusted. Typically, cases in crisis and new assessments demand more time than cases where an agreed care plan is in place. One case can sometimes monopolise a worker's time for a while. The status of a case can also change very quickly. It can go into crisis, demand reassessment or more intensive work.

Monitor and enable workers' competence to assess, plan, implement and review their work

The case management process is outlined below (Figure 6.1).

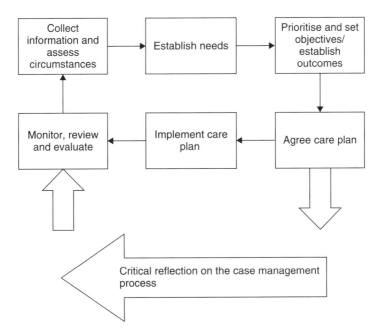

Figure 6.1. The case management process

The National Occupational Standards of Social Work (Topss England, 2002) give this process depth and can provide a useful basis for auditing practice. It can be useful to review these standards with your team, identifying areas of strength and weakness in their practice. Key roles 1–4 are the most pertinent in reviewing and evaluating case management, but as they consist of 13 units this can be quite daunting. It therefore might be a good idea to focus on one of the key roles at a time. Don't let the fact that your team will have been assessed using these standards as part of their qualifying training deter you. They offer a detailed and useful breakdown of good practice that can be used by a practitioner, no matter how experienced they are, to review and improve their practice. Crucially, if you are to effectively develop practice through methodical review and analysis you need a model of good practice to work with. There are other national standards that can be worth exploring, depending on who you are supervising. For instance, the National Occupational Standards that support NVQs in Care can be helpful (see **www.skillsforcare.org.uk/developing_skills/National_Occupational_ Standards/ National_Occupational_Standards_(NOS)_introduction.aspx**). Service standards are also an important point of reference in reviewing practice with your team.

Ensure supervisor and workers are clear about accountability and the limits of their individual and organisational authority and duties

Cameron (2003, p 54) defines accountability as, *being obliged to give an explanation or being held to account for one's actions or inactions*. To be accountable, you are in a position where you hold power and the limits to your authority and decision making, including the use of resources, must be clear to protect vulnerable users and organisational and public interest.

Cameron (2003) identifies six stakeholders to which social workers are accountable.

- The employer.
- Other agencies.
- The law.
- The public.
- Service users.
- The profession.

How do you become clear about accountability? Perhaps superficially it is about ensuring someone is aware of their responsibilities as outlined in their job description and other legal policy, procedural and professional code of practice requirements. Supervision is in itself an exercise in accountability and clarity comes from joint reflection and discussion of individual cases that explores the extent to which accountabilities have been met.

Banks (2002) points out that accountability can be about determining responsibility when something has gone wrong or else a more general explanation or reporting. She suggests that there is technical, procedural, managerial and ethical accountability.

- Technical – professional accountability with reference to models of good practice.

- Procedural – organisational accountability in terms of policy and procedures that must be followed.

- Managerial – implementation of decisions made by managers.

- Ethical – with reference to professional, personal or more general social values.

Putting Cameron and Bank's typologies together sets the agenda for a dialogue that is at the heart of supervision. Accountability to each of the domains in Figure 6.2 shapes the discussion and the analysis, providing points of reference.

As we discussed earlier in Chapter 4, accountability is problematic in that there can be conflicts of interest e.g. between an employing organisation and professional codes of practice or the expressed needs of people who use services. Supervision plays a crucial role in grappling with these dilemmas, agreeing ways forward and recording disagreements on

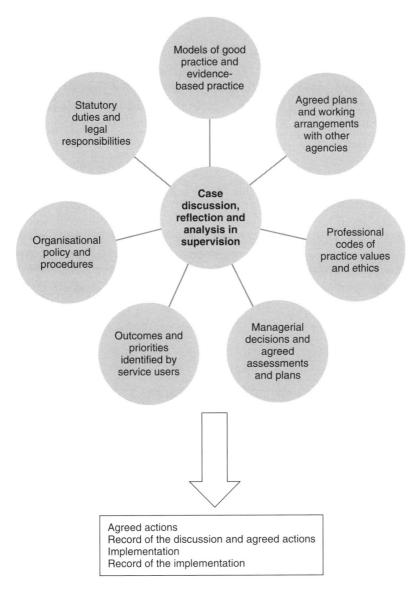

Figure 6.2 Accountabilities and case discussion and decision making

how accountability should be exercised. The key question for a supervisor is, are you in case discussion and decision making using these domains of accountability as points of reference?

Apart from shaping practice in the light of accountabilities, supervision also offers opportunity to gate-keep, determining any areas where responsibilities and authority are unclear or where procedures have not been followed or authority has been exceeded. This involves exploring why a problem might have occurred and rectifying the situation or, if the problem lies with the procedure or policy, seeking to clarify or adjust it. This may mean you as a manager having to raise issues and seek resolution at a higher level.

Ensure workers understand and demonstrate anti-discriminatory practice

In exploring what leaders and managers in social care do Skills for Care suggest they should:

> *treat people with respect and dignity and support them in overcoming barriers to inclusion. Services should be tailored to the cultural, ethnic and religious needs of individuals in the context of their communities. Their leaders and managers should focus on positive outcomes and wellbeing, and work proactively to include the most disadvantaged groups.*

(SfC, 2008, Appendix 1, p26)

This constitutes a considerable challenge to you as a leader and supervisor, as Carr (2004) points out:

> *Exercise of choice as an individual 'welfare consumer' remains restricted, particularly if you are from a black or minority ethnic group or are lesbian or gay. The ability to make choices can be limited by a lack of information about options and a lack of support for decision making. Professionally led assessment of eligibility for services can pose difficulties for exercising choice and control.*

(Carr, 2004, pvi)

In exploring the characteristics of organisations that promote diversity Butt identifies some formidable barriers to success; see Table 6.1.

Overcoming these barriers generates an organisational agenda (SCIE/Butt, 2006, pix) consisting of:

- implementing a policy framework that promotes diversity and provides clear objectives;

- implementing an ethnic record keeping and monitoring system that produces information that is used to plan and improve services;

- recruiting a diverse workforce that can help engage communities and encourage and lead change;

- a needs-led approach whereby workers with a knowledge of the needs of diverse communities engage service users and black and minority ethnic voluntary organisations to determine community need;

- providing resources and planning for the delivery of services that promote diversity.

Table 6.1 Organisational barriers to promoting diversity (SCIE/Butt, 2006, pviii)

Barriers to success	Evidence
Lack of knowledge among black and minority ethnic communities about available support	Families with disabled children are coping with limited resources and a lack of support.
Lack of appropriate services	Few appropriate family support services, such as parent and toddler groups for Somali families, in safe and convenient locations.
Poor quality services	An assumption that the lack of service take-up by black and minority ethnic families with disabled children is the result of a lack of need.
Lack of choice	The provision of homes for black and minority ethnic disabled people that meet the 'Lifetime Homes' standard, are either too small to accommodate larger family groups or are based in an area where existing social and support networks cannot be maintained.
Workers without effective communication skills	Workers carrying out assessments when they are unable to speak the same language as the service user.
Workers without the skills and experience to work with racially and culturally diverse communities	White managers are unable to provide direction to black and minority ethnic workers.
Direct and institutional discrimination	Prevailing stereotypes about particular communities leads to the assumption that informal or family support is always available, resulting in communities having to 'look after their own'.

This organisational agenda sets the context for supervision in that the quality of frontline practice is an essential feature of organisations that are successful in promoting diversity (SCIE/Butt ,2006). Supervision is the central point where frontline practice is managed. In organisations demonstrating effective frontline practice:

Confident and competent workers communicate effectively, use their knowledge in a non-stereotypical manner and demonstrate flexibility in their approach. Workers draw on available resources and have access to managers who are knowledgeable about diversity and are competent supervisors.

(SCIE/Butt 2006, pix)

From this we can develop an agenda for supervision.

• Ensuring awareness of policy and organisational objectives on diversity.

- Playing a part in engaging communities and engaging individuals to determine their needs.

- Ensuring needs identified at a local level are fed into organisational development agendas.

- Contributing to service improvements and developments that respond to need.

- Meeting the needs of black and minority ethnic workers to ensure they are retained and practice effectively.

- Ensuring staff and supervisors develop their knowledge and skills including communication and language skills.

And crucially:

- ensuring people who use services and carers are engaged in assessments that identify their needs and developing care plans and access to resources that meet their needs.

This is complemented by the *Statement of Expectations From Individuals, Families, Carers, Groups and Communities Who Use Services and Those Who Care For Them* (Topss England, 2002) that forms part of the National Occupational Standards for Social Work. Given the broader context outlined above, supervisors and supervisees should:

a. *[demonstrate] awareness of your own values, prejudices, ethical dilemmas and conflicts of interest and their implications on your practice;*

b. *[demonstrate] respect for, and the promotion of: each person as an individual, independence and quality of life for individuals, whilst protecting them from harm, dignity and privacy of individuals, families, carers, groups and communities;*

c. *recognise and facilitate each person's use of the language and form of communication of their choice;*

d. *value, recognise and respect the diversity, expertise and experience of individuals, families, carers, groups and communities;*

e. *maintain the trust and confidence of individuals, families, carers, groups and communities by communicating in an open, accurate and understandable way;*

f. *understand, and make use of, strategies to challenge discrimination, disadvantage and other forms of inequality and injustice.*

(Topss England, 2002)

Ensure work with people who use services is outcomes-focused and that their views are taken account of in service design and delivery

This is a crucial but challenging and problematic dimension of practice that too easily is dealt with superficially. It is the heart of the government's transformation and personalisation agenda (see *Putting People First* (DH, 2007a), *Every Child Matters* (DfES, 2004) and *High Quality Care for All* (DH, 2008d)). It means making sure a focus on outcomes includes the views of people who use services and involving them in service design and delivery.

Outcomes refer to the impacts or end results of services on a person's life. Outcomes-focused services therefore aim to achieve the aspirations, goals and priorities identified by service users – in contrast to services whose content and/or forms of delivery are standardised or are determined solely by those who deliver them. Outcomes are by definition individualised, as they depend on the priorities and aspirations of individual people.

(Glendinning *et al.*, 2006, pv)

This needs to happen at all levels from policy development to frontline practice.

Crucially, Lord Laming has stressed the importance of placing the child at the centre of all that we do. That means understanding the perspective of the child, listening to the child and never losing sight of the child. Just as the centrality of the child drives our policies so too should it drive day-to-day practice at the frontline.

(DCSF, 2009 p4)

The Centre for Excellence and Outcomes in Children and Young People's Services (C4EO) provides an Outcomes Based Accountability (OBA) toolkit (Gill *et al.*, 2009). They note that an outcomes-orientated service is a major cultural change that demands leadership. Included in the toolkit is a supervision tool that encourages an exploration of the effectiveness of casework in relation to the Every Child Matters outcomes (DCSF, 2008). They point out that performance measures do not necessarily lead to outcomes for people who use services. Some measures can militate against outcomes.

Glendinning *et al.* (2006, pvii) have identified a number of factors that adversely effect the delivery of outcomes-focused services for older people; these include irregular service-led assessments that do not offer choice or overlook psychological and other needs. They cite Qureshi (2001; cited in Glendining *et al.*, 2006, p18) who has developed documentation that strengthens assessment plans and evaluations by providing:

- *a summary of needs;*
- *expected changes that could affect future service delivery;*
- *a summary of agreed outcomes;*
- *options and preferences for achieving these outcomes.*

Carr (2004) notes how there is a tendency to engage people who use services in an initial assessment but then not to review how effective the care plan has been or any new needs (Carr, 2004, citing Crawford *et al.*, 2003). Effective practice management needs to ensure care plans are developed alongside people who use services, clearly identifying needs and outcomes that are then used as the basis for shared review and evaluation. This is the heart of the personalisation agenda.

Personalisation
There are two broad dimensions to involving people who use services in service design and delivery: contributing to social care planning and development; and participating in planning and evaluating their own service.

Therefore, practice comes to be seen as a joint project (Beresford and Croft, 2002). This shift is the essence of personalisation and one that demands leadership and a major change in supervision to be successful (O'Leary and Lownsbrough, 2007). SCIE have published

Personalisation: a rough guide that offers a concise review of the personalisation agenda. While it is facilitated by individual and personal budgets, personalisation means:

> *. . . services should respond to the individual instead of the person having to fit with the service. This traditional service-led approach has often meant that people have not received the right support for their circumstances or been able to help shape the kind of help they need. Personalisation is about giving people much more choice and control over their lives.*

(Carr, 2008, p3)

What does the agenda demand from practitioners? Skills for Care suggest:

> *The primary implication for staff skills and knowledge is an understanding that their role has shifted, from following the recipe of a care plan, to understanding what the core ingredients of a person's care plan are and being able to reorganise the recipe of care according to a person's needs. To do this effectively, care managers have to empower their staff and staff need to know the parameters or limits and opportunities that they must work within. Managers who succeed in creating a climate of learning and trust are most likely to succeed.*

(SfC South West, 2000, p60)

Primarily, personalisation demands traditional social work skills and values (GSCC, 2008). Carr (2008) cites Henwood and Grove who suggest, *some social workers view the person-alisation developments as an opportunity for them to return to the traditional social work role of enabling vulnerable people to achieve their potential. However, this is not what more recently qualified staff have been trained to do and competition for scarce social work skills is likely* (Henwood and Grove, 2006, pp 7–8). This means that in reviewing and evaluating practice in supervision we can draw on the *Statement of Expectations From Individuals, Families, Carers, Groups and Communities Who Use Services and Those Who Care For Them* (Topss England, 2002). As part of the National Occupational Standards for Social Work supervisors and supervisees should:

a. have respect for:

    individuals, families, carers, groups and communities regardless of their age, ethnicity, culture, level of understanding and need for the expertise and knowledge individuals, families, carers, groups and communities have about their own situation;

b. empower individuals, families, carers, groups and communities in decisions affecting them;

c. be honest about:

    • the power invested in them, including legal powers;

    • their role and resources available to meet need;

d. respect confidentiality, and inform individuals, families, carers, groups and communi-ties about when information needs to be shared with others;

e. be able to:

    • challenge discriminatory images and practices affecting individuals, families, carers, groups and communities;

    • put individuals, families, carers, groups and communities first.

Participation in service design and development

While the main focus of supervision will be case management, you and your team should also be involved in working with people who use services to design, review and improve services. SCIE have published a number of reports (Danso *et al.*, 2003, Barnes *et al.,* 2003, Glendinning *et al.,* 2006, Doel *et al.,* 2007) reviewing the effectiveness of the participation of people who use services in service design and development. Carr (2004) identifies a number of key problems, some of which are listed below.

- A lack of research into the effectiveness of participation.

- A tendency to judge the effectiveness of participation by perceptions of the process rather than objective measurement of outcomes.

- Lack of organisational responsiveness to suggestions.

- Failure to address power issues that undermine participation such as professional attitudes.

- Negative judgements about the ability of people who use services to contribute.

- Not valuing contributions that aren't based on professional understandings and expressed in professional terms.

- Working to timetables and timescales that effectively exclude people.

- Not covering the costs people incur in participating.

- Failure to fund and support user groups to provide a critical viewpoint.

- Not preparing, briefing and supporting people so that they can participate with confidence and understanding.

To be successful in building partnership and participation in service design and development you will need to plan initiatives carefully, making sure you have adequate resources and accept this is a long-term and demanding change. You should seek to plan initiatives with service users from the outset so that they own and commit to them. Time and effort is also required around the practical aspects of involvement i.e. transport, payment, personal support before and after involvement. Having a dedicated person who co-ordinates involvement and is the point of contact is essential as is the need to review the effectiveness of involvement and give feedback regularly.

REFLECTION POINT *6.1*

Ensuring work with people who use services is outcomes-focused and that their views are taken account of in service design and delivery can be a considerable challenge for any manager and their team.

- *Can you identify an initiative you can take that will involve people who use services more closely in service design and delivery?*

- *How will you involve the team?*

- *How will you avoid the problems identified above by Carr (2004)?*

Identify risks to users of services and workers and take appropriate action

You are likely to have organisational procedures and guidance to adhere to that will shape your practice. In addition, there is a best practice guide for risk management in adult services (DH, 2007b) available from: **www.dh.gov.uk/en/Publicationsandstatistics/ Publications/PublicationsPolicyAndGuidance/DH_074773**.

The importance of adopting a person-centred approach in assessing risk and the importance of a degree of risk to a good quality of life is noted in this guide. Recording discussion and decisions in complex situations is essential. The 'Supported Decision Tool' is included in Appendix 3 of this book. This offers a good practice guide of the issues to be explored and how they should be recorded. Situations can arise where there is disagreement within multi-disciplinary teams on risk and how it should be managed. The Department of Health recommends that organisations have a resolution procedure to respond to these situations but as a manager you may need to liaise with other managers to broker an agreement. The NSPCC provides a useful summary of research into risk assessment in child protection (Cleaver *et al.*, 1998a), which is available from: **www.nspcc.org.uk/Inform/publications/Downloads/assessingriskinchildprotection_ wdf48173.pdf**. The authors point out the importance of risk assessment based on professional knowledge and skills, and the need to:

- avoid being diverted into other features of the case;
- maintain objectivity;
- obtain information from as wide a range of sources as possible;
- escape preconceptions.

Ten common pitfalls of risk assessment are noted alongside guidance on how to avoid them (Cleaver *et al.*, 1998b).

Obtain and give timely feedback on workers' practice, including feedback from people who use services

Having evidence to inform judgements about staff members' practice is essential but can be a difficult area of practice. Depending on your setting, you may or may not have the opportunity to observe your staff member at work. Rather you may be making judgements and giving feedback on the basis of records, self-reports from the staff member, discussion, feedback from others and activities you are involved in e.g. case planning and reviews. Feedback from others is important, especially feedback from users, but this can be difficult to gain. There are a number of issues to be aware of.

- Overtly seeking the views of others can be very threatening and disempowering.
- Even if you don't seek views openly you can still pick up information about someone's practice. However, when you have not made it clear what you are doing, how do you know whether any feedback is simply impressionistic? Also, what point of reference will others be using in gauging someone's performance?

- You need to be able to focus feedback on areas identified as areas for development. Feedback that only identifies strengths is useful, but doesn't permit improvement.

- At key points users can be too hostile or angry or too distressed to give feedback and asking them for it can undermine your staff member and divert the intervention from its objectives.

- To what extent is the practice the staff member's and to what extent is it the organisation's? Procedures and resources and the network of provision can mean that there are many variables that are beyond the practitioner's control.

How can you get around all this? To some extent you cannot. Necessarily you will have to make judgements on the basis of a range of information from a number of different sources and this will include making judgements about the validity of information and gradually building a picture. In effect, what makes supervision a skilled activity is the need to make a judgement on the basis of a complex and fragmented picture. What makes it so important is that it allows these sources to be drawn together. So, what can you do?

- Evidencing practice and making judgements about it is a shared responsibility. Staff can't fulfil their professional responsibilities for CPD if they aren't making judgements about their own practice, so make it shared responsibility – not something that is done to people.

- Try and make obtaining feedback from users and others who are part of the network of provision something that is part of case planning and review processes and applies to all staff.

- Be clear that you will be given and will ask for feedback from others on someone's practice and that you will bring the information into supervision.

- 360 degree feedback is used by managers to judge their performance (see Chapter 10) so why not extend it to social workers and work together to obtain feedback about their performance.

- Make use of natural opportunities to observe or build occasional observations into supervisory practice for everyone.

- Make use of opportunities and requirements on post-qualifying programmes to observe practice and obtain witness/third party testimony.

- Use and emphasise positive feedback to motivate and encourage. Don't just look at the negatives.

- Give opportunity to people to disagree with feedback and be heard.

Identify learning needs and integrate them within development plans

It is important that supervision is used to identify learning needs as they arise from case discussion and integrate them into development plans. If this doesn't happen, and development planning is separated out as an activity, needs and their context can be lost and development planning can be ill-informed and lose meaning. Learning needs should be included regularly in the supervision contract and to really join things up a supervision learning agenda should appear in personal development plans. As in social care practice do try and identify the need not the development plan or method e.g. 'for x to improve the quality of their report writing' rather than 'for x to go on the report writing course'. The former allows a range of possible learning opportunities to be considered and will create a richer learning experience and a more productive one as methods that appeal to the staff member and their learning style can be chosen. Learning can be directly related to practice situations and experiences and the full depth of a team's learning resources can be mobilised.

Remember that it is the staff member's professional responsibility to identify their learning needs, so give them space to do this. There is a section in the reflective questions in Appendix 1 that can be used to encourage staff members to identify learning needs for themselves and plan how to meet them. Obviously you will need to help less experienced staff with this and sometimes even experienced staff will not see a learning need, but you need active learners and leading your own learning is motivating and makes it more effective. Remember also to evaluate learning and give positive feedback on improved practice.

Create opportunities for learning and development

Supervision sessions are in themselves a valuable opportunity for learning and development. This may come from the dialogue and reflection on particular cases or activities but you may also be directly coaching team members and it can be worth considering dedicating sessions or parts of sessions to coaching. However, supervision is also the place to explore other training and development opportunities and to plan for them. Skills for Care (SfC, 2006b) offer a guide to managers on the use of the National Occupational Standards for Social Work (Topss England, 2002). They point out that the standards provide the basis for a more methodical review of practice in determining learning needs. While there is benefit in identifying learning needs as they arise in supervision, a more thorough and methodical audit of practice is desirable. Some general questions worthy of consideration are:

Am I finding enough time to look at personal development?

In managing my team's personal development, am I responding to their individual styles and needs as learners and professionals or offering standardised responses?

Are portfolios and development plans used and referred to in supervision or left mostly on the shelf?

Are we making use of a good range of developmental methods?

Can I see evidence of individuals, as they develop over time, taking an increasing role in enabling and developing colleagues?

Am I helping staff with coaching to carry what they have learnt into practice?

Are we giving feedback and guidance to trainers of the quality of courses and their application and transfer into practice?

Are we identifying new training needs and requesting that courses are provided?

Again, try and identify needs and objectives as this allows a choice to be made from a range of development methods rather than always reaching for a training course e.g. coaching, shadowing, learning sets, e-learning and taught components and programmes. Users and carers can also make a valuable contribution to learning and development, offering to less experienced staff an insight into their experiences and needs. Remember to evaluate the effectiveness of learning experiences together and to give positive feedback on improvements. Also explore how learning can be shared as some of it can be developmental for the whole team not just the individual. It can also be useful for you to identify your leaning needs and for your staff member to explicitly share their learning with you. The GSCC are actively trying to encourage staff to include more than just training courses in their PRTL when they re-register (Keen *et al.*, 2009, Chapter 4), so a broad look at learning will assist in meeting requirements and should be recorded. Evaluating development and development planning becomes a richer experience if you have identified learning needs or objectives and used a range of methods. Otherwise it can degenerate into simply agreeing that people have or have not attended a training course. Chapter 9 explores the management of training and development in detail.

Assess and review performance, challenge poor practice and ensure improvements in standards.

Having your performance judged by someone else is uncomfortable, even if you admire their expertise. So assessing and reviewing your team's performance demands not only professional expertise and knowledge on your part but also careful handling, given its potential impact on the relationship. Performance management needs to be ongoing and part of every supervision session, but formal methodical appraisal is also desirable. This can draw together issues identified in individual supervision sessions but it also affords opportunity for a careful audit of practice against benchmarks and drawing on a range of evidence. In our experience, appraisal is not viewed positively by either staff or managers. There are perhaps a number of reasons for this, including:

- it is an uncomfortable power exercise for both parties especially if it is linked to performance related pay;

- it is imposed by the organisation;

- insisting on a format that applies to all staff may be unhelpful;

- it demands a lot of work from manager and staff member;

- it is often done under pressure and deteriorates into a formality;

- training opportunities for staff and managers can be limited.

Yet a lot can ride on this rather unhappy experience, notably improvements in practice, successful staff development and people's long-term commitment and motivation. As in the above discussion on development planning, one of the main outcomes of appraisal, method is important as is choosing the benchmarks you will use to judge performance. Job descriptions, National Occupational Standards, Codes of Practice, business plans, Quality Improvement or team development plans are all possible options. Your organisation may determine benchmarks for you, especially if they have introduced performance related pay.

Remember though, we need to reach for method *and* improved approaches. The following bullet points offer some options for you and your team.

- Have team discussions on appraisal and how it can be made more rewarding. Training or coaching as a team can also be valuable.

- Regularly discuss individual's performance in supervision so that there are no surprises when it comes to appraisal.

- While identifying areas for improvement always also look for good practice to give positive feedback on. If performance management and appraisal celebrate success as well as identifying problems, they are more likely to be valued. Practice improvement can also come from doing what we do well more often as well as responding to deficiencies.

- Try and let your staff member lead and take control, where possible, identifying areas for improvement themselves. If you have identified an area for improvement check out your staff member's views and whether they can own it and work with you to bring improvement.

Enable multi-disciplinary, integrated and collaborative working as appropriate

Quality problems often occur at the interface between services. With services now dependent on partnership working for effective delivery, multi-disciplinary, integrated or collaborative working relationships need constant attention. Every social worker, in negotiating, implementing and reviewing care plans, is at the hub of several teams that need to co-ordinate their activities if they are to provide a high quality service. You have a role in this, actively liaising with the managers and leaders of other services, but you also need to engage and enable your staff team in leading and managing their collaborative work. Reflect on the following questions in reviewing your own practice as a broker between teams and services and in supervising your team in their collaborative work.

- Am I clear on the range of teams that my staff and I need to work with?

- Is collaborative working getting sufficient attention in supervision or is it getting neglected?

- Is the effectiveness of collaborative working reviewed in your supervision with your manager?

- Do teams get opportunity to meet with each other and discuss quality issues?

- Are there joint planning opportunities for both individual cases and business plans?

- Are all members of your team fully aware of and mobilising all the resources available in their care planning?

- Are you exploring the quality of working relationships with your staff, identifying breakdowns and blockages and planning for improvement with them and the leaders and managers of other teams?

Managing the supervisory team and managing projects and development work

Although the Effective Supervision Unit does not cover managing a supervisory team, if you lead one it is worth exploring the following questions.

Are we avoiding staff members being supervised by too many people?

Are we co-ordinating our activities to avoid confusion e.g. briefing each other on issues and decisions?

Are we clear on our roles and responsibilities?

Have members of the team been trained as supervisors?

Are we using the Effective Supervision Unit to guide our practice?

Are supervisors supported and supervised so they can develop their practice as supervisors?

Are we providing a consistent quality of supervision across the team?

Do we review and evaluate our supervisory team practice and plan for improvement?

Are there individuals who are taking advantage of being supervised by several people to achieve their own agenda?

You should be involving your team in service development work or projects and so you will need to review your practice and monitor how the implementation of project and development work is proceeding, stepping in to help if they are hitting any problems. The following questions will help you to review your practice in supervising project and development work.

Do all staff have opportunity to be involved in project and developmental work?

Do I allocate project work according to developmental needs and experience?

Do I ensure staff members are clear on their objectives?

Do we develop implementation plans together?

Do I regularly review progress, giving more time and contact to less experienced staff?

Do we regularly reflect on and evaluate implementation together, learning from the process?

Chapter summary

- Some performance criteria of the Effective Supervision Unit are easier to meet than others e.g. the participation of people who use services and outcomes-focused services are very challenging for managers and staff if practice is not to be tokenistic.

- The Effective Supervision Unit (SfC/CWDC, 2007) does not cover all the dimensions of supervision e.g. managing the supervisory team and managing service development projects.

ACTIVITY **6.1**

Given our discussion, which of the performance criteria for this element (listed below) are a strength of your current practice? Which areas are priorities for improvement? What would the view of your team and your manager be?

Performance criteria

a. *Ensure workloads are effectively allocated, managed and reviewed.*

b. *Monitor and enable workers' competence to assess, plan, implement and review their work.*

c. *Ensure supervisor and workers are clear about accountability and the limits of their individual and organisational authority and duties.*

d. *Ensure workers understand and demonstrate anti-discriminatory practice.*

e. *Ensure work with people who use services is outcomes-focused and that their views are taken account of in service design and delivery.*

f. *Identify risks to users of services and workers and take appropriate action.*

g. *Obtain and give timely feedback on workers' practice, including feedback from people who use services.*

h. *Identify learning needs and integrate them within development plans.*

i. *Create opportunities for learning and development.*

j. *Assess and review performance, challenge poor practice and ensure improvements in standards.*

k. *Enable multi-disciplinary, integrated and collaborative working as appropriate, manage the supervisory team and manage projects and development work.*

- Accepting the value of National Occupational Standards in shaping practice and building your own good practice model are essential.

FURTHER READING

Cleaver, H.,Wattam, C. and Cawson, P. (1998a) *Assessing Risk in Child Protection – Summary of Research Findings.* London: NSPCCInform. **www.nspcc.org.uk/Inform/publications/Downloads/assessingriskinchildprotection_wdf48173.pdf**.

Cleaver, H.,Wattam, C., Cawson, P. and Gordon, R. (1998b) *Children Living at Home. The Initial Child Protection Enquiry: Ten Pitfalls and How to Avoid Them.* London: NSPCCInform. **www.nspcc.org.uk/Inform/publications/Downloads/tenpitfalls_wdf48122.pdf**.

Demos, the think tank behind the personalisation agenda. **www.demos.co.uk**.

Department of Health personalisation web pages. **www.dh.gov.uk/en/SocialCare/Socialcarereform/Personalisation/index.htm**.

Chapter 7

Managing change and developing the team and the organisation

Ivan Gray with a contribution from Liz (person who uses service)

CHAPTER OBJECTIVES

This chapter will help you address the following National Occupational Standards for Management and Leadership.

- C5 Plan change.
- C6 Implement change.
- D1 Develop productive working relationships with colleagues.
- F8 Work with others to improve customer service.

This chapter will also help you address the following Principles of Social Care Management.

- Promote and meet service aims, objectives and goals.

Introduction

Leaders are often distinguished from managers in terms of their contribution to organisational change (Kotter and Cohen, 2002). While managers are seen as concerned with routine operations, a leader is seen as someone with the attributes necessary to instigate and bring to fruition changes that improve service quality. This can be approached in a number of ways. A leader's ability to change the organisation can be explored in terms of their influencing or interpersonal skills or, as an alternative, their strategic ability. In evaluating your management practice it can be useful to ask yourself how effective are you in managing change. This is especially the case as we live in a world where change is endemic and policy initiatives are legion.

We will explore in this chapter two contrasting models. The first is a model that looks at the psychology of change; the second is a model that takes a more strategic approach. We then explore how to go about developing the team and the wider organisation.

Change as loss

One way of approaching change is to try and understand the psychological processes that it engenders. This allows us to revisit our professional knowledge base since very often as social workers or health care practitioners we help people cope with personal change. If these changes are viewed as loss then the transition or loss curve (Adams et al., 1976) can give us an insight into the impact of change on an individual (see Figure 7.1).

Anyone experiencing change will go through seven stages (Adams et al., 1976). The depth of the initial curve in Figure 7.1 and the impact or stress on the individual will vary according to the nature of the change or transition. Holmes and Rahe's (1967) social readjustment rating scale illustrates the impact that different life events can have (Table 7.1). More severe events both deepen the curve and increase the degree of immobilisation, minimisation, etc., and increase their impact on morale. They also increase the overall time it takes to adjust.

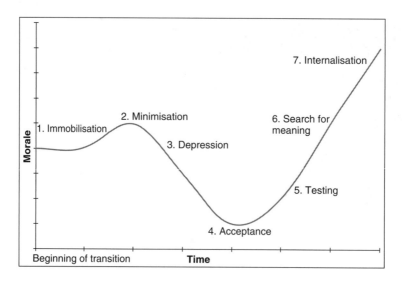

Figure 7.1 The transition curve taken from Adams et al. (1976, p81)

Table 7.1 The Holmes and Rahe social readjustment rating scale

Life event	Mean value
1. Death of a spouse	100
2. Divorce	73
3. Marital separation from mate	65
4. Detention in jail or other institution	63
5. Death of a close family member	63
6. Major personal injury or illness	53
7. Marriage	50

8.	Being fired at work	47
9.	Marital reconciliation with mate	45
10.	Retirement from work	45
11.	Major change in the health or behaviour of family member	44
12.	Pregnancy	40
13.	Sexual difficulties	39
14.	Gaining a new family member e.g. through birth, adoption, oldster moving in, etc	39
15.	Major business readjustment e.g. merger, reorganisation, bankruptcy	39
16.	Major change in financial state e.g. a lot worse off or a lot better off than usual	38
17.	Death of a close friend	37
18.	Changing in a different line of work	36
19.	Major changes in the number of arguments with spouse e.g. either a lot more or a lot less than usual regarding childbearing, personal habits, etc	35
20.	Taking on a mortgage greater than $10,000 [£6,000] e.g. purchasing a home, business, etc	31
21.	Foreclosure on a mortgage or loan	30
22.	Major change in responsibilities at work e.g. promotion, demotion, lateral transfer	29
23.	Son or daughter leaving home e.g. marriage, attending college, etc	29
24.	In-law troubles	29
25.	Outstanding personal achievement	28
26.	Wife beginning or ceasing work outside the home	26
27.	Beginning or ceasing work outside the home	26
28.	Major change in living conditions e.g. building a new home, remodelling, deterioration of home or neighbourhood	25
29.	Revision of personal habits (dress, manners, association, etc)	24
30.	Trouble with the boss	23
31.	Major change in working hours or conditions	20
32.	Change in residence	20
33.	Change to a new school	20

Table 7.1 (continued)

	Life event	Mean value
34.	Major change in usual type and/or amount of recreation	19
35.	Major change in church activities e.g. a lot more or a lot less than usual	19
36.	Major change in social activities e.g. clubs, dancing, movies, visiting, etc	18
37.	Taking on a mortgage or a loan less than $10,000 [£6,000] e.g. purchasing a car, TV, freezer, etc	17
38.	Major change in sleeping habits (a lot more or a lot less sleep or change in part of day when asleep)	16
39.	Major change in number of family get-togethers e.g. a lot more or a lot less	15
40.	Major change in eating habits (a lot more or a lot less food intake, or very different meal hours or surroundings)	15
41.	Vacation	13
42.	Christmas	12

Before exploring the management of the stages people experience in adjusting to change it is worth making some general points.

- Sometimes people don't make any adjustment to change, instead getting stuck in depression and anger.

- A series of uncompleted changes, even minor ones, can build on each other, increasing stress levels and creating distress.

- Working through the curve takes time and energy. There is only so much change an individual can cope with.

- More traumatic life events take longer to adjust to than minor ones.

- Transition is easier if the change is chosen, meaningful and purposeful.

- All professional and personal development is dependent on managing transition.

- Successful transition engenders personal growth and builds self-esteem.

Successfully working through transitions is dependent on several factors. Schlossberg (1981) identifies four: the situation, personal characteristics, available support and the strategy an individual adopts. As a manager you can influence all of these variables as demonstrated in Table 7.2.

Table 7.2 Managing change situations (based on Schlossberg, 1981)

Make it meaningful	Be clear about the reasons for the change. Present it positively, identifying the improvements and gains. Be clear about why previous practices needed to change. Put the change in its policy context. Link it to professional values and point out the benefits to users. Relate it to team and organisational history. Remember that different people are motivated by different things, so reframing a change so that it appeals to their agenda can make a big difference.
Give control	At best let them initiate and manage change themselves. Otherwise consult and involve them as much as possible in managing it.
Give or help find direction	Ensure the broad objectives are clear and there is a plan. Make sure people know what is expected of them and progress is reviewed.
Recognise loss	Accept the initial periods of minimisation or depression and be patient. Recognise what people will be giving up. You may need to celebrate the past and remind people of their previous successes and, if people have lost their team and/or colleagues in major change they may need time to grieve. Keep the transition curve in mind and ask yourself regularly how far along it your team are.
Allow negative emotion	Let people express the negatives openly so that they can move on.
Managing the person and accept difference	The same change will affect each member of your team differently. They will move through a transition at different speeds. Remember, that experiences outside work will also present them with change. This may reduce their capacity to respond to workplace change.
Listen and enquire	Listen carefully to what people are saying or not saying. They may need to express things they feel they cannot share with the team. Actively enquire how they are coping with the changes.
Challenge	Sometimes people need to be challenged in order to move on. This should not be confrontational but can often consist of reminding them of inconsistencies or asking them pertinent questions.
Encourage reflection and personal development	If people reflect on how they are managing or have managed change they can identify approaches that work for them and make use of them in future.
Manage yourself	Remember you are also subject to the stages in the transition curve. Reflect on where you are in the change process and how you have managed change in the past. Make sure you are supported too.

Table 7.2 (continued)

Providing support and guidance	People need to be clear on what they have to achieve and guidance on how they get there. This can be provided by coaching from you or an expert colleague or they may need written briefing materials or procedures.
Provide training and development	Training courses or workshops that introduce new policies and practices can be invaluable in developing the knowledge and skills people need to manage change. However, bear in mind they still have to apply it to the workplace.
Monitor progress	Build in regular review points where you monitor progress and respond to problems. Uncompleted transitions can be painful and if change isn't taken to completion people can stop taking it seriously.
Give feedback	Remind people of achievements and praise them. Be honest when things aren't quite right and identify ways forward together. Praise them when they succeed.
Mobilise the team	Being in it together can make the unbearable bearable. Encourage team members to take the lead and to learn from each other. Let them evaluate progress and troubleshoot problems.

Strategies for managing change

Within the psychological model there are at least six concurrent strategies to ensure the change is introduced successfully and all of your team make the transition. It is worth making these explicit (Table 7.3).

Table 7.3 Strategies for managing change

Strategy	Purpose
Managing meaning	Make sure people understand the reasons for the change, value it and are motivated to succeed.
Managing direction	Establish clear objectives, team and individual action plans; monitor and review progress.
Problem solving	Identify problems as they arise and mobilise the team and other resources to find ways forward.
Manage emotion	Make sure the emotional impact of change is not ignored. This involves both negative and positive emotions. Remember to celebrate and recognise team and individual successes; personal growth and development.
Develop	Ensure people have the knowledge, skills and guidance they need to manage the transition.
Individualise	Make sure you recognise and respond to individual needs.

Advantages of this approach to change

- It individualises change. Each person experiences change differently. The model allows managers to recognise these different needs and respond to them.

- Effective change management is dependent on managers being able to offer individual contact and time – professional supervision can be mobilised to this end.

- It is humanistic and engages the whole person. It recognises our common human responses to change and does justice to the interplay of meaning, control, knowledge, skills and emotion in changing behaviour. It accepts our limitations.

- It can be useful in periods of rapid, frequent, top-down change.

- It is part of our professional knowledge base. Managers and staff can readily understand the approach and contribute to change management.

A critical perspective on this approach to change

- Managers can get sucked into counselling staff.

- Its original purpose was to help people cope with grief and loss where this was creating depression. Its application to changes in organisational life can be considered less appropriate and overemphasise the importance of emotion.

- People are presented almost as victims of change when in fact it is natural.

- People are innovative and actively choose change to seek to improve organisational practices.

- It can be very time consuming and can become self-indulgent, directing managers away from the tasks essential to managing practice.

REFLECTION POINT 7.1

How effective are you at managing the six dimensions of a psychological approach to change?

- *Managing meaning*
- *Managing direction*
- *Problem solving*
- *Managing emotion*
- *Developing people*
- *Individualising change*

Managing change proactively and strategically

In contrast to responding to change psychologically as loss, Kotter and Schlesinger's (1979) approach is task and outcomes-focused and aims to manage change proactively and strategically.

Kotter and Schlesinger's approach to change management was developed out of a concern that senior mangers were failing to manage resistance in organisations and the validity of Machiavelli's view of innovation:

> *And let it be noted that there is no more delicate matter to take in hand, nor more dangerous to conduct, nor more doubtful in its success, than to set up as the leader in the introduction of changes. For he who innovates will have for his enemies all those who are well off under the existing order of things, and only lukewarm supporters in those who might be better off under the new.*

(Machiavelli, 1992, p13)

Kotter and Schlesinger believed that senior managers were launching new initiatives and policies without thinking through how changes could be implemented. Managers were therefore ignoring people and processes, and thinking they could simply command change and that it would happen. This often led to failure in introducing change or generated unnecessary conflict and wasted energy. So, Kotter and Schlesinger outlined a methodical process allowing for resistance, determining the speed for change and choosing between broad strategies. We offer a depiction of this process in Figure 7.2 below.

Carrying out a stakeholder analysis makes a useful start to the management of any change. You need to identify all the groups of people and significant individuals who might be affected by the change and make a judgement about their ability to influence

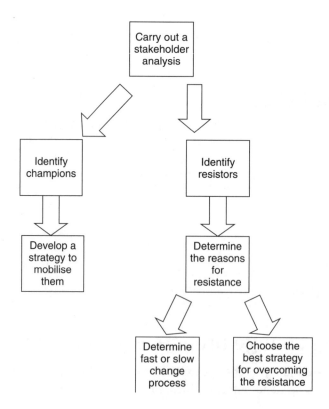

Figure 7.2 Managing resistance to change (based on Kotter and Schlesinger, 1979)

the process and the outcome. Some groups and individuals will support the change more than others. It is worth identifying supporters and deciding how you can best work together to help sell and manage the change.

Crucially, the stakeholder analysis will allow you to identify likely resistors. As with champions or supporters you need to make judgements about their comparative influence. Conceivably there may be a number of reasons for resistance (see Table 7.4).

If you are able to identify the resistors and the likely reasons for resistance, it is useful to make a judgement about the speed with which the change can be implemented. Five variables need to be taken into account (see Table 7.5).

Table 7.4 Causes of resistance to change (based on Kotter and Schlesinger, 1979)

Cause of resistance	
Self interest	Change doesn't necessarily bring benefits to everyone. People resist simply because the change will have negative effects upon them.
Misunderstanding and lack of trust	It easy for people to misunderstand the purpose of change. If there is a lack of trust the worst possible interpretation will be placed on the change and the worst of motivations assumed.
Different assessments of need or the situation	People can simply disagree with the change on rational grounds. Change is always contended so people can review and analyse a proposed change and prefer a different solution or way forward.
Low tolerance to change	Some groups are less able to take on change than others. For instance, an organisation in a resource or political crisis cannot cope readily with major change and if a group has been subject to relentless change initiatives people can be burnt out.

Table 7.5 Variables of change (adapted from Kotter and Schlesinger, 1979, Exhibit II)

Variable		
The amount and kind of resistance	Fast 1	Slow 5
The power difference between you and the resistors	Fast 1	Slow 5
The need to get commitment and information from others	Fast 1	Slow 5
The degree of risk to the organisation if the change is not implemented quickly	Fast 1	Slow 5
The possible benefits to the organisation if it is implemented quickly	Fast 1	Slow 5

Given the nature of the resistance and the desired pace of change the final and crucial consideration is the most effective strategy to follow. Kotter and Schlesinger identify a number of possible approaches and explore their advantages and disadvantages and the circumstances under which they are best used (see Table 7.6).

Table 7.6 Methods for dealing with resistance to change (Kotter and Schlesinger, 1979, p111)

Methods for dealing with resistance to change

Approach	Commonly used in situations	Advantages	Drawbacks
Education and communication	Where there is a lack of information or inaccurate information and analysis	Once persuaded, people will often help with the implementation of changes	Can be very time consuming if lots of people are involved
Participation and involvement	Where the initiators do not have all the information they need to design the change, and where others have considerable power to resist	People who participate will be committed to implementing change, and any relevant information they have will be integrated into the plan	Can be very time consuming if participators design inappropriate change
Facilitation and support	Where people are resisting because of adjustment problems	No other approach works as well with adjustment problems	Can be time consuming, expensive and still fail
Negotiation and agreement	Where someone or some group will clearly lose out in a change, and where that group has considerable power to resist	Sometimes it is a relatively easy way to avoid major resistance	Can be too expensive in many cases if it alerts others to negotiate for compliance
Manipulation and co-optation	Where other tactics will not work, or are too expensive	It can be a relatively quick and inexpensive solution to resistance problems	Can lead to future problems if people feel manipulated
Explicit and implicit coercion	Where speed is essential and the change initiators possess considerable power	It is speedy and can overcome any kind of resistance	Can be risky if it leaves people mad at the initiators

Crucial to their approach is not managing every change in the same way but varying your approach according to circumstances. You can also combine several different strategies together. A benefit of this more strategic approach is not attempting to educate people when the change is simply not in their interest or trying to coerce people when you need their participation and involvement.

Again, this strategic approach has a number of advantages and disadvantages. Although explicitly intended for senior managers, it offers a different approach to the psychological model we examined earlier and could even be seen to compliment it. Its main advantage is that it encourages managers to think about the social context of change and to be flexible. This is particularly valuable given the need to often manage change across a network of providers, as a manager is encouraged to give attention to each of the groups that need to be part of the change and handle each one differently.

Its downside is that it could be seen to encourage top-down, controlling and manipulative change. It puts senior mangers in the driving seat making judgements about others with no real regard to any ethical considerations. For instance, there is no suggestion that people should be consulted and involved on principle, but rather only if it is necessary or expedient – otherwise coercion is equally acceptable as a strategy.

REFLECTION POINT 7.2

Take some time out and ask yourself how effective you are at managing change.

- *What strategies do you use?*
- *Do you take time to plan changes in advance?*
- *Do you identify key stakeholders who must be involved in the change?*
- *Do you identify resistors and champions?*
- *Do you adopt different change strategies according to the nature and the type of resistance?*
- *Do you mobilise champions to help with change?*
- *Do you allow different timescales for implementation allowing for risks and resistance?*

Developing the team and the organisation

The final part of this chapter focuses on developing your team and the organisation. Rather than just administering everyday activities or responding to changes as these arise, another expectation placed on leaders and managers is that they should actively develop and improve the organisation and its performance. So, instead of only responding to change, effective leadership means that you should initiate change. This can at one end of the spectrum mean improving the effectiveness of the team you lead or it can also mean helping improve organisational structures, systems, processes and cultures. We begin by exploring team development.

Developing your team

A crucial responsibility for a team leader or manager is developing the team itself. Team development consists of intervening in the team to influence behaviours and relationships in order to improve efficiency and effectiveness. A typical way to develop the team is through team away-days and other team development activities, but a common criticism is that team development is all too often not methodical or purposeful. This means that there is necessarily no way the development activity can be designed to meet particular objectives or can be evaluated to judge if objectives have been met.

To make team development methodical we need to determine the characteristics of an efficient and effective team and compare current team behaviours and relationships with this model. Therefore, team developmental objectives need to be based on proper analyses. Team development activities can then be directed towards objectives that improve team functioning. There are several theories or models of team functioning that are commonly referred to – we list six below.

- Stages of team development. Teams are seen to go through a number of distinct stages from the point of formation until their termination. Each stage is progressive and leads towards increasingly better performance (Tuckman, 1965). Each has particular characteristics and demands a particular type of leadership if a team is to steadily improve its performance. Making a judgement about what stage a team is at allows a leader to determine the appropriate leadership and actions to help a team progress to higher levels of performance.

- Team roles. The most influential theorist here is Meredith Belbin (1993) who has identified nine essential team roles for a team to function effectively. The absence from a team of a member who fulfils a particular role can explain problems in a team functioning effectively. Aware of a gap in a team, other members can compensate for the deficiency or another team member can be recruited with the right characteristics – visit the Mind Tools (2009) website **www.mindtools.com/pages/article/newLDR_83.htm** to explore Belbin's team roles. The site is also a useful resource for other management tools and theories.

- Appropriate leadership. Leadership that responds to the needs of the team allows it to improve its performance over time. Inappropriate leadership can lead to a team that is 'stuck' or result in deviant and unhelpful behaviour. Situational leadership theory (Hersey and Blanchard, 1974, 1993) can be seen to mirror the stages of team development with a leader adjusting their style as the team 'matures' (see Chapter 3).

- A mixture of conflict and consensus. Without sufficient trust and consensus to hold the team together, disagreements over its direction or decisions can lead to damaging conflicts that can reduce effective functioning or even lead to the break up of the team. A lack of conflict can mean that team members do not contribute different perspectives and so discover creative options to improve team functioning and problem solving. A balance of the two is essential for an effective team (see Mullins, 2007 p310).

- Stuck teams. Irving Janis (1971) coined the term 'Groupthink' to describe a team stuck in unquestioned consensus. However, there are a range of 'stuck' scenarios. A team can develop a blame culture that scapegoats an individual in the team or blames 'people out there' for its problems. It can be stuck in conformity because of an over-dominant leader or locked into rebellion. It can be split into sub-groups that feud or its problem solving can be distorted by hidden unspoken agendas. It can be so lacking in trust, positive relationships or sense of direction it is almost impossible to get the team to even meet together. Irving Janis's original paper on Groupthink is available from: **www.er.uqam.ca/nobel/d101000/JanisGroupthinkPolicyMakers.pdf**.

- Clear objectives and a sense of direction. Teams need to know what they are working together to achieve and this needs to be set in a broader vision that gives their objectives meaning. So, a team needs a business planning or unit planning process made meaningful by a shared value base and a team commitment to improving service quality.

ACTIVITY 7.1

Review each of the characteristics of an effective team below and make some notes about the extent to which they are a feature of your team. What evidence do you have for your conclusions? What actions will you take to improve team effectiveness? You may wish to involve your team in this process.

A purpose, value base and sense of direction that is meaningful to its members

Objectives that integrate with the plans of the wider organisation and are regularly reviewed

Trusting relationships between its members and positive regard

A climate where problems can be raised and practice challenged

Responsive and flexible leadership

A good range of personalities and roles

Procedures and ways of working that allow it to work effectively, including resolving conflicts

Good relationships and established working relationships with co-providers

Good relationships and established working relationships with the rest of the organisation

Continuous team development and improvement

Some other useful questions in determining how you might build team effectiveness are:

What stage of development do I think the team is at and why? What might move the team on to a higher stage of performance?

Could the team be seen to be in any way 'stuck' in unhelpful behaviours?

What might I do to help them move on?

Do I have a team development plan that has been discussed and agreed with the team?

Is it based on an analysis of team effectiveness and functioning?

Has it clear objectives that can be evaluated?

Is it reviewed regularly?

Improving organisational systems and processes and developing organisational culture

Apart from managing organisational practices, procedures and systems on an everyday basis there is opportunity as a manager to contribute to improving practices, procedures and systems. For instance, some systems and policies you might seek to improve are personal development planning/CPD and appraisal, management development policy and practice, business planning, budget management, etc. The basis of this book is to assist you to improve service quality and performance by problem solving and hopefully the outcome of each chapter will be an improvement plan that you and your team can work on. It is a good idea to pull activity together as a business or team development plan working to the business planning process (see Figure 7.3).

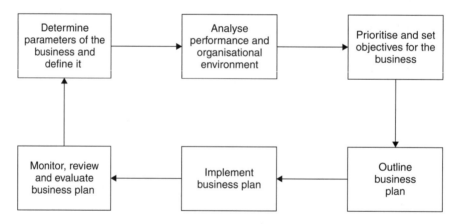

Figure 7.3 The business planning process (Keen et al., 2009, p103)

In analysing performance and the organisational environment to set objectives for your business plan there are a number of sources you can draw on. These can then be used to establish strengths, weaknesses, opportunities or threats in what is often called a 'SWOT' analysis (see Figure 7.4 and chapter 8 for a detailed discussion of this important analytical tool and guidance on how to use it).

There are a number of things to note in how we have represented Figure 7.4.

- We have emphasised the involvement of all stakeholders. Each has a part to play in the service, either as contributors or beneficiaries. Not only are they the best source of information but are crucial in agreeing and implementing any future plans. People who use services are your most important stakeholders.

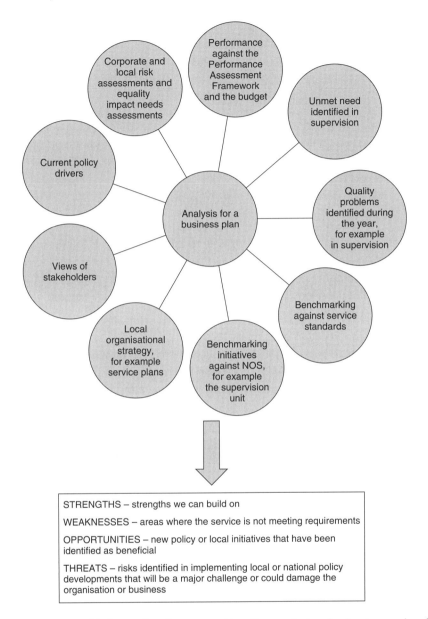

Figure 7.4 Sources of information for supporting the analysis of a business plan (Keen et al.,2009, p113)

- Making judgements about previous organisational performance involves collecting information. Some is readily available as performance measures but some will need collecting as it arises e.g. out of supervision.

- As a team you will need to keep abreast of national policy initiatives.

- You should have available to you information about organisational performance against Performance Assessment Framework indicators. This may provide you with an obvious target e.g. reducing the time it takes to complete an assessment or you may need to problem solve with your team to determine the factors that might be preventing you meeting a performance target. For example, what elements of the team's practice might be contributing to the breakdown of foster placements?

- There may be local organisational strategies and service plans that you need to incorporate into any business planning.

- You will probably need to carry out some benchmarking activity e.g. reviewing team performance against service standards like the Commissioning Standards that can be accessed on the CWDC (**www.cwdc.org.uk**) and Skills for Care (**www.skillsforcare.org.uk**) websites.

- Some general 'good practice models' are worth considering (see section below on learning organisations).

- If you and your team are not ready or able to get involved in a full business planning process then try and identify a simple team service improvement plan to which you can all contribute. Sometimes, once you start reviewing some aspects of service provision and thinking about options that might better meet need, it can become part of how a team works and can develop over time.

A business plan also needs to encompass the general level of activity of the team and the team budget needs to support this level of activity as well as service improvements you identify (see Chapter 8 for detailed guidance on business planning). Before we move on to the final part of the chapter on learning organisations consider auditing your business planning process below.

ACTIVITY 7.2

Auditing business planning

Do you have a business planning process that the team own and contribute to?

Do you draw on the range of possible sources in determining objectives as in Figure 7.4 above?

Have you involved the range of possible stakeholders in business planning?

What role do users play in business planning?

Do you have clear objectives based on identifying strengths, weaknesses, opportunities and threats?

Do you have a delegated plan of action that identifies who is responsible for activities and when they will be completed?

Is your business plan monitored and reviewed as circumstances change?

Learning organisations

While business planning is essential we could attempt to develop the organisation as a whole to achieve the characteristics of a 'learning organisation'. A learning organisation is one which mobilises all its resources to continually learn and develop itself. Senge's (1990) influential work identifies the features of a learning organisation as being systems thinking, personal mastery, overcoming mental models, shared vision and values, team working and learning. SCIE (2004) have developed an audit tool that is designed to help managers develop their organisation as a learning organisation. There is an adapted version of this audit for you to use in Activity 7.3 at the end of the chapter.

It is worth noting, however, that there are a number of approaches or models of learning organisations. One can see different models associated with different learning cultures found in organisations (see Chapter 9). In a professional learning culture where learning and development is primarily a professional responsibility, a learning community might be developed and led by professionals, perhaps with an emphasis on learning processes. In a managed learning culture, where learning and development are directed towards organisational ends led by managers, an approach to developing a learning organisation might be planned from the top down and might emphasise systems, procedures and evaluation of outcomes. A humanistic learning culture might result in a learning organisation that is much nearer to a therapeutic community in its characteristics and focused on personal growth and development (Hinshelwood and Manning, 1979).

Mobilising the team to contribute to developing services

Individual practice cannot really be distinguished from organisational practices. Rather, we are perhaps all best seen as members of a 'community of practice' (Wenger, 2006) in which our individual perspectives, aspirations and actions form part of these wider systems and relationships, and, in social work, these are underpinned by our explicit value base (see GSCC, 2004). This makes influencing the broader context in which practice is set central to high quality professional practice.

The National Occupational Standards for Social Work in England (Topss England, 2002) emphasise the need for social workers to contribute to the development of services and to maintaining service quality. Unit 15 identifies the need to, *contribute to the management of resources and services* and describes four key activities:

15.1 Contribute to the procedures involved in purchasing and commissioning services

15.2 Contribute to monitoring the effectiveness of services in meeting need

15.3 Contribute to monitoring the quality of the services provided

15.4 Contribute to managing information

Unit 17 expects social workers to *work within multi-disciplinary and multi-organisational teams, networks and systems* and as part of that work to:

17.2 Contribute to the identifying and agreeing of the goals, objectives and lifespan of the team, network or system

and

17.3 Contribute to evaluating the effectiveness of the team, network or system

So, rather than taking sole responsibility yourself, create opportunities for the team to work with you in enhancing service quality. In fact, social care professionals are well placed to act as a broker in bringing service improvements and you play a crucial role in facilitating this (see Figure 7.5 below).

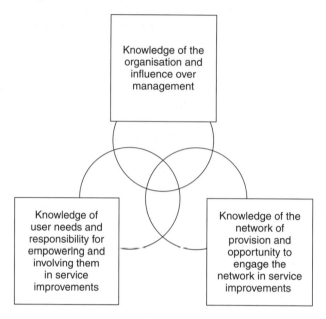

Figure 7.5 The role of the social worker as broker for service improvements (Keen et al., 2009, p101)

User involvement in enhancing service quality

Herein lies an important point. If, as the theory of distributed leadership (Watson, 2002) suggests, leadership should be diffused as much as possible within an organisation, it raises the question as to whether it should be distributed to people who use services. This is the thrust of the current participation agenda, allowing users to lead and manage their own services (DH, 2007a). As a manager or supervisor you will play a key role in engaging people who use services and carers in service improvements through identifying problems, designing improvements and implementing solutions. This can be achieved by evaluating the effectiveness of services they receive or by working with representatives to use their expertise to bring about service improvements (see Liz's (pseudonym) experience in the case study below). To ensure this involvement is genuine is quite a challenge and will require you and your team to question and change your practices.

CASE STUDY **7.1**

Liz's involvement in service development

Involving the public, users of services and carers, in health and social care development initiatives has been increasingly promoted in recent government policies in the UK and is high on the agenda of regulatory bodies (DH, 2002; DH, 2006; Lowes and Hulatt, 2005).

My own experience of involvement has developed over many years; from being a silent voice at a formal strategy meeting, to participation as one of many stakeholders; and now

CASE STUDY 7.1 (CONT.)

to an expert in my own field. As a user of mental health services, I wanted to do something positive to 'make a difference.' Initially, I was thrust into an alien environment which excluded me through its structures and jargon. The professionals did not know what to do with me. I sat at a meeting and then left. To continue, I had to question my purpose and function.

Through a user forum, I began to accept invitations to speak about my experiences. I spoke to others so that I could offer a balanced perspective of how people experienced services. I came to conclude that often what people were offered was 'service led' rather than 'needs led'. I wanted to communicate that the voice of the 'consumer' was key. Receiving a service, appropriate to individual need made sense and was surely more cost effective? My aim was not to be critical, but to simply report 'how it is' and offer constructive input on how it could be better – for both the practitioner and person using services. The practicalities of being involved proved to be a challenge. These included:

- being required to attend meetings at 9 am which involve a long journey by public transport;
- having no prior discussion/training to be able to participate from an informed perspective;
- waiting months to receive any payment for expenses;
- finding myself sat next to my own Psychiatrist at a service review!

It is only by voicing these difficulties that change can occur. It is not always easy when fluctuating mental health can bring periods of acute anxiety and withdrawal. In spite of this, I have worked hard to gain respect and credibility in my involvement activities and have begun to engage in meaningful dialogue with all stakeholders. I am encouraged when I have tangible evidence that I have been heard and taken seriously.

The gains of involvement are rarely financial, so what motivates me? I want services to be of a high quality and to provide good outcomes for those who use them. I want to use my years in the system in a positive way; to give something back. Through this, my confidence and sense of self-worth have significantly increased.

I started out as the token user of services – wheeled in and out at the appropriate time and my involvement was meaningless. This has developed into what I would describe as inclusive and productive partnership working.

This chapter ends with an opportunity for you to reflect on your organisation.

ACTIVITY 7.3

Learning organisation audit

Use the Learning Organisation Audit below to audit current organisational practices and plan for improvement. You might want look at both your team and the wider organisation when using the SCIE audit tool as, while your team culture and practices will be influenced by the wider organisation, they are not necessarily congruent.

Learning organisation audit

On a five-point Likert scale ranging from strongly agree to strongly disagree, rate how the following statements apply to the information systems used in your organisation.

- There are effective information systems for both internal and external communication.
- The organisation makes good use of IT to improve information exchange and management.
- Information is freely available.
- Where possible, information is shared openly with people who use services and their carers.
- Policies and procedures are meaningful and understood by all.

Using the same Likert scale rate how the following statements apply to the structure of your organisation.

- Feedback and participation of people who use services and carers is actively sought.
- Team working, learning and utilising all staff skills are integral to the organisation.
- There is cross-organisational, collaborative and partnership working.

Again, using the same Likert scale rate how the following statements apply to the culture of your organisation.

- There is a system of shared beliefs, values, goals and objectives.
- Development of new ideas and methods is encouraged.
- An open learning environment allows the opportunity to test innovative practice.
- New evidence and research are considered and incorporated into practice.
- Ideas and proposals can come from any part of the organisation – not just 'top down'.
- People who identify problems are not blamed.

Again, using the same Likert scale rate whether the following statements apply to learning and development in your workplace.

- There is a commitment to continuous personal and career development for all staff and by all staff.
- Individual learning styles and learning needs are responded to.
- A good range of formal and informal learning opportunities are open to all.
- A high quality of individual supervision and support is offered.

And finally, using the same Likert scale, rate whether the following leadership strengths are established in the organisation you work for.

- *The organisation develops and improves services wherever it can.*
- *Leaders model the openness, risk-taking and reflection necessary for learning.*
- *Leaders ensure that the organisation has the resources and capacity to learn, change and develop.*
- *Learning and development opportunities are linked to organisational objectives.*

These statements have been adapted from the SCIE website and are used with permission within this book (see SCIE, 2006).

Chapter summary

- Managing organisational change is a key leadership function and change is rife in our organisations.

- There are many different perspectives on change, some look at the psychology of change, which can be very helpful in managing our teams.

- Other approaches to change, such as Kotter and Schlesinger's (1979) take a more strategic and proactive approach.

- Developing team effectiveness can be a valuable activity that improves service quality.

- You can also work with your team to formulate a business or improvement plan that will directly improve service quality.

- Involving people who use services, carers and patients in service and quality improvement initiatives is essential but needs a lot of investment by you and your team to be effective and not merely tokenistic.

- A currently popular approach to organisational development supported by government policy is developing the features of the organisation so that it becomes a learning organisation.

FURTHER READING

Everitt, A. and Hardiker, P. (1996) *Evaluating for Good Practice.* Basingstoke: Macmillan.

Offers a critical approach to the evaluation of practice and services.

Senge, P.M. (1990*) The Fifth Discipline. The Art and Practice of the Learning Organisation.* London: Random House.

The classic text on learning organisations.

Chapter 8
Planning and budgeting

Richard Field

CHAPTER OBJECTIVES

This chapter will help you address the following National Occupational Standards for Management and Leadership.

- C5 Plan change.
- E1 Manage a budget.

This chapter also helps you address the following Principles of Social Care Management.

- Promote and meet service aims, objectives and goals.

Introduction

The future operating context for public service leadership is such that efficiency and effectiveness will become even more important than now. Planning and budgeting processes will be critical to ongoing success.

This chapter explores planning and budgeting, offering ideas intended to help the reader develop competence and confidence. Planning can be defined as:

the process by which a desired future state is conceived and an effective way of delivering this developed and resourced (Field, 2007, p2).

Budgeting is the process by which the resources required to support planned activity are secured and managed.

Although often seen as separate processes the case is made for integrating planning and budgeting, which in many organisations means that managers will need to become more involved than is currently the case. The planning and budgeting sub-sections of this chapter conclude with self-audit and reflection tasks.

Planning

The earlier definition of planning makes three important points; that planning is a design process, is future based and seeks to ensure the desired future state is delivered.

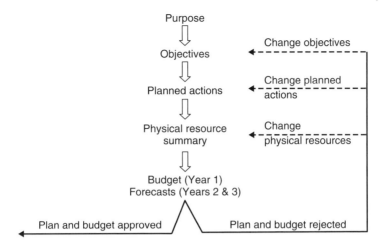

Figure 8.1 Integrating plans and budgets (Field, 2007, p5)

While all people plan in respect of their personal lives we differ in the extent to which we plan, the detail we engage in and our overall approach. Organisational planning differs from personal planning in that it normally involves preparation of a planning document, the use of planning techniques and approval by a more senior person or body. Organisational planning should be an integral part of the performance management process and flows from strategic analysis and synthesis.

Plan and budget integration is illustrated in Figure 8.1, where an annual planning process leads to the preparation of a three-year rolling plan with the first year expressed as a detailed budget and years two and three as broader financial forecasts.

Accepting the idea of plan and budget integration it follows that:

• planned activity cannot be changed without this affecting the budget;

• a change in budget will impact on the quantity and/or quality of planned activity;

• managers start the project or year with sufficient money to resource approved plans;

• approval or rejection decisions apply to both the plan and the budget.

As public sector resources are limited there will inevitably be occasions when a perfectly good plan will be rejected. If an attempt is made to approve the plan but with a reduced budget, the manager should stay true to the principle of integration, identifying changes in planned quantity and/or quality of activity, or deploying different physical resources such that the cost of required resources reduces to the point that the plan and budget once again match.

Planning and budgeting processes should go far beyond the simple preparation of action points and the calculation of the budget required to purchase physical resources. Effective planning involves strategic thinking and significant challenge regarding the level and quality of resources required, where and how these are purchased – all with a view to ensuring value for money.

However, this integrated approach, despite its associated logic and attractiveness, is relatively rare in practice. Continuous pressure to increase service quantity and quality while reducing or at least constraining budgets has led to years of budgets based on figures for previous years rather than what is needed. This rather crude approach often results in poor service prioritisation, gains in economy and efficiency at the expense of effectiveness, game playing, poor value for money and undue managerial stress.

Why plan?

Undertaken with enthusiasm and care the planning process should ensure that services and activities continue to be relevant to the community, service development is stimulated, value for money is achieved and management control facilitated, all of which contribute to sustainable performance improvement.

Types of planning and plan documents

Approaches to organisational planning and the preparation of plan documents differ between organisations, vary over time and change to reflect managerial fashion. Such variations include the organisational scope, plan format, the extent to which planning is strategic or operational, and the time period addressed.

The format of a plan is often determined by another agency or by managers operating at a more strategic level within the organisation. Where there is freedom regarding plan format the broad structure outlined in Figure 8.2 should be considered. It features three main sections (analysis, direction and action), which combine to make planning proposals in a coherent and persuasive way.

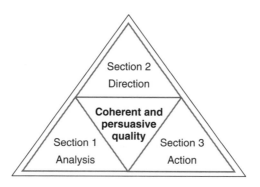

Figure 8.2 Planning to plan (Field, 2007, p9)

The analysis section should include relevant historic, current and forecast information regarding various aspects of the service which helps the reader understand the current and likely future context for the plan.

The direction section explains why the service exists, identifies key objectives for the planning period and explains in broad terms how these will be achieved.

The action section should convince the reader that proposed actions will deliver the objectives, are realistic and will happen if the plan is approved.

What constitutes a good quality plan?

The quality of a plan can be assessed using a number of criteria presented as questions in Table 8.1.

Table 8.1 Criteria – quality plans

Plan evaluation questions
1   Is the plan written in a way that can be understood by the intended reader(s)?
2   Does the plan have a persuasive quality?
3   Are short- and long-term outcomes recognised and balanced?
4   Do the planned objectives and actions fit the current situation?
5   Is the plan of appropriate length?
6   Does there appear to be sufficient analysis?
7   Does the plan flow?
8   Does the plan contain sufficient detail regarding the internal and external context?
9   Does the plan appear to be the product of a sound planning process?
10   Does the plan show how this links to other plans?
11   Is the plan self-critical?
12   Does the plan take account of the views of key stakeholders, balancing the different desired outcomes?
13   Is there evidence that planned performance is being stretched, yet realistic?
14   Does the plan include a clear statement of direction and SMART objectives?
15   Does the plan indicate the level of resources required to support activity?
16   Does the plan reassure the reader that planned actions will happen?
17   Have risks been considered?

What constitutes a good planning process?

Good quality plans arise from an effective planning process, which typically involves six steps as shown in Figure 8.3 below.

The first stage concerns planning to plan and involves addressing ten questions (see Table 8.2.

The second stage, analysis and strategic thinking, is at the heart of the planning process and is covered in more detail later in this chapter. With the content of the plan generated, attention turns to the third stage, which involves writing the document in preparation for the fourth stage; approval and feedback. Once approved, the plan is implemented leading to the final stage involving periodic performance review.

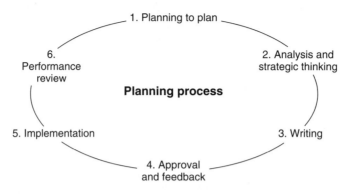

Figure 8.3 The planning process

Table 8.2 Planning questions (Field, 2007, p15)

Planning to plan

1   Who will receive the plan and for what purpose?

2   What plan format will be used?

3   Who should be involved in planning, and how?

4   What guidance and support will be given to those involved?

5   What will be communicated to those not directly involved in planning?

6   What timetable will be adopted for planning?

7   What criteria will be used to evaluate the plan?

8   How does the plan link with other systems?

9   Who will write the plan?

10   Who will present the plan?

Thirteen key questions – analysis, direction and action

The thirteen key questions in Table 8.3 offer a framework for analysis, direction and action planning.

Analysis

Questions 1–7 in Table 8.3 provide a framework for completing the analysis section, the quality of which can be greatly enhanced by using planning tools such as a strengths, weaknesses, opportunities and threats analysis (SWOT) or environmental scanning (SPELT). These two tools, which are in widespread use, are explained below.

Table 8.3 Thirteen key planning questions

Question	Purpose and approach
Analysis	
1. What do we know about how we operate?	Most services have strengths that contribute to successful operation which, depending on the future environment and direction, will be important to maintain in the immediate term. Similarly, most services have one or more weaknesses that if sufficiently serious should be addressed within the plan.
2. What do we know about our performance?	Plan readers need to understand how successful a service is, whether performance is improving or reducing and how this compares with similar services or organisations.
3. What restraints affect our planning?	Most plans are prepared within frameworks that in effect limit the actions planners can propose.
4. What do we know about the environment?	The plan should reflect the environment within which the service will operate, how this might change in the future and the implications this poses for the service.
5. What do we know about those that use our services and the services we provide or contract?	The plan should identify current service users and their level of satisfaction together with targeted future users and the needs that should be addressed. The resource implications of running these services together with the associated unit costs should also be included.
6. What do we know about organisations that provide similar services?	Understanding how this service compares to similar ones is important either because of operating in a competitive situation or because there is potential to learn from other organisations.
7. What do we know about opportunities and threats?	Arising from the earlier analysis will be opportunities and threats, which should be drawn together and the implications explored.
Direction	
8. Why do we exist or act as we do?	The plan should include a succinct statement that captures the purpose of the organisation.
9. What do we want to achieve?	The plan should include a small number of key objectives some of which are likely to relate to ongoing service delivery, others to one-off initiatives or specific required actions. These should flow from the earlier analysis, be consistent with the purpose statement and expressed in SMART terms (Specific, Measurable, Achievable, Realistic and Timed).
10. How will we achieve what we want?	This section outlines the broad approach to achieving each key objective expressed as headline actions with more detail appearing later in the action section.

Table 8.3 (continued)

Question	Purpose and approach
Action	
11. How will we ensure that the plan will happen?	This section identifies the detailed actions required to make the plan happen, the person responsible for taking action and how progress will be monitored.
12. What resources are needed to support the plan?	It is important that the level and cost of resources needed for planned activity are clearly stated.
13. What risks are plan activities exposed to and how will these be managed?	The plan should identify the risks to which the service is exposed, the potential impact, likelihood of occurrence and the approach proposed for managing this risk.

SWOT

A SWOT analysis is used to capture the internal strengths and weaknesses of a service together with the external opportunities and threats, typically presented as four cell matrix as shown in Figure 8.4.

Strengths	Weaknesses
Opportunities	Threats

Figure 8.4 SWOT analysis

A variation on the traditional approach to SWOT is to split this analysis into two further tools; a strengths and weaknesses analysis undertaken at the start of the analysis section and an opportunities and threats analysis, completed towards the end. This split is adopted in the following material.

Strengths and weaknesses analysis

Any service is likely to have a number of strengths and weaknesses, some of which will be key to ongoing success and others of relatively minor importance. As a general rule a strength or weakness should only be included in the plan if it is relevant to the service, significant in size and its impact differential when compared to other services. When stating strengths and weaknesses it is important to avoid the common practice of simply producing a list (e.g. our staff are a strength) as this leaves readers unaware of why a factor is a strength or weakness, the impact this has on service performance and so on. The analysis can be improved by using the grid included as Table 8.4, which contains five questions intended to help determine which strengths and weaknesses feature in a plan.

Table 8.4 Strengths and weaknesses analysis

Strength/ weakness	How does this impact on the service?	Is the significance high, medium or low?	How do similar organisations compare?	Is the significance increasing/ decreasing/ or static?	What evidence is there to support this view?
E.g. Well equipped staff – all have high specification laptops, PDAs, etc.	Staff are in constant touch with the office, information is entered once only and efficiency is high. Responses to client enquiries can be immediate. Staff feel that they are well equipped for the work they undertake	Medium	A number of similar organisations appear to have failed to make this investment	Decreasing as technology costs fall and other organisations invest	Customer response times and qualitative feedback. Staff feedback from annual Attitude Survey

Where a strengths and weaknesses analysis is undertaken prior to completing an environmental scan and determining future service direction there is a risk of focusing on factors that will be less important in future or failing to identify ones that will be important given the future environment and direction. The initial strengths and weaknesses analysis should therefore be reviewed once the proposed direction is known.

Environmental analysis

Understanding the environment and how it might change provides the context for planning. Environmental scanning is a process which helps develop this understanding, one version of which (SPELT) provides a framework for identifying five major sources of environmental influence; sociological, political, economic, legal and technological, and three timeframes; influences that are impacting now, those expected to impact over the next three years and those that might impact in the longer term as shown in Figure 8.5.

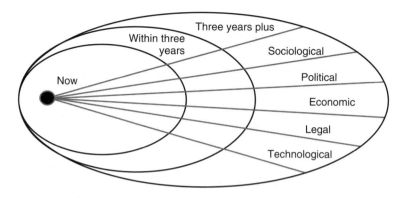

Figure 8.5 SPELT analysis (Field, 2007, p22)

When using SPELT the first stage is to identify environmental influences that might impact on the service under consideration. This might affect all organisations, all public services or only those offering, receiving or employed within a particular service. The five sources are used to prompt rather than constrain thinking across the environment and an influence will often relate to two or more categories.

The second step in using SPELT is to identify the likely impact of each influence on the service concerned using low, medium and high descriptors to indicate the extent of the impact and the probability of it occurring. Table 8.5 illustrates how one significant economic influence can impact on a service, in this case a large General Practice.

Table 8.5 SPELT influences – economic example

SPELT Category and influence	Impact	Possible implications	Impact and probability
Economic recession	High levels of unemployment	Increased demand for services – particularly related to treatment for stress and depression	Medium impact and high probability
		Reduced levels of staff turnover and easier recruitment – more applicants with greater experience	Low impact and high probability
	Reduced public sector funding	Reduced funding and an increased emphasis on efficiency	High impact and high probability

The final step is to use the impact/probability assessment to determine whether to:

- respond to the influence in this plan;
- consider this influence during the period covered by the plan;
- monitor this influence during the life of the plan;
- ignore the influence.

Opportunities and threats analysis

Opportunities and threats face all organisations, the implications of which range from minor to very significant. Considering opportunities and threats at the end of the analysis stage allows this to be influenced by factors that have emerged while considering key questions 1–6 (see Table 8.3). However, it is also worth allowing time and space for more opportunities and threats to be identified – perhaps via the use of a creativity technique, such as brainstorming.

As it is likely that there will be a significant number of opportunities and threats it is help-ful to filter these to isolate those that are both potentially significant and likely to materialise. This process of filtering can be assisted by the use of a grid such as the one included as Table 8.6, where the first column identifies opportunities and threats and the second, its potential impact. Columns 3 and 4 record the significance and likelihood scores using a scale of 1–10 where 10 is high. Where those planning decide that an opportunity or threat looks significant, Column 5 should be completed, describing one or more possible responses.

Table 8.6 Opportunities and threats analysis

Opportunity/ threat	Potential impact	Potential significance (Score 1–10 where 10 is high	Likelihood of occurrence (Score 1–10 where 10 is high)	Possible responses
(1)	(2)	(3)	(4)	(5)
Imposed efficiency target	Need to increase efficiency year on year	8	9	Establish a rolling efficiency review programme

Direction

Having addressed the seven key questions relating to analysis, attention turns to stating the purpose, key objectives and the high level actions associated with direction.

All plans benefit from the inclusion of a high level statement of purpose, which helps the reader understand why the service, unit, organisation, etc. exists and provides a focus for objectives and planned actions. The following is an example of such a statement for a home care service.

> *We aim to provide a range of tailored services to users in a way that promotes their independence, secures an improved quality of life and helps them remain in their own homes.*

Statements of purpose, mission or vision are usually expressed in general terms and are a high level expression of direction. More specific information about direction is normally provided in the form of key objectives such as:

To undertake a rolling programme of service reviews resulting in savings of:

- *£0.5m in 2011/12*

- *£1.5m in 2012/13*

- *£2.5m in 2013/14*

While there are potentially numerous objectives relating to a service, only those that are key to success should be included in this part of the plan. When stating objectives care should be taken to ensure that they are stated in SMART terms (Specific, Measurable, Achievable, Realistic and Timed).

The direction stage of planning concludes with the identification of high level actions needed to achieve the key objectives. Both the objectives and high level actions can be captured in a grid as shown in Table 8.7, the preparation of which is completed during the action planning stage. Identifying the purpose, defining the objectives and stating highlevel actions answers key questions 8, 9 and 10 in Table 8.3, which concern the direction phase of planning.

Action planning

The action plan element should reassure the reader that thought has been given to how the plan is to be achieved, that risks have been considered and contingency measures are in place. The first stage of action planning is to identify the detailed actions that will lead to the achievement of each high level action, thereby ensuring that each key objective is met. The action grid included as Table 8.7 and started during the direction phase can be used to record detailed actions together with information regarding responsibility and monitoring. The grid is completed by:

Table 8.7 Action grid

Objectives	High level actions	Detailed actions	Detailed action – key dates	Responsible person	Monitoring arrangements
(1)	(2)	(3)	(4)	(5)	(6)
Undertake a rolling programme of service reviews resulting in savings of; • £0.5m in 2011/12 • £1.5m in 2012/13 • £2.5m in 2013/14	Develop a three-year review programme by 31st March 2011	Identify full list of reviews Prioritise reviews Submit priorities list for approval by senior management team	By 25th February 2011 By 14th March 2011 By 16th March 2011	Director of Operations	Monthly line management monitoring and consideration by senior management team

- breaking high level actions down into detailed actions and inserting these in Column 3;

- entering key dates in Column 4;

- stating in Column 5 the name of the person responsible for ensuring each detailed action occurs;

- specifying monitoring arrangements in Column 6.

Completing this action plan addresses key question 11 in Table 8.3.

Question 12 in Table 8.3 concerns the identification of resources needed and the associated budget, the process for calculating which is detailed later in this chapter.

When approving a plan those involved need to be assured that potential risks have been identified, assessed and will be managed. This information can be conveyed via the grid provided as Table 8.8, completion of which involves:

- describing risks in Column 1 indicating the source;

- describing the likely impact in Column 2;

Table 8.8 Risk grid

Description of risk and source	Description of likely impact	Impact (Score 1–10, where 1 is low and 10 is high)	Likelihood (Score 1–10, where 1 is low risk and 10 is high)	Risk score (Column 3 x Column 4)	Risk management
(1)	(2)	(3)	(4)	(5)	(6)
Level of cuts imposed is greater than planned budget reductions, arising from planned service reviews (Source: Environmental – Economic)	Likely to be even tougher financial targets imposed by senior managers, probably on a pro-rata basis Possible failure to achieve cuts with subsequent overspend	8	6	48	Priority will be given to services expected to yield more significant resource savings Second optional schedule will be prepared with a much faster pace of review

- indicating in Column 3 the potential severity of this impact, using a score of 1–10 where 1 is low;

- indicating in Column 4 the likelihood that this risk will occur, using a score of 1–10 where 1 is low;

- multiplying the impact and likelihood scores to give a total risk score and entering this in Column 5;

- indicating in Column 6 the management arrangements in respect of risks where scores are considered high.

REFLECTION POINT 8.1

Planning is a significant management process, competence in which will be important to future organisational survival and leadership success. The following five questions comprise a framework for reflecting on current competence in the workplace, the application of learning and planning further personal and organisational development.

1. *To what extent do the plans you prepare, contribute to or work with:*

   a) *meet the evaluation criteria identified in Table 8.1?*

   b) *address the 13 key questions detailed as Table 8.3?*

2. *If you undertake strengths and weaknesses analysis is the output meaningful to the user (Table 8.4)?*

3. *If you undertake environmental scanning is the potential impact of each factor clear and the likelihood that it will occur stated (Table 8.5)?*

4. *If you undertake an opportunities and threats analysis is this:*

   a) *informed by the answers to key questions 1–6 (Table 8.3)?*

   b) *presented in a way that clearly identifies the potential impact and likelihood (Table 8.6)?*

5. *What is your experience of using other planning tools and how could you improve the value these yield?*

Budgeting

Budget management is a key responsibility for most managers and one which with career progression, tends to become more significant. The exact responsibilities, organisational rules that apply and the processes by which budgets are managed vary significantly between and even within some organisations. The experience that an individual budget manager will have of budget management depends on a number of factors including the:

- number of budgets they are responsible for and the extent to which they can exercise control – at its simplest this responsibility will be limited to a small number of budgets over which reasonable control can be exercised. At its most onerous budget responsibility includes budgets that relate to all the resources used by the manager irrespective of controllability;

- extent to which the financial regulations or rules of the organisation allow managerial control – for example the degree to which the manager is free to make purchases from wherever they wish, whether they can switch money between budgets, have permission to carry forward under/overspends, etc.;

- nature of budget responsibility, this generally being devolved or delegated.

It is essential that budget managers are clear about which budgets they are responsible for, the rules they are required to operate within and whether they have devolved or delegated responsibility.

Devolved and delegated responsibilities

Devolved budget management is defined by Bean and Hussey (1996) as being

> *the process whereby budgets are devolved to an individual who becomes the budget holder and who will be totally responsible and accountable for that budget. Ideally management and financial responsibilities are aligned such that the budget holder is accountable for the financial implications of his/her management decisions*

(Bean and Hussey, 1996, p5)

By contrast the delegated approach is defined as being

> *where budgets are delegated to nominated budget holders who are responsible for monitoring the budget, but are not accountable for the budget as they will have little or no control over its construction and its usage*

(Bean and Hussey, 1996, p6)

Devolved budget managers have total responsibility and are expected to exploit opportunities or remedy problems as they arise during the year. However, the word 'total' is somewhat misleading as there are circumstances where the only responsible action a manager can take is to escalate the budget situation to a more senior budget manager. For managers of a delegated budget, responsibility is limited to ensuring they spend appropriately, monitor levels of income and expenditure regularly, investigate apparent problems and report these to the person who holds devolved responsibility.

Devolution, which is currently quite popular, requires:

- organisational leaders to relinquish a degree of power, which some find quite difficult;

- managers to engage appropriately in budget setting;

- all those involved to understand their role, responsibilities and rights;

- managers to have reasonable managerial and financial freedom.

Where these conditions are not met budget managers will tend to feel responsible for a budget they do not understand or believe to be sufficient and in respect of which they have little freedom to act.

While managers tend to have some understanding of their role and responsibilities with regard to budget management relatively few are aware of their rights. The following questions provide a framework for addressing rights.

1. What rights do I believe I have with regard to budget management?

   Table 8.9 includes some rights typically identified by budget managers.

2. Are these rights being met?

3. What can I do to help my employer meet these rights?

Regarding competence, budget managers with delegated responsibility should be able to monitor a budget, identify causes of variance between budgeted and actual figures, correct errors and propose possible actions. Those managers with devolved responsibility should also be able to prepare and negotiate a budget, complete a year end forecast, interpret financial performance in the wider context, take thoughtful action and escalate issues promptly when necessary. All managers should understand the responsibilities and rights associated with their post, the financial regulations and procedures relevant to their responsibilities, the budget reporting process and budget reports.

Table 8.9 Budget manager rights

The right to:

- Proper involvement in preparing, negotiating and agreeing a budget

- Know the amount of the agreed budget before the financial year starts

- Know the financial regulations and procedures within which they are required to work

- Budget management training before assuming responsibility

- Good quality information

Budget management

In practice, budget management comprises two important interlinking processes; preparation and control. Budget preparation involves calculating how much resource is needed and negotiating this in the light of planned activity and available budget. Budgetary control involves periodically checking the reported financial position, investigating any worrying variances, projecting a year end position and taking action.

Effective planning leads to a greater understanding of service operation and costs, which can greatly assist in budgetary control. Similarly, good budgetary control involves analysis of actual spending and service operation, which in turn can improve the next cycle of plan and budget preparation.

For planning and budgeting to be effective preparation needs to begin well before the start of the period covered by the plan. Early preparation means starting the process before the total available resource is known, so early drafts of the plan and budget may need to be revised several times in the lead up to the start of the new financial year. Final plan and budget approval tends to occur just before the start of a financial year after which attention turns to monthly performance monitoring, including budgetary control. Towards the end of the financial year and continuing into the early part of the following year attention turns to preparing final performance statements and annual accounts.

Budget preparation

Effective budget preparation results in budgets that are challenging yet sufficient to resource planned activity and budget managers who understand how the figures have been calculated. A robust process and the active involvement of budget managers is essential to effective budget practice.

Robust budget preparation leads to budgets being agreed that match planned activity and managers who understand how the budget has been calculated and who are likely to be committed to staying within the agreed sum. Where the preparation process is poor agreed budgets may be too generous or insufficient, managers are unlikely to know how their budget is calculated and will probably suspect it is insufficient. Stress, delayed spending, game playing and low morale can be expected.

Ineffective budget preparation is caused by a number of factors including:

- budget managers who not are involved in preparation;
- little or no opportunity for budget managers to negotiate the plan and budget;
- budgets being calculated by reference to historic spending levels rather than what is required;
- percentage budget cuts being applied.

In practice, budget managers are often presented with a budget that has been calculated by someone else; in which case they have three options.

Option 1: Accept the budget figures given to them, which will probably have been calculated on an historic basis.

Option 2: Calculate the budget they believe necessary to resource the plan, compare this with the budget provided and negotiate accordingly.

Option 3: Check that the budget looks broadly reasonable given performance so far this year and what they know about the service to be delivered next year.

The first option is risky as provided budget figures may bear little relation to planned activity and the second option can be time consuming. In practice, a mix of options two and three tend to be adopted and can work reasonably well providing that: the environment is reasonably stable and no significant changes in service demand or provision are envisaged; the budget manager has reasonable knowledge of their service and is willing to assert their resource needs in the event that they consider the budget to be inadequate; and whenever there is a significant change in the service the budget is recalculated to identify the resources needed (option two).

Budgets can either be prepared with regard to planned activity (rational) or by reference to budgets set for previous years or projects (historic or incremental).

Rational approaches

Rational approaches to budget preparation involve identifying the cost of resources needed to act in a planned way to achieve the set objectives and ultimately the purpose of the service. Policy-based budgeting, thematic, plan-led, needs-led and zero-based are all forms of rational budgeting, each of which should result in a budget that is sufficient to resource planned activity.

While the financial calculations involved in rational approaches are typically straightforward calculating the quantity of physical resources required can be challenging. Clarity about the purpose of the service, the objectives and actions required is essential to successful rational budgeting. Once the actions are known the following five questions need to be addressed.

1. What types of physical resource are needed to act in the way we plan?

2. What minimum quantity of physical resources is required?

3. What is the minimum quality of physical resource needed?

4. What is the cheapest way of securing the required volume and quality of physical resources?

5. How much will these physical resources cost?

The quality of rational budgeting depends on the rigour of the whole process, in particular the extent to which assumptions have been challenged and radical delivery options explored. As a consequence, rational approaches to budget preparation tend to be time consuming and expensive.

Incremental approach

Incremental or historic budgeting is a simple approach to budget preparation whereby the budget for next year is based on the budget relating to the current year. In its purest form the current budget is adjusted up or down to reflect the financial implications of anything which is likely to be different next year e.g. changes in planned service volume and quality, organisational form, processes and inflation.

In practice, many organisations, particularly in times of budget pressure, use a poor variant of incremental budgeting where appropriate downward adjustments to budgets are made but necessary upward adjustments are ignored or under-provided for, resulting in a mismatch of plan and resources. Where the mismatch is relatively minor managers usually try to cope by improving economy and efficiency. If minor mismatches occur over a number of years or there is a large mismatch in any one year, sufficient improvements in economy and efficiency are unlikely and the quantity and quality of services are likely to reduce or physical resources may be allowed to deteriorate. With incremental budgeting there tends to be a lack of challenge with budgets evolving slowly over time, lagging behind service development. There is widespread use of incremental budgeting in public service organisations accompanied by the occasional use of rational approaches.

Inflation

All budgets reflect two factors; the volume of physical resource to be purchased and the price to be paid for each unit of resource. A gas budget therefore comprises a number of kWh to be purchased at a particular tariff or rate. At the point at which budgets are prepared the price that will be paid per unit is difficult to estimate due to inflation. Inflation can be accommodated either by:

- setting budgets at prices that apply when the budget is prepared and updating the value of these as and when actual prices change; or

- including within the budget an allowance for the anticipated impact of inflation between the date the budget is calculated and the end of the year to which it relates.

In practice, the second approach is widespread with budget managers given an estimated allowance for inflation together with responsibility for handling the impact of any difference between estimated and actual inflation. The ability to predict inflation is crucial as there is an attendant risk of under-inflating budgets which, unless the manager reduces the volume and or cost of purchases, will lead to overspending.

Example 1 – Gas budget on a rational basis and allowing for 3% inflation

It is estimated that next year 215,000 KWh of gas will be needed to deliver a planned service, the price of which is 5p at the point the budget is prepared. The budget has to include an allowance for future inflation and the best estimate of this is 3% for the period.

	£
Estimated consumption * current rate (215000*5p)	10,750
Inflation adjustment * £10,750 * 3%	322
	11,072

Whether in practice this budget proves to be sufficient will depend on whether the estimated volume of required gas proves accurate and whether future inflation is 3.0%.

Example 2 – Postage budget on an incremental basis and allowing for 2.5% inflation

Using the incremental basis the budget for next year is based on the current year rather than on an estimate of how much postage is likely to be required. Assuming future inflation is likely an adjustment is required to re-price the current budget. The rate to be used is normally provided by finance staff and in this example is assumed to be 2.5%. If the current postage budget is £800 re-pricing this for 2.5% will result in a budget of:

	£
Current budget	800
Add effect of inflation 2.5%	20
	820

Whether in practice this budget proves to be sufficient depends on the current budget being adequate to meet the cost of current consumption, the volume of postage remaining constant and inflation proving to be 2.5%. As a budget manager it is essential to know how inflation is treated and where budgets include an inflation allowance, the rate used. If the rate and/or the overall budget appear incorrect this should be challenged at the earliest opportunity.

Budgetary control

Budgetary control is the process by which managers check and respond to the evolving position on actual income and expenditure budgets during the year. Effective budgetary control is an integral part of performance management, provides early warning of emerging underspends or overspends and helps budget managers spot opportunities as they arise and act if needed. Figure 8.6 shows budgetary control as a five-stage process.

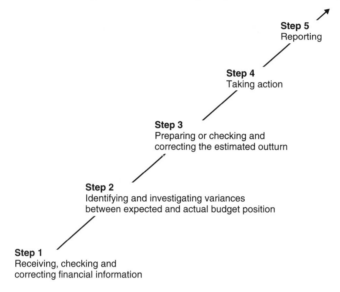

Figure 8.6 Five-stage budgetary control process

Knowledge of the budget profile or the rate at which income is expected to be earned or expenditure incurred over the budget period is crucial. While this rate might be even over time it often varies according to one or more driving factors such as service demand, contract terms or weather, etc. Up-to-date information regarding actual income and expenditure is also vital. Where the accounting system records expenditure at the point payments are made it will be necessary to manually take into account the value of orders placed in respect of which invoices have yet to be received.

Once financial information has been received the manager should check and correct this for errors before identifying and investigating any variances they consider significant. The next step involves either preparing a projected year end/project end budget position or checking and correcting year end figures that have been generated elsewhere. This figure, which may be referred to as a year end forecast, budget forecast or estimated outturn, relates to the key performance measure of keeping within the approved budget for the whole year or project. Many organisations require estimates of the likely year end position for each budget at the end of each month, producing these either by:

- scaling up actual income or expenditure at a particular point in the year or life of the project. If, for example, postage spending three months into the year is reported at £1,000 the estimated outturn will be £4,000 (based on (1,000/3*12). This approach can be risky as it assumes that the rate of income and expenditure is the same each month, which is not the case for many budgets; or

- combining current actual income or expenditure figures with estimates of how much is expected to be earned or spent over the rest of the project or financial year.

Irrespective of approach it is essential that the budget manager is involved in either checking, agreeing and amending the scaled up figures or preparing an estimated outturn.

The final steps in the budgetary control process are to take action and report performance as required. While budget responsibility normally rests with the manager it is likely that an accountant will be involved in providing financial information and offering technical advice. It is important that accountants do not become too involved, otherwise there is a blurring of accountability with a risk that managers disengage from the process.

Understanding budget reports

Budget information is central to the budgetary control process and tends to take the form of a regular print out showing the financial position based on transactions recorded by the main accounting system. While the exact layout of these reports varies (Case Study 8.1) they tend to include as a minimum:

- the budget for the project or year in question;
- the expected budget position at this point in the project or year (profile);
- actual income and expenditure to date, the latter based on payments made or payments made plus outstanding orders for goods and services;
- the variance or difference between the expected budget position and actual income or expenditure;
- estimated year end position – either based on scaled up figures or a year/project end estimate.

CASE STUDY 8.1

Below is an example budget report prepared in respect of the period 1 April to 30 June. The budget relates to telephone expenditure and is profiled according to the predicted pattern of spend, which for the first three months is £300. The projected year end figure is £1300 based on the actual to date which has been scaled up for the full year.

Central Services Budget Report 1st April to 30th June

Budget Detail	Annual Budget	Budget to Date	Actual to Date	Variance	Estimated Year End
	(£)	(£)	(£)	(£)	(£)
Telephone	1200	300	325	25	1300

This report shows that after three months the telephone budget is overspent by £25. By the end of the year it is estimated that this overspend will have grown to £100. Investigation reveals that service activity is higher than planned and inflation is slightly higher than allowed for when the budget was set. As there is nothing that can be done about inflation and little about call volume other actions must be considered including, for example, transferring money in from another budget.

When interpreting financial information it is essential the budget manager understands how:

- each budget has been prepared, the volume of activity it relates to and how inflation is being treated;

- the profile has been calculated and whether this appears realistic;

- actual income and expenditure is recorded – whether it is up to date or it is necessary to adjust for transactions that relate to the period covered by the report but which are not yet included in the figures;

- favourable/unfavourable variances are shown which might include the use of minus signs, brackets or colour. There is no standard approach to how variances are shown so it is good practice to check understanding before interpreting;

- if an estimated outturn is included how this has been provided and calculated, and to have a view as to its accuracy.

ACTIVITY 8.1

Budgeting is a significant management process, competence in which will be important to future organisational survival and leadership success. We end this chapter by asking you to answer nine key questions:

1. *If you are a budget manager is your responsibility devolved or delegated?*

2. *With regard to budget management:*

   a) *What rights do you consider you have?*

   b) *To what extent are these met?*

   c) *What might you do to help your employer meet these rights?*

3. *Do you engage in budget preparation and negotiation either by:*

   a) *Independently calculating the budget you need to resource planned activity, or*

   b) *Checking provided figures to see if they are broadly reasonable given current budget performance, recalculating these where this is not the case?*

4. *Do you integrate your plan and budget?*

5. *Do you seek to negotiate your plan and budget at the same time?*

6. *On what basis are your budgets prepared – rational or historic?*

7. *Do you know how inflation is treated with regard to your budgets and do you consider this to be adequate?*

8. *Does your budgetary control practice appropriately match estimated and actual income and expenditure for the same period?*

9. *Do you either:*

   a) *prepare estimated outturns, or*

   b) *check and correct estimated outturns prepared by others?*

Chapter summary

- Plans and budgets must be integrated recognising that a change in one will lead to a change in the other.

- Effective business planning ensures services and activities are relevant to our communities.

- Good plans arise from an effective planning process.

- Good use of planning tools improves strategic thinking and analysis that underpin an effective plan.

- Budgetary control is essential to performance management.

The next few years are likely to see significant development in our understanding of what effective planning and budgeting looks like due to factors such as the widespread adoption of commissioning and the challenging economic context. The competencies associated with these key processes will evolve as the context within which they are practised increasingly moves from being within an agency or a simple formal partnership to more complex partnerships, in respect of whole communities and beyond this to multiple linked communities. There is a need for continual review of what competence looks like, periodic self-assessment and planned development to ensure that leaders are equipped to meet this challenge, confident of their ability.

Bean, J. and Hussey, L. (1996) *Managing the Devolved Budget.* London: HB Publications.

One of a useful financial series, this short book offers a good introduction to budget management.

Field, R. (2007) *Managing with Plans and Budgets in Health and Social Care.* Exeter: Learning Matters.

This is a practical guide for managers engaged in planning and budgeting within a health and social care context.

Johnson, G., Scholes, K. and Whittington, R. (2008) *Exploring Corporate Strategy.* 8th edition. Harlow: Prentice Hall.

This best-selling book is an essential text for anyone involved in developing, implementing or evaluating strategy.

Chapter 9

Managing training and development

Ivan Gray

C H A P T E R   O B J E C T I V E S

This chapter will help you address the following National Occupational Standard for Management and Leadership.

- D7 Provide learning opportunities for colleagues.

This chapter will also help you address the following Principles of Social Care Management.

- Value people, recognise and actively develop potential.

- Provide an environment and time in which to develop reflective practice, professional skills and the ability to make judgements in complex situations.

- Take responsibility for the continuing professional development of others.

Introduction – why invest?

There is an established viewpoint that sees investing in the training and development of staff as perhaps the best way to improve organisational performance (DH, 2000). A variant of this sees such investment as making good 'business sense' as it provides an organisation with competitive advantage. It can have a direct impact on service quality, efficiency and effectiveness, some would argue more impact than any other activity area, and it can also have a powerful influence on innovation and service improvement. It can improve the ability of your team to respond flexibly to new policies and practices and to the ever-changing service environment.

> *An organisation's employees are a major asset, not only in themselves, but also because the organisation's whole reputation and future success depend on them. Consequently it is a false saving to skimp on staff support and development. These are arguably the most direct ways to influence the quality of organisational performance as well as retaining and fostering the best employees.*
>
> (Coulshed *et al.*, 2006, p161)

If your team is likely to be a crucial focus for you in managing training and development you will also need to meet the needs of the wider organisation and the network of providers and activities that make up service provision. For instance, colleagues will need induction opportunities to understand the work of your team and co-operate with you in delivering the service. You will need to reach out beyond your organisation and become involved in the training and development of partner organisations. Partner organisations may also need to influence your work, i.e. offer training and development activity to you and your team.

Your organisation may also be an Investor in People (IiP). The IiP Award is an award made to an organisation whose management of training and development meets certain, nationally determined standards (IiP, 2009). When the government introduced IiP they did so because they saw training and development activity as *the* most important management activity for many service organisations. In addition to this, *Options for Excellence* (DfES/DH, 2006) puts training and development at the centre of current government plans for improving care services. So there are good reasons for giving training and development careful consideration. Beyond its possible benefits, it is a complex and challenging activity area that managers need to give time and attention to in developing their practice.

Another way to approach this issue is to see personal growth and development as essential features of being human. Through this more critical perspective, if people are deprived of learning and development opportunities their personal wellbeing is undermined as well as the greater social good. Also, contributing to the learning and development of others, so that their values, knowledge and skills are improved, can be seen as a crucial 'value creating' activity that enhances the human condition and is a vocation in its own right.

Learning and development can also be seen to empower in that it gives individuals opportunity to achieve more and take control of their lives. In social contexts where learning and development opportunities are not evenly distributed, learning and development can be seen as a way of empowering disadvantaged individuals and groups. In other words, there is good reason for seeing learning and development as positive affirming activities. Movement towards user-led service provision (Beresford, 2003) has increased the involvement of people who use services and carers in training and development processes – in particular within qualifying and post-qualifying social work education (Levin, 2004).

What are your responsibilities in managing training and development?

Your leadership and supervisory practice as explored in Chapters 4 and 5 is at the heart of managing training and development. However, it does help to break this broad project of managing training and development down into its component parts. We can then examine each part and determine the priorities and actions that are most likely to bring about improvement.

To begin with, it is worth remembering that training and development has several distinct stages that together can map an individual's career. At any one point in time you will have staff in your team at these different stages and therefore with different needs to respond to. It is also worth making the point that they will also have different abilities and needs as learners. They will be at different stages of professional development and will need to be offered different training and development experiences and given different types and levels of support by you and others who may be supervising them (Figure 9.1).

There are key processes we use to support and help people through these stages. Also, training and development needs to be linked to the wider organisation and the network of service provision. Figure 9.2 offers a reasonable representation of the key dimensions that make up the management of training and development. In the following pages we explore each of these dimensions.

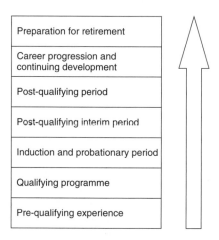

Figure 9.1 Training and development stages of an individual's career

Figure 9.2 Key dimensions of managing training and development

Managing training

There are three broad activity areas that constitute the management of training.

- Training audit and evaluation.

- Managing nominations and release.

- Integrating learning into practice.

Training audit and evaluation

Determining what a training department should provide, whether by using an in-house training team or by commissioning training from a provider, is a crucial activity. Managers are key players in this process as they are well placed to make judgements about training need. Some have argued that healthy training and development provision is where responsibility for training and development shifts away from training managers to line managers (Figure 9.3).

So, the expectation could be that you focus on determining what is provided and play a central role in delivering training and development activity. However, in most organisations the process is one of negotiation, with specialist trainers and training managers facilitating the process of determining training needs and then delivering training, with you making an important contribution along the way. Often, an incremental approach is taken that brings only slight variations from previous years' activity.

Another dimension to the effective determination of training needs is ensuring that training activity supports service strategy or business planning. This is also identified as a sign of well developed training and development provision (Figure 9.3). Giving priority to planned and essential changes in service provision makes a lot of sense and ensures the menu does not become static. Training managers will usually have a role in planning training to respond to or contribute to organisational strategies but you also have a role in ensuring that needs arising from your local business plan are conveyed to the commissioning team. Apart from your plan containing initiatives that respond to local conditions you will also have a better idea of what a team may or may not be able to respond to and where they will need assistance.

A team's training needs analysis needs to encompass a number of dimensions.

- New policy and legislation that staff need to be prepared for.

- Training needs that arise from service and business plans.

- Analysis of individuals' performance against occupational standards, definitions of good practice and job descriptions, i.e. personal audit that is the basis for personal development planning.

- Identified service quality problems the team need to respond to.

- Career aspirations and succession planning.

- Core or essential training for new appointments including induction.

- Maintenance training for essential activities, i.e. staff need refresher courses or people need to be trained up as others leave.

- Feedback from key stakeholders.

- Organisational performance set against performance measures.

1 *The fragmented approach*

- Training is not linked to organisational goals.
- Training is perceived as a luxury or a waste of time.
- The approach to training is non-systematic.
- Training is directive and does not focus on continuous development.
- Training is carried out by trainers and takes place in the training department.
- Emphasis on knowledge-based courses.

2 *The formalised approach*

- Training becomes linked to HR (human resources) needs and appraisal systems.
- The emphasis is still on knowledge-based courses but the focus of courses broadens, with greater emphasis on skill-based courses.
- The link that is made between training and HR needs encourages organisations to adopt a more developmental approach.
- Training is carried out by trainers, but the range of skill demands placed on a trainer develops with the new breadth of courses offered.
- Line managers become involved in training and development through their role as appraisers.
- Pre- and post-course activities attempt to facilitate the transfer of off-the-job learning.
- Training is carried out off the job, but through career development the value of on-the-job learning gains formal recognition.
- There is more concern to link a programme of training to individual needs.

3 *The focused approach*

- Training and development and continuous learning by individuals is perceived as a necessity for organisational survival in a rapidly changing business environment.
- Training is regarded as a learning process and a competitive weapon.
- Learning is linked to organisational strategy and to individual goals.
- The emphasis is on-the-job development so that learning becomes a totally continuous activity.
- Specialist training courses are available across the knowledge/skills/value spectrum.
- Training is generally self-selected and non-directive.
- New forms of training activity are utilised, e.g. open and distance learning packages, self-development programmes, etc.
- More concern to measure effectiveness of training and development.
- Main responsibility for training rests with line management.
- Trainers adopt a wider role.
- Tolerance of some failure as part of the learning process.

Figure 9.3 Approaches to training and development (based on the Ashridge model by Barham et al., 1988, p75)

It may well be that your organisation already has a particular approach, with policy and procedures that shape training needs analysis. If not, you may like to use the Investors in People model (IiP, 2007, see **http://diagnostic.iipuk.co.uk/**).

Training evaluation

Training evaluation is potentially as expensive and as complex as needs analysis. The Skills for Care Leadership and Management Strategy (SfC, 2004) puts forward a five- stage model for organisations to use in gauging the effectiveness of management development activities, but the same model can readily be applied to training activity more generally (Table 9.1).

Table 9.1 Five levels of evaluation (SfC, 2005, p7)

Level 5 Stakeholders' outcomes	What has been the impact on stakeholders of the training or developmental activity? What has been the impact on service users, their carers and families? What measures were used? What has been learnt that will contribute to future development? How have partnerships been improved and maintained? What changes have been made to benefit stakeholders?
Level 4 Organisational outcomes	What has been the significant impact on the organisation's performance? What has been learnt that will contribute to future development? What changes have been made to how the organisation operates? What are the outcomes from changes in performance? What is the overall cost-benefit of the investment in training and learning?
Level 3 Individual outcomes or application of learning	Has the learning produced any changes in culture, behaviour, relationships, equal opportunities and service delivery? To what extent has the learning transferred to the team or network? To what extent was the individual able to put into practice what was learnt? Has the learning improved performance?
Level 2 The learning outcomes	How effectively were health and social care values integrated into the learning? What learning outcomes were achieved? Did participants achieve the learning objectives in their Personal Development Plan and if so how? How will the learning objectives that have not been met be addressed? What has been learnt that would contribute to the development of future learning opportunities including training, qualifications and work-based learning? What new learning needs were identified?
Level 1 Reactions to the learning process	What were the reactions of participants to the training or learning opportunity? What were the reactions to the trainers, mentors/assessors, content or methods? What changed as a result of ongoing feedback? What else could be provided?

A danger for a manager and their team is that evaluation can too readily be focused entirely on the participant's immediate response to the training event, often collected at the end of the event on a simple tick box form. This only really evaluates the participant's experience not the application of what has been learnt in practice, nor its impact on service outcomes. So, the questions for most managers are, what is your team's current approach to evaluating training activities and does your methodology encompass the impact of training on practice and on service outcomes?

Do bear in mind that making evidenced judgements about the impact of training on service outcomes is very difficult, which is why evaluation is often superficial. Trying to move up the ladder from Level 1 is a worthy endeavour although you might have to accept your limitations and be only able to make crude judgements beyond Level 3.

Managing nominations and release

While allowing staff to select themselves for training courses can be seen as an advanced form of practice where individuals are totally committed to and in control of their own learning (Figure 9.3), most managers will want to maintain some oversight of nominations. In part this consists of ensuring that people's development plans are on track and that they have completed core or required training. One crucial consideration is to ensure you have sufficient staff on the ground to keep the service running. It is common practice to have a wall chart or some other means where nominations and leave are recorded to ensure a reasonable team establishment at all times. It is also important to make sure individuals are not over-committing themselves, which can result in cancellations.

A further issue is making sure both your team and yourself are aware of available training inside and outside of the organisation. Necessarily this means being able to get a good idea about a course's content so that relevant parties can make a judgement about whether it responds to needs. It is also important that the system for making nominations is efficient. Staff need to be nominated promptly to make sure courses requested and provided are not then left half-empty. Staff also need to be clear whether they have been accepted onto a course and therefore will receive pre-course materials as a reminder and information about venue, times and comfort factors such as parking and whether lunch is provided. This all may seem obvious or even trivial but they frequently go wrong and actually play an important role in determining the quality of training provision.

Many organisations have a history of staff not attending courses they are nominated for, which is wasteful. Often there are monitoring systems that feedback to line managers on non-attendance. If there isn't one in place for your team, consider setting one up. Given the frequent crises we face in our work, training is often given second place in our priorities. If staff are cancelling nominations, managers usually seek to ensure this is done as early as possible so the place can be offered to another colleague.

Another problem for staff is being interrupted on a training course or even being required to return to the workplace. Sometimes this is unavoidable but ensuring, where you can, that adequate cover is available so that staff are fully released and make the best use of the learning experience, is important.

It can sometimes be useful to ask a suitable member of staff to take on responsibility for liaising with your training and development section. The personal touch always helps and they can often develop considerable expertise in understanding training section systems and quality issues. They can also assist in training needs analysis, managing nominations and evaluating training.

Integrating learning into practice

Line managers have a crucial role in ensuring that learning is applied to practice. In leading and managing supervision you stand at the interface between the training event and practice and are able to identify any problems and respond to them. Taking time to discuss application with staff is important as they may need support to do so. Coaching can often greatly improve the impact of training and drawing on the team's experience to help with this is essential.

Sometimes, it can be a struggle for staff to see the application of training into practice. They may report back favourably on the training event but can't really say how it has or will change their practice. As discussed above, it might be that they need assistance or it could be that the course has provided them with essential information or knowledge and the application is obvious. Sometimes, problems with application are a sign that a course needs re-designing or is redundant. In exploring application you move in effect from Level 1 evaluation to Level 3 learning outcomes (Table 9.1).

Beyond exploring whether training has met an individual's needs, the experience of attendees is a resource that you may be able to mobilise for team benefit. In discussing learning outcomes with an individual it may be possible to identify learning that can be disseminated to or shared with the team. This may include the team member running a team training event – a valuable exercise that can carry individual learning into team practice. Returning again to Table 9.1 it is perhaps now easier to see how crucial a line manager is in facilitating the higher levels of impact that training can have on service outcomes. It can be argued that the training event is only a small part of the process and that the bulk of real learning, which is married to application, is down to line managers and team leaders, not trainers.

Another way of ensuring the relevance and applicability of training to practice is involving experienced practitioners and specialists in training design and delivery. This can have a big impact on the quality of training. Involvement in training can be very rewarding for individuals and can open up career options that allow practitioners to have a beneficial impact on training and education.

Investors in People (IiP)

IiP was introduced as a quality assurance system for service industries dependent on personal service from staff in meeting the needs of customers. It was introduced because other quality assurance systems such as the British Standards Association (BSO) and the International Standards Association (ISO) were considered to be too strongly orientated towards manufacturing. By focusing on how effectively an organisation trains and develops its people the idea was that the key activity area that impacts most on service quality would be addressed.

IiP, therefore, offers a good structure against which to audit training and development activities. Part of its website contains diagnostic tools that can be used by organisations to audit their current practices (IiP, 2007). You could also use the IiP standards to audit your management of training and development. You may already be doing so if your organisation is an IiP organisation or is seeking accreditation.

Although it isn't usually described as such, IiP could be seen as a learning organisation model. Given its emphasis on linking learning and development to business planning processes, auditing, analysis and improvement planning, it could also be seen as taking a managerialist approach. That is, it attempts to formally manage learning to achieve organisational outcomes.

ACTIVITY 9.1

Auditing the management of training

Review Figure 9.3 – which approach do you think is closest to your organisation's practice? What improvements could be made to help move the organisation towards a 'focused approach'?

Review Table 9.1 and the five levels of evaluation. At what level does your team currently operate? How could you improve the evaluation of training?

Is application to practice discussed in supervision and do staff share training course material and experiences with others?

Training and developing the network of service provision

Working in partnership to deliver services appears repeatedly as a government policy objective because of its impact on service quality. Quality problems are likely to occur at the interface of social systems whether we are talking about where two departments meet or the meeting place between sub-systems within one organisation. This is because different systems have differing cultures, objectives, working practices and procedures that can all militate against integration or co-operation. Group dynamics can also often mean that the team orientation that motivates team members excludes or even generates distrust or hostility towards non-team members. So reaching beyond team boundaries can be a way to find the quality initiatives that are likely to have the most impact on service quality.

Just as training and development can be seen as a powerful means of influencing behaviour and therefore service quality, it is also a valuable way to seek to develop partnership working. It is not hard to see that it can be categorised according to the level of co-operation it requires. So, for instance, sharing each others' training events is a relatively superficial level of co-operation, while joint planning and delivery of training including shared training needs analysis can be seen as a more advanced approach. Corporatism in the delivery of training, i.e. the development of shared Personnel or Human Resource Management (HRM) services including training, can be seen to work against or form a barrier to partnership working.

In Total Quality Management, quality circles should be developed at the interface of departments and supplier organisations (Ishikawa, 1985). In the same way, more advanced forms of training and development embrace the network of service provision and can involve joint problem solving and planning with partners and shared provision.

Joint training and development planning is probably the first step on this road, but it is important that initiatives involve other learning and development methods e.g. practitioners working together on projects and action learning. It is worth remembering that working outside your organisation can generate resistance and reaction from formal and informal systems (Corley and Thorne, 2006). That is why the 'silo effect' of organisational structures is so powerful in the first place; it is supported actively by group dynamics, perceptions and behaviours within the system.

REFLECTION POINT **9.1**

Training and developing the network of service provision
Is your training open to partners, co-providers and sub-contractors?

Do you make good use of partners, co-providers and sub-contractors as training and development resources?

Do you co-operate in planning and delivering shared training including induction?

Managing CPD

Skills for Care and the CWDC have a CPD strategy. They identify clear benefits for people who use services and workers but note that:

the objectives that are particularly relevant for employers are to:

- *support continuous improvement and delivery of integrated services to put individuals and their families at the centre of care;*
- *improve recruitment and retention and provide career pathways;*
- *provide employers with structures that support their responsibilities for developing a competent workforce and to achieve training and qualifications requirements;*
- *support the development of learning organisations;*
- *meet requirements for registration and re-registration with the General Social Care Council and other regulatory bodies;*
- *improve the effectiveness, quality and relevance of learning;*
- *encourage the use of a range of flexible learning and development approaches to strengthen work-based learning;*
- *align CPD activities with the national qualifications framework and national occupational standards.*

(SfC/CWDC 2006a, p16)

They point out that while it is a joint responsibility, with individual professionals having to demonstrate CPD if they wish to maintain their registration with the GSCC, employers have a crucial role to play in facilitating CPD through the management of training and development. Skills for Care/CWDC offer a CPD framework that breaks the process down into seven stages (Table 9.2). This process offers in itself a basis for reviewing our current

Table 9.2 CPD processes (SFC/CWDC, 2006b, p10)

CPD process	CPD methods	Examples of CPD activities
Stage 1 Assessment of individual worker and organisational need.	Develop person profile.	Review learning needs against competences to develop a personal CPD profile.
Stage 2 Identify development needs.	Assessment of development needs against the person profile.	Can be done in supervision and appraisal or larger organisations can make use of: • diagnostics, e.g. 360° feedback • skills benchmarking.
Stage 3 Identify learning.	Identify learning objectives.	Identify types of learning to meet objectives: work-related learning, action learning, networking, mentoring, secondments, e-learning, attending events, external learning, formal study, networking.
Stage 4 Plan development opportunities.	Identify goals.	Identify strengths, weaknesses, opportunities and threats that might help or hinder these goals such as lack of basic skills or access to resources.
Stage 5 Implement learning opportunities.	Experience different types of learning – both planned and *ad hoc*.	Have a learning log or reflective diary for workers, which they can complete. It could be an on-line recording system.
Stage 6 Record outcomes.	Reflect upon and record development.	Record of achievement or record of learning outcomes in practice, summarised in CPD portfolio.
Stage 7 Review, accredit and refine learning.	• Review person profile and include any additional responsibilities or roles. • Evaluate learning. • Back to stage 1.	• Use supervision to review learning outcomes in practice. • Review learning against updated competences and update CPD profile. • Accredit CPD through regulatory and professional bodies. • Review and refine learning in teams.

practices. Set in a broader framework it also offers us a useful basis for auditing organisational systems (Table 9.3).

Table 9.3 The CPD framework (SFC/CWDC, 2006b, p3)

---

1 **Principles** – a set of principles and values and information on relevant codes of conduct or practice for the range of staff in the organisation. The principles should inform CPD policy.

2 **A learner-centred approach for implementing CPD.**

3 **Learning culture.**

4 **CPD processes** – the seven-stage cycle.

5 **Documenting CPD** – recording CPD practice for workers and employers, use of appropriate systems.

6 **Funding, resources and access to learning and qualifications** – access to the range of learning activities, qualifications and support, including mentoring, assessment and coaching.

7 **Guidance and processes for registration** – the role of appropriate regulatory or professional bodies.

8 **Career pathways** – flexible routes to career enhancement.

9 **Monitoring and evaluation of CPD** – systems and processes which focus on the impact on and benefits for the people who use the service.

ACTIVITY 9.2

Auditing CPD

Review the Skills for Care/CWDC models of the CPD process and framework (Tables 9.2 and 9.3). Do these reflect your current organisational and team practices? Where can improvements be made?

Are your staff keeping updated portfolios ready for GSCC registration?

Does your team own and take pride in their personal professional development and are they able to make use of a range of training and development opportunities?

Managing qualifying education

The quality of qualifying education is largely dependent upon placement provision. Students regularly identify their placement experiences as offering them the most learning opportunities. However, the quality of placements and practice teaching is not necessarily that consistent – breakdowns and unhappy experiences are not unusual.

Shortages of placements have not helped problems of quality with less satisfactory placements continuing to be used despite difficulties because of a lack of other options. Poor placement experiences can do a lot of damage to a student's learning.

So, the number of placements available and their quality are crucial determinants of the impact of qualifying training. The management of placements by line managers and teams is therefore a crucial activity where improvements can have a very positive effect on the profession and the service.

Close liaison with providers of qualifying education is crucial in maintaining and enhancing placement quality; they are likely to have quality management systems you can engage with. Their systems are not likely to be as effective as managers and teams leading quality assurance and improvements. There are models available for reviewing the quality of placement provision (GSCC, 2002) but it is important that you and your team have thought through and developed your own approach to this essential activity.

A useful point of reference is the GSCC's (2002) *Guidance on the Assessment of Practice in the Work Place*. This offers an outline of key dimensions and is divided into three sections. Domain A focuses on organising a learning experience. Domain B centres on the relationship between the practice educator and student, and Domain C the assessment of practice. If no other quality standards are available this will provide a useful starting point in reviewing placement quality. Co-operating with Higher Education Institutions (HEIs) and other organisations in judging and responding to placement demand is also essential to avoid shortages and inappropriate placements. Usually there are forums that will assist in this co-operation and attempt to manage supply and demand.

Quality standards for placement provision are currently being piloted and these will bring clarity to auditing and improvement planning and should be incorporated into your practice when they are introduced. Apart from the general contribution placement provision makes to the profession there are also considerable benefits to placement providers. It can for instance be a good way of identifying and recruiting future colleagues and while some students can be challenging, in general they stimulate a team's learning and development. Often most of the team are involved not just the practice educator. In helping the student develop their practice they often end up reviewing and reflecting on their own.

Traffic between placement providers and HEIs should not be one way. Practice educators need to be kept briefed on the curriculum if they are to do their job well and it is important that practitioners are enabled to influence the curriculum as well. Contributing to management and teaching on qualifying courses including recruitment and assessment processes is also important and again offers stimulating learning opportunities to the

---

REFLECTION POINT 9.2

Auditing placement provision

Are you regularly training and developing practice teachers and work-based supervisors and assessors to respond to identified needs?

Is the quality of placement provision regularly and methodically reviewed against agreed criteria and improvements made?

Are practice educators and work-based supervisors properly supported and helped to reflect on their work as practice educators and is the wider team contributing effectively to the learning process?

team. So, a healthy relationship with HEIs is important and worth investing in. In the next chapter we will explore the importance of your own training and personal development to service quality and identify some good practice models.

Managing post-qualifying education and work-based learning

Work-based practice learning goes beyond the provision of placements for students on qualifying courses. There is also a more fundamental and complicated issue here though. We all learn from and develop our practice through work-based learning. Training provision and qualifying and post–qualifying education all have parts to play in personal development, but it can be argued that it is work-based learning that carries knowledge and skills into practice. So, managing work-based learning goes beyond managing and providing placements to how we all as a team make the best use of 'natural' work-based learning opportunities.

Taking the opportunity to reflect critically on our practice is crucial. Williams and Rutter suggest that this goes beyond ensuring competence to developing professional capability or 'dynamic competence' (see Williams and Rutter, 2007, pp15–27). Effective and balanced supervision has also got to be a crucial factor in developing professional capability and facilitating work-based learning. It is also possible to take a more holistic view and try to develop a team and perhaps even a wider organisation that has a culture of learning (see Hawkins and Shohet, 2000, pp167–81).

Significantly, the revised post-qualifying social work framework could be seen as reaching for this approach to work-based learning in expecting all professionally qualified social workers to contribute to enabling others (GSCC, 2005a). All social workers studying at a post-qualifying specialist level will be introduced to practice education skills and their practice as enablers assessed. Hopefully this will build a larger population of practice educators and contribute towards developing learning cultures (Williams and Rutter, 2007).

By exploring training and development from a range of perspectives and developing improvement plans that will impact on a number of interrelated variables and activities, we are attempting to influence your team as a whole and to improve it as a learning community or learning organisation. By encouraging you towards a participative and development-orientated leadership style we are also attempting to mobilise your team individually and collectively to work towards this end (see Chapter 7, p118 for a Learning Organisation audit tool).

Managing post-qualifying training

The challenge for managers will no doubt be getting up to speed with the new pathways (GSCC, 2005a). Many of you should already be involved in consultation and briefings as HEIs validate new awards.

Keeping your team briefed on the revised post-qualifying training framework should be on your agenda. Experiences of past post-qualifying education can vary considerably from organisation to organisation. Limited research is available, some of which is very informative (Brown *et al.*, 2005 pp75–80); problems that might benefit from improvement include:

- poor completion rates;
- lack of information;
- unclear and unequal nomination processes;
- lack of support from line managers and more generally in the organisation;
- lack of knowledge and understanding in the organisation of post-qualifying provision;
- post-qualifying experiences not being integrated into supervision, personal development planning and CPD before, during and after the programme;
- not being able to bring new practices back to the team and implement them;
- problems with release and lack of time;
- lack of monitoring and evaluation;
- lack of IT skills and access to IT;
- lack of time to reflect;
- lack of study skills including reflection on practice;
- unrecognised learning needs, e.g. dyslexia;
- lack of support and follow up if candidates are not successful.

REFLECTION POINT **9.3**

Post-qualifying training

Look back with the team on their experiences of post-qualifying training. What were the strengths and weaknesses in how it was provided? How will you manage differently or try to influence HEIs?

Are your staff on post-qualifying training courses encouraged and supported by colleagues? Are they able to implement new practices? Are they helped with study skills and special learning needs?

Is there time put aside in supervision to discuss and reflect on practice and to support the post-qualifying experience?

Chapter summary

- Investment in training and development has a direct impact on organisational performance and service quality.
- People at different stages in their career have different training and development needs.
- There are different approaches to training and development that can be seen as different levels of organisational development.

- More sophisticated approaches link training and development to organisational strategy and service development and evaluate outcomes.

- If training and development is to be effective we must manage:

  - training processes e.g. audit and evaluation;

  - CPD;

  - qualifying training and placement provision;

  - post-qualifying education.

FURTHER READING

Coulshed, V., Mullender, A., Jones, D.N. and Thompson, N. (2006) *Management in Social Work*. Basingstoke: Macmillan.

This book has rightly become a popular introductory text for social work managers. It is full of useful guidance and insights. It is very comprehensive and for an outline of the work of some of the key human relations theorists see pages 35–39.

We need a good practice model for CPD in order to shape our own personal development and to support and manage CPD for our teams. Take a look at:

SfC/CWDC (2006b) *Continuing Professional Development for the Social Care Workforce – the Framework*. Leeds: SFC.

www.skillsforcare.org.uk/developing_skills/Continuing_Professional_Development/Continuing_ Professional_Development_(CPD)_strategy.aspx.

Chapter 10

Managing your own development

Ivan Gray

CHAPTER OBJECTIVES

This chapter will help you address the following National Occupational Standard for Management and Leadership.

- A2 Manage your own resources.

This chapter will also help you address the following Principle of Social Care Management.

- Take responsibility for the continuing professional development of self.

Introduction

The Overview of Seven Years of Joint Reviews by the Audit Commission (Audit Commission, 2004) came to the conclusion that the quality of leadership and management in social care are key factors in providing quality services. Effective leadership and management are essential to manage the complexity of social care arrangements. This can mean managing staff from different professions and disciplines across integrated and multi-agency settings and within a range of partnerships.

(SfC/Topss, 2004, pp8–9)

More recently, *Options for Excellence* (DfES/DH, 2006) also put training and development at the centre of current government plans for improving care services, and leadership and management development is emphasised as a key activity area in workforce development strategies (SfC, 2008).

Skills for Care have recently updated their national leadership and management strategy (SfC, 2008). The Children's Workforce Development Council originally adopted the same strategy as Skills for Care but are now reviewing it to ensure that it responds to the needs of integrated children's services (Hartle *et al.*, 2008). The revised General Social Care Council's (GSCC) post-qualifying framework for social workers has introduced a new leadership and management pathway (GSCC, 2005 a & b). In the NHS, the Leadership Qualities Framework (LQF) (DH, 2009a) and *Inspiring Leaders; Leadership for Quality*

(DH, 2009b) provide the foundation for their leadership development strategy. David Nicholson points out:

It is imperative that we align what we are doing with leadership with what we want to achieve on quality. . . . The NHS is only just beginning to grasp the importance of leadership. We have not systematically identified, nurtured and promoted talent and leadership

(DH, 2009b, p5)

In their strategy update Skills for Care argue:

There is therefore a clear business case for investment in leadership and management development, so that all managers acquire the necessary knowledge, skills and understanding. Such an investment is not an unaffordable luxury but an essential prerequisite for providing quality services. Employers need to ensure that policies and systems are in place to deliver effective ongoing development of all managers. The specific responsibility for making this happen will normally rest with the manager of each individual manager, who will need to be able to access a wide range of resources, as available locally.

(SfC, 2008, p28)

So, with management development taking centre stage in government policy, this chapter offers you the opportunity to critically review your leadership and management development practice to date and plan to meet your future needs. These exercises aim to make a direct contribution to your personal development and, if you are a qualified social worker, shape the fulfilment of your post-registration training and learning (PRTL) requirements (GSCC, 2005c). At the heart of this chapter is an invitation for you to explore your effectiveness as a learner and to seek to improve your approach, not just for your own benefit but also for the benefit of the team and the service you lead. Developing a model of good practice and being seen to work towards it is essential given your responsibilities for managing the learning and development of others and acting as a professional role model. As above, there is good argument for seeing investment in your personal development as having more impact on service quality than any other activity.

That is not to say, however, that we think leadership and management development is only a matter for the individual. On the contrary, we invite you to look at the working relationships you have with colleagues within your organisation and in the network of organisations you work with to explore your effectiveness in developing management practice. That is, to explore your *community of practice* (Wenger, 2006) and your contribution to the joint development of leadership and management skills.

This is also an opportunity to take a critical approach and ask, as objectively as you can, how well existing developmental processes are working or have worked for you and others. Obviously you will want to take existing opportunities and experiences into account but please don't let current procedures and practices limit your thinking or approach.

The following structure (Figure 10.1) should facilitate an audit of your CPD and any improvement plans. We will explore each of these dimensions in turn.

159

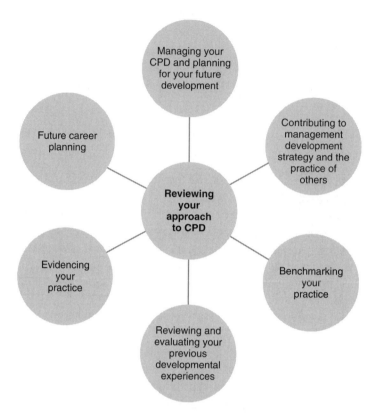

Figure 10.1 Possible approaches to reviewing your CPD

Managing your CPD and planning for your future development

CPD is a joint responsibility (Brown *et al.*, 2006; SfC/CWDC, 2006a). Social work professionals have to demonstrate CPD if they wish to maintain their registration with the GSCC (2005c) and employers have a crucial role in facilitating CPD through development processes. In the support materials for the national leadership and management development strategy SfC break the CPD process down into seven stages that we explored in Chapter 9 where we used it as a model for reviewing how you managed your teams CPD (see Table 9.2, p152). Although these stages offer a basis for reviewing our individual experiences and practices, they are set within a broader framework that offers us a model of good practice for organisational processes and systems as well (see Table 9.3 p153). This SfC model offers a very managed approach to learning and development and some people may not respond well to such a planned approach to personal development (Megginson, 1994).

There are in fact a range of approaches to CPD that orientate around a number of variables (Table 10.1). An argument can be made that current compulsion, prescription, organisational needs, defined outcomes and planned learning hold sway and need balancing with more personal control, choice and greater emphasis on values and informal leaning processes. Thankfully, it is possible to balance each of these possible approaches in their application.

Table 10.1 Different approaches to CPD (based on Joy-Matthews et al., 2004, pp138–39)

Managed	Author commentary	Learner-centred
Compulsory	Voluntary	Some theorists emphasise the importance of freedom to effective learning (Rogers and Freiberg, 1993). However, government, professional bodies and organisations seek to manage learning and development and ensure that it occurs.
Prescribed	Designed by the individual	Professional bodies often prescribe suitable training or education e.g. the post-qualifying leadership and management pathway. This can militate against personal control and also over-emphasise the importance of formal learning events compared with work–based learning opportunities.
Focused on organisational need	Focused on individual need	There is a strong current driver to direct learning to organisational ends so that it supports business plans and strategy. This may not accord well with an individual's priorities, perceived needs or ambitions.
Evaluated against defined outcomes	Value driven	Good practice can be defined e.g. by occupational standards, and controlled by organisational procedures. Alternatively, individuals can be expected to take responsibility for practice, shaping their actions according to a value base e.g. GSCC Codes of Practice.
Planned	Emergent	Some people like to approach learning in a planned way with clear objectives. Others prefer learning to emerge out of activities through personal reflection.

To illustrate, a manager might be told her performance will be judged against a set of competencies or standards by an assessor and that this process will generate her learning objectives and therefore the training courses she will attend. Alternatively, they could be given a choice or a mixture of benchmarks against which to evaluate their practice, including values, and given control of the assessment process. They could be encouraged to develop their own learning plan using a number of development methods. The latter approach does not exclude use of competencies or organisational outcomes or a development plan, but it might generate higher levels of motivation and more effective personal and organisational development. There are a number of factors that can help you generate learning objectives alongside any benchmarks. There is perhaps a tendency to see auditing against benchmarks as 'scientific' and the best way forward, yet this can readily be contested. Personal reflection may be a better way of developing practice. Feedback from staff, users of services, colleagues and other stakeholders might be more important to a community of practice in determining learning objectives.

Perhaps the secret is to develop a mixture of sources that are meaningful and motivating for you. If you are a benchmarking 'fiend' and this works for you in identifying learning objectives that give direction, then go for it. Otherwise, it is worth considering the range of options that are outlined in Figure 10.2 below.

Figure 10.2 Generating management learning objectives

ACTIVITY **10.1**

Continuing professional development

Which of the approaches to CPD typifies your experience of management development so far (Table 10.1)? Could you find a more balanced approach?

Looking at Figure 10.2, what are the current challenges for you in your management practice and what are your key learning objectives?

Contributing to management development strategy and the development of others

The National Leadership and Management Strategy

A GSCC requirement for the post-qualifying leadership and management pathway is that it supports SfC's and the CWDC's National Leadership and Management Strategy (SfC, 2004). Accepting that CWDC are currently reviewing it (Hartle *et al.*, 2008) this strategy offers us a 'good practice' model for management development that has development agendas at three levels (Table 10.2).

Table 10.2 Three-level good practice model (SfC, 2004, pp22–23)

Level	Issues
Individual leader or manager	• Effective recruitment, selection and induction should allow early identification of learning needs • Access to a variety of on and off the job learning activities – shadowing, placements, coaching, mentoring and projects • 360 degree feedback involving service users • Good supervision and appraisal • Personal development plan based on learning needs analysis and career planning • Monitoring and evaluation of learning
Organisation	• Links between business plan, leadership and management competences and learning and qualification needs • Leadership and management development policy • Systems for monitoring and evaluating the impact of learning • Funding streams to support management learning • Commitment to Investors in People standard • Link between leadership and management learning and quality systems such as the European Foundation for Quality Management (EFQM) • Clarity about values and behaviours expected of managers and the link to organisational culture • Succession planning • Use of national occupational standards to audit learning needs
Partnerships	• Development of strategic partnerships with local training and education providers • Creating joint management learning opportunities with other agencies such as health, education, private and voluntary agencies • Identifying and channelling funding to support leadership and management learning and qualifications • Using partnership networks as opportunities to extend on the job learning through work exchanges, shadowing, projects, placements and meetings

These three levels encompass the individual's experience, organisational context and requirements for effective strategic partnership. As a whole, they offer valuable points of reference to view your own and your team's management development practice and any improvement plans. A number of prerequisites are required for this model.

- *Commitment from the top to a proactive approach to the development of all leaders and managers.*

- *Linking managers' learning to wider business objectives and targets.*

- *Involving and engaging service users.*

- *Developing clarity about the beneficiaries of leadership and management learning.*

- *Scale – it should be possible to scale down a model of learning that is applicable to large organisations so that it can be applied to small agencies as well.*

- *Equality – access to learning and qualifications needs to be fair and based on clear criteria.*

- *Infrastructure – the need for systems and structures to support learning.*

- *Funding – clarity about the resources that can be invested in leadership and management development.*

(SfC/Topss, 2004, p22)

For this strategy to work it is essential that it is not left to Human Resources but that it is taken on and progressed by leaders individually and collectively. As Skills for Care put it:

Stakeholders are keen that we raise the stakes for leadership and development with an approach that fosters a culture of learning and learning organisations at its heart.

(SfC/Topss, 2008, p19)

Therefore, there is good argument for engaging teams you are a part of by putting the implementation of the national management development strategy on their agenda. Remember that leadership and management development should perhaps not just be confined to those in formal management positions. Watson (2002) re-frames management as 'the management of work' suggesting that everyone is involved, not just managers. This concept of 'distributed leadership' allows for expertise to be located anywhere in the organisation and be mobilised for communal purposes (Mehra *et al.*, 2006). Some writers view distributed leadership as particularly suited to social care organisations (Hafford-Letchfield *et al.*, 2008).

So, you could argue leadership and management training should be available to every social care professional, not just those with formal management responsibilities. Beyond this, direct payments or individual budgets mean that people who use services and their families will increasingly shape and commission their own services (DH, 2007a). In the future, it may be the case that people who use services require management training. Already Skills for Care have developed a toolkit to help people who employ their own personal assistants (SfC, 2009). More generally, management and leadership training and education could be seen to address how human beings change the world and influence others – essential knowledge and skills that until now had been reserved for the privileged few and only shared with those in management positions. In effect, leadership and management development could be seen as an important empowering activity that should be more widely shared. This broader humanitarian vision is congruent with social care values.

The good practice model for management development offers us a useful framework against which to audit current organisational practice and plan for improvement.

ACTIVITY 10.2

Contributing to leadership and management development strategy and practice development

Using the SfC/CWDC good practice model for leadership and management development as a point of reference (Table 10.2), what are the strengths and weaknesses of your organisation's approach to leadership and management development? What changes would you recommend?

Are you contributing to the development of leadership and management in the network of provision that makes up the service?

What can you personally do to improve your contribution to developing the leadership and management development practice of others?

Benchmarking your practice

In social care we currently have a number of points of reference or benchmarks we can use to explore the role and responsibilities of a manager and make judgements about our own practice. The GSCC identify five sets of standards and codes that must be integrated into the post-qualifying leadership and management pathway – they also expect other sector skills standards to be incorporated into programmes as these are produced, such as the Effective Supervision Unit (SfC, 2007).

Some organisations have produced their own statements or standards to direct management development activity. Job descriptions and person specifications are often the basis for appraisal and so must also be taken into account. In addition, there are standards for specialist services e.g. registered managers of residential services, youth justice, housing and commissioning. Furthermore, different professions have produced their own standards e.g. Head Teachers and in the NHS the Leadership Qualities Framework (DH, 2009a). Standards for commissioning managers in social care have also just been introduced (CWDC, 2008). The NHS has developed its own standards for commissioning managers (DH, 2007c). In short, this field is complex.

If you are a social worker and manager the benchmarks you should consider in auditing your current practice and planning for improvement as determined by the GSCC consist of:

- the National Occupational standards for Social Work (Topss England, 2002);
- the Code of Practice for Social Care Workers (GSCC, 2004);
- the Code of Practice for Employers of Social Care Workers (GSCC, 2004);

- the National Occupational Standards for Managers (MSC, 2008, see Appendix 4);
- the Ten Principles of Social Care Management (SfC/Topss, 2004, see Appendix 5);
- the Effective Supervision Unit (SfC/CWDC, 2007, see Chapters 4, 5 and 6).

In addition you may also need to take into account any:

- management standards produced by your organisation;
- job descriptions and person specifications;
- standards for commissioning, procurement and contracting;
- specialist standards for particular services;
- new standards as they are introduced;
- the Leadership Qualities Framework (if you manage a service integrated with Health these will be useful – see Appendix 6).

Life is a little easier for managers in the NHS who only need to refer to the Leadership Qualities Framework (DH, 2009a), the Knowledge and Skills Framework (DH, 2004) and the National Management Standards (MSC, 2008).

Why spend so much time and effort to define management practice? Definition is at least in part a response to a problem that was apparent before 1988 when the first version of the generic National Occupational Standards for Managers was produced (MSC, 2008). The standards were part of the Management Charter Initiative (MCI), which sought to respond to national inadequacies in management development and provide standards to help define good management practice. Before that time, appraisal and development planning for managers was hindered by the lack of a common frame of reference that could be used as a comparator in making judgements about management practice. These standards also formed the basis of National Vocational Qualifications (NVQs) for supervisors, first line managers, middle and senior managers and were intended to encourage work-based learning and the assessment of practice. Since this first set of standards was produced, the Management Standards Centre has taken over responsibility for them. They have been revised several times and the latest edition was produced in 2008 (MSC, 2008).

In two decades we can be seen to have lurched from a dearth of benchmarks that clearly limited the effectiveness of management development, to a positive glut. A rather embarrassing surplus of options confuses managers and may inadvertently have the same effect as having no point of reference at all. We may also have become over-reliant on standard setting as a way of changing practice. It perhaps gives us a false sense of confidence, as defining outcomes appears 'scientific'. But standards don't actually *make* anything happen and their impact on learning and development has been criticised. For instance, NVQs have been criticised for poor completion rates, focusing too much on assessment rather than learning, for being too bureaucratic and time consuming, and failing to demonstrate organisational impact (Torrington and Hall, 1998, pp421–22).

The National Leadership and Management Strategy (SfC/Topss, 2004) recommends that, *all managers should have their own person management specification and this requirement should be included within National Minimum Standards* (SfC, 2004, pvii). They propose that this profile should be based on a range of current competencies taken from the generic and the specialist standards (see SfC/Topss, 2004, p25).

If you have a 'person management specification' already, then obviously make use of it. Do bear in mind our discussion about the effects of too managed an approach and other benchmarks might still be well worth exploring. If you don't have one, then here is an opportunity for you to take control of your management development experience by exploring and determining helpful definitions of good practice and the role of a manager.

ACTIVITY **10.3**

Benchmarking management practice

What are the points of reference you have used in benchmarking your management practice in the past? How helpful have they been?

Explore the possible benchmarks you could use as outlined above (we have included an overview of the less familiar National Management Standards, the Ten Principles of Social Care Management and the Leadership Qualities Framework in the appendices to help with this).

Which of the benchmarks might offer you a new reference point in benchmarking your practice?

Reviewing and evaluating your previous developmental experiences

There is value in reviewing your previous learning experiences to identify the features of those that have been most valuable to you. While this should not hold you back from experimenting with new ways of learning, it is useful to identify what has worked for you in the past in terms of learning processes and establishing the building blocks of knowledge, understanding and skills that support your current practice. To help you review your learning experiences we have identified some useful questions in Figure 10.3 below.

Evidencing your practice

It is good practice to evidence your practice and your learning because it is important that your identification of learning needs is as objective and informed as possible, otherwise you could be working on areas that will not achieve best outcomes. Getting learning objectives right is not only about what you compare your practice with i.e. benchmarking as above, but also about the evidence you draw on in making, what is called, a gap analysis (Figure 10.4).

So, what are the options open to you in obtaining evidence? Broadly, they are workplace artefacts, feedback from stakeholders, observations, assessment exercises and personal reflection, as explored below.

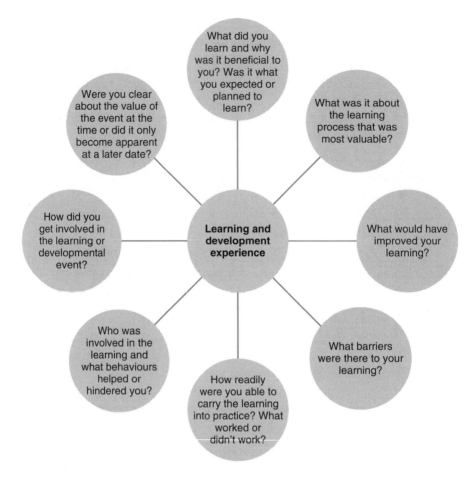

Figure 10.3 Reviewing and evaluating learning and development experiences

---

ACTIVITY 10.4

From the list below identify the learning experiences that have been most meaningful to you.

When you have established the key events for you, use the questions in Figure 10.3 (above) to review the experiences and reflect on the impact of the experience on your learning and development.

Table 10.3 Key learning events

Key learning events

- *Project work*
- *Learning from everyday events*
- *Coaching and one-to-one discussion*
- *Shadowing a colleague or colleagues*
- *Sitting in on planning meetings, reviews and conferences, etc.*

ACTIVITY 10.4 *(CONT.)*

- *Consultation and advice*
- *Personal research*
- *Visits and short placements*
- *Guided reading*
- *Distance learning*
- *E-learning*
- *Policy and supporting documents*
- *Secondments*
- *Taught course, programmes and workshops*
- *Qualifying training*
- *Mentoring by colleagues*
- *Group work and learning sets*
- *Conferences*

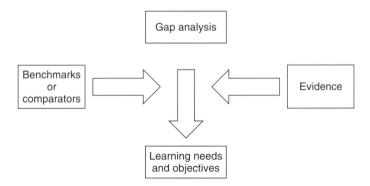

Figure 10.4 Gap analysis

Workplace artefacts

Evidence of your management practice naturally occurs in the workplace e.g. a report on a service development. If you lead your team in putting together a business plan or lead a project group or working party, there can be valuable and tangible outcomes that offer evidence of your management practice. Layers of evidence or several sources of evidence that confirm evaluations of your practice are stronger and have more depth than just one artefact.

An approach that can be helpful in this respect, in building a case for the evaluation of your practice, is triangulation. Triangulation is a principle of navigation that is borrowed and applied in research (Figure 10.5). If you can locate yourself in relation to three land-marks on a map then you will know precisely where you are. If three pieces of evidence support the same picture of your practice, then you have a good case for claiming that your conclusion is evidenced.

Figure 10.5 Triangulation of evidence to support practice evaluation

Feedback from stakeholders

As illustrated by Figure 10.5 a rich source of objective evidence can be provided by the stakeholders involved in your practice. Stakeholders are all the individuals or groups who benefit from or work with you, both inside and outside of your organisation, in managing and delivering the service. A rigorous approach to collecting feedback from key stakehold-ers is 360° feedback.

The idea of 360° feedback is very similar to triangulation (Figure 10.6). A 360° or an 'all round' scan of stakeholders' views is useful to provide evidence of a manager's practice and develop a learning agenda. This usually involves collecting evidence from senior man-agers, colleagues, the team you manage and patients or users.

There are a number of different ways of approaching 360° feedback. At its simplest, it can be managed by seeking feedback from different groups on your management practice. At its most sophisticated, a third party manages this process for you, determining who will be consulted, structuring the consultation, summarising the information while maintain-ing anonymity, sharing the information with you, supporting you in determining your learning needs and formulating a development plan and objectives – the Leadership Qualities Framework (DH, 2009a) advocates working in this way.

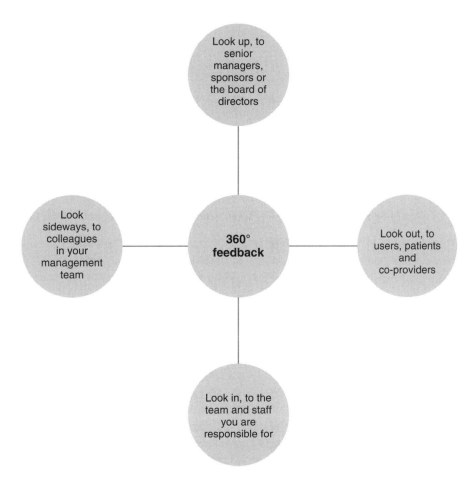

Figure 10.6 360° feedback

If you do not have access to formal 360° feedback provision there are a number of options open to you. You could ask a trusted colleague to help co-ordinate it for you, perhaps doing the same for them. You could manage the process yourself, either accepting that it won't be anonymous or else perhaps asking an administrator to collect feedback and type it up for you so that you cannot identify who has responded.

The main problem with completing this process yourself is that some personal support is advisable when receiving feedback. While 99 per cent of the time the feedback experience is one of being given the positive comments that people normally never share, or else save until we leave or retire, the odd anonymous comment can be quite disturbing. You can end up trying to guess who said it; you may find several different ways of interpreting it, or it can hit a sensitive spot. A facilitator, mentor or colleague can offer some protection from this and help keep it in perspective, which is why their role is so valuable. If you receive negative feedback from a 360° feedback exercise bear in mind that:

- it probably isn't a new perspective. It was out there before, you just didn't know about it;

- you have a choice as to whether you 'own' it or not. Just because someone said it, doesn't make it true or something you must take on board;

- people's perceptions can be based on a one-off incident that you may not even have been aware of at the time and it may have never occurred since;

- people do hold grudges and can totally misunderstand situations and actions;

- it may be prudent to check it out if anyone else holds the same view, if it is better evidenced it is more valid and deserves to be taken more seriously;

- it has been known for those giving the feedback to give it to the wrong manager!

So, there is a risk to undertaking 360° feedback and it might not be entirely comfortable. Remember that you do have some control of the risk in determining who you ask. Though it might be a waste of time to only ask people who you know hold a high opinion of your practice, it might be a step too far to only ask for feedback from colleagues who you don't get on with! So, make some choices of the range of relationships you, in effect, audit.

If seeking feedback can be hazardous for you, it can also be difficult for the people you have asked to provide it. They can find it quite anxiety provoking to be asked to comment on your practice and can find it hard to determine a point of reference if they have little understanding of management. Users and patients can be particularly vulnerable in this respect and while it is good if they can be included, be cautious, especially if you have little face-to-face contact. On the other hand, in seeking feedback and giving your personal development attention, you are making an important statement. The dialogue that can ensue with people can improve relationships and open doors to further discussion. But remember not to ask too many people. Too much information can be problematic – perhaps confine yourself to feedback from seven or eight people at the most.

To help people who you ask for feedback to respond effectively there are a number of options open to you.

- You can give them a simple pro-forma that has headings such as 'What do I do as a manager that you find helpful?'; 'What could I improve on?'; or 'What could I do more of?'. Also include an 'any other comments' category and ask if you can get back to them to discuss their feedback.

- Alongside the pro-forma, a letter explaining why you are doing this and how this process will be useful to you is to be recommended. This should also say whether anonymity can be protected and the date you need to get the feedback by. A stamped addressed envelope can help if you are not asking them to complete the forms electronically. Remember to thank them for their time and effort!

- If you have had previous feedback and have been working on improving your practice you may wish to ask specific questions about particular areas, or you may wish to focus on personal or business priorities. If you choose approaches like these, please make sure you elicit more general views as well.

- Sometimes it can be helpful to take the pressure off individuals by making it a group exercise. For instance, leave a team meeting early and ask your team to complete a feedback form together – one manager who led a residential unit asked their deputy to complete one with a group of patients after a resident's meeting.

If at this point you are thinking that 360° feedback is hard work – you are right. It is a very good way of getting a picture of how others perceive your practice as a manager, but you have to invest time and energy to get the information. It is also not just a passive piece of information gathering. It demands a new stance from you on how you develop your practice and then it impacts, whatever the results, on the relationships and perceptions of your community of practice and on your own perceptions. So approach it thoughtfully. If you choose to undertake it, seek advice. If you find yourself in difficulties, talk to someone about it – don't agonise over it alone.

If 360° feedback is too demanding an option, one alternative could be discussing your practice with a range of selected stakeholders. As with 360° feedback you may well have to prompt them with questions or a frame of reference, or perhaps even take an analysis of your practice to a meeting to get them started. Make sure the focus is your practice, not the quality of the service more generally, although this is bound to figure. A well-informed appraisal is also a good starting point and constitutes feedback from a key stakeholder. Some appraisals, especially for senior managers, are based on consultation with a number of stakeholders and can be shared and owned by them. Another option for obtaining evidence is observation.

Observations

The strength of an observation is that it is an immediate account of what someone has actually seen. As with a 360° feedback, asking someone to observe you can be daunting. You will need to spend some time briefing them – here are some suggestions for good practice.

- Select your observer carefully. They need to have sufficient understanding of leadership and management practice to be able to comment in a constructive manner.

- Brief them carefully and share your agenda – what you think your strengths and weaknesses are, what you are pleased with, what you would like to improve and so on.

- If your observer would not normally be part of the event you will need to ask the permission of others involved to introduce the observer and explain their role. Remember this can be a bit daunting as, although you are the focus of attention they will also be observing the other people involved. Also, having somebody silently watching an activity can be a bit unnerving. So, asking a trusted colleague who would be involved in the activity anyway might well be the best way forward.

- Set up the observation in good time.

- Meet with the observer after the event and debrief them.

Personal reflection and assessment exercises

Another source of evidence for gap analysis is personal reflection and other self-assessment exercises. Methodical personal reflection can offer you a valuable way of developing evidence about your practice (Stein, 2009).

One option is to keep a reflective diary of your practice but it is important that your reflection is critical and analytical. This involves thinking about your practice in the light of a particular perspective on management practice or a particular theory and drawing an evaluation from it that gauges your strengths and weaknesses as a professional manager and helps determine how you might develop your practice. The reflection points and activities provided throughout this book have offered you opportunities to reflect on and analyse your practice in this way and provided some self-assessment exercises.

REFLECTION POINT 10.1

What evidence can you already draw on in reviewing and evaluating your management practice?

What might give you a clearer picture of your practice to help you determine your learning needs?

Reviewing the activities and reflection points in this book and the notes you have made, what learning and development needs can you identify?

Future career planning

The final section of this chapter helps you to consider future career planning – what you might do and achieve in the longer term. Some organisations take it seriously under the guise of 'succession planning', but organisations are mostly interested in retaining and developing your talent to ensure they have the management resources they need for their future. In other words, they are not necessarily interested in you as a person and your needs.

Succession planning is now appearing as a component of workforce planning and in leadership and management strategies. Skills for Care note that *High Quality People Management is imperative in the sector. This must include succession planning and 'growing' of managers* (SfC, 2008, p19).

Look for opportunities to engage your manager and if possible build a long-term development agenda that meets your future needs as well as responding to the immediate demands of the workplace. Asking your manager about their career pathway and plans, what has most helped them and what they see as your options is not a bad place to start.

As with CPD it is worth considering a 'softer' approach that contrasts with the more technocratic world of management standards, processes and plans. Joy-Mathews *et al.* (2004, p141) have designed a useful way of thinking about this. They contrast the conventional SMART formula for good objectives (see Chapter 1) with SPICE:

- **S**piritual

- **P**hysical

- **I**ntellectual

- **C**areer

- **E**motional.

They suggest it is important to approach CPD and career planning as a whole person and in a balanced way. This demands giving attention to aspects of your character that the organisation does not. So, beyond specific learning objectives you should have goals that will help you meet not just your career ambitions but your spiritual, physical, intellectual and emotional needs.

Another way to express this is to suggest that you determine what makes you happy. You may find it useful to visit the work of Csikszentmihalyi (1998, 1990, 2008), a positive psychologist who has researched what gives people happiness. You can find a talk by him on YouTube (**http://uk.youtube.com/watch?v=fXIeFJCqsPs**), in which he points out how important it has been for chief executives he has worked with that their work is meaningful to them and that they take pleasure from the process as well as outcomes. Just as you have reviewed and reflected on your developmental history it may pay you to also think back over your work experiences and identify posts, projects and roles that have given you particular satisfaction or in which you have been particularly successful. You may have identified skills that are particular to you, challenges you thrive on, work that most motivates you and also activities or responsibilities to avoid. There are also some fundamental value issues here about what you want to achieve in your life and questions about your work-life balance. If you think it important that your career planning has this added depth, there are still some practical things that you can do to help set goals and find direction.

Get advice

Human Resources or Personnel may be able to offer you advice and guidance on career prospects and pathways. Succession planning is figuring more and more in public service thinking, so you may find their approach helpful. Alternatively, your manager or someone else in the sort of post you might be interested in could be a useful port of call. Think about asking them:

- what attracted them to their job?

- what do they think was key to them being appointed?

- what have been the challenges for them?

- what have they found most enjoyable?

- what have they not enjoyed?

- what they see as their next step?

- what would they advise someone like yourself to do if they are aiming for a similar appointment?

If possible, shadow them for a day or sit in on some key events, for example, senior strategy or team meetings. Think about asking to be delegated some development responsibilities that would not normally be in your remit. What can be really helpful is if a senior manager agrees to be your mentor. If this isn't possible perhaps ask if your manager would meet with you on a few occasions during the course to discuss issues that come up but are not in your area of responsibility.

Research opportunities

Determine where the type of posts you are most interested in are advertised and scan them regularly. Get the job descriptions and person specifications and do a gap analysis against your current experience, skills and knowledge. Perhaps also explore the training and development provision that is offered to people in those posts. When benchmarking your practice, look at senior as well as middle manager standards. Employment agencies and consultants can also offer career guidance.

Plan

By setting your longer-term career goals you can plan development activities to help you get there. You may need a short-, medium- and long-term plan. It might be an idea to build in some contingency and/or alternative pathways and options. If you can persuade your organisation to take on these longer-term development needs as part of a succession planning initiative then you should be in an even better position.

REFLECTION POINT 10.2

Are you clear about your career ambitions and intentions?

If you aren't clear, what could you do to help you explore options?

If you are clear, have you a development plan to help you succeed?

Chapter summary

- Leadership and management development strategy is finally getting the attention it deserves with major new initiatives in both health and social care.

- Reviewing and improving your own CPD is a good way to further your career and have a positive effect on service quality and service development.

- It is important that you personalise your approach to CPD as a manager, finding ways forward that work for you and motivate you.

- Taking opportunity to plan for your career is beneficial and our organisations are now improving their approach to succession planning.

- Contributing to leadership and management development strategy and the learning of others is important, as this is best led by leaders and managers rather than Human Resource specialists.

The Birmingham & Solihull Learning & Skills Council's (LSC) Centre for Excellence in Adult Social Care offers a valuable 'Quality in Care' e-portal that provides a good point of access to leadership resources including a map of leadership and management standards in social care that can be used to develop a person specification. **www.quality-in-care.co.uk/leadership.htm**.

Hartle, F., Snook, P., Apsey, H. and Browton, R. (2008) *The Training and Development of Middle Managers in the Children's Workforce – Hay Group Report to the Children's Workforce Development Council.* London: Hay Group. **www.cwdcouncil.org.uk/assets/0000/2362/Training_and_development_of_middle_managers_in_the_children_s_workforce.pdf.**

This report produced by the Hay Group consultancy for the CWDC on middle manager experiences offers a valuable insight into current practices and some useful ways forward.

Accepting that the good practice model we introduced in this chapter offers a valuable summary, take a look at the national management development strategy in full.

Skills for Care (SfC) (2008) *Leadership and Management Strategy Update 2008.* Leeds: Skills for Care. **www.skillsforcare.org.uk/developing_skills/leadership_and_management/leadership_and_management_strategy.aspx.**

This report refreshes and updates the original 2004 report.

Chapter 11

Further key theoretical perspectives

Keith Brown

CHAPTER OBJECTIVES

This chapter will help you address the following National Occupational Standards for Management and Leadership.

- A2 Manage your own resources and professional development.
- B6 Provide leadership in your area of responsibility.
- D1 Develop productive working relationships with colleagues.

This chapter will also help you address the following Principles of Social Care Management.

- Inspire staff.
- Value people, recognise and actively develop potential.
- Develop and maintain awareness and keep in touch with service users and staff.
- Empower staff and service users to develop services people want.
- Take responsibility for the continuing professional development of self and others.

Introduction – the development of management theory

Leadership is about getting extraordinary performance out of ordinary people

Sir John Harvey Jones (cited in Adair, 2005, p61)

This chapter is a review of some of the more influential approaches to the study of people in organisations and organisational behaviour to help you broaden your understanding of what might constitute effective leadership and management and supervision in health and social care.

The serious and detailed study of people in organisations is relatively recent. Before F.W. Taylor (1911) burst upon the scene with his concept of 'scientific management' in the early years of the 20th century there was little coherent management thought of any kind.

Business was generally in the hands of individual entrepreneurs who saw no need for management theory to assist them in their pursuit of commercial self-interest. Taylor was not an industrial psychologist but his work was based on certain assumptions about man's nature and motivations, and it is probably fair to state that these represented the general view of people in organisations at that time. Although Taylor's assumptions are perhaps psychologically naïve, they are by no means altogether misconceived. They are based on the predominance of the financial incentive and on the 'rationality' of man's response to it (Taylor, 1911).

The most influential refutation of the simple view of industrial man came from Elton Mayo's Hawthorne experiments in Chicago in the 1920s (Mayo, 1933). These lengthy and impressive studies produced telling evidence of complex motivations other than those of a financial nature and demonstrated the importance of group pressures in determining individual behaviour.

Following Hawthorne, the study of groups became paramount and for a period one might have wondered if the individual still existed. In the last three decades the related disciplines referenced by the term 'behavioural sciences' have contributed much to our knowledge of human behaviour in organisations. Emphasis has been on a changing concept of man's essential nature (viewpoints expressed broadly by McGregor's (1961) Theory X and Theory Y– see below) and on the needs, drives and motivations which explain man's often apparently irrational behaviour. Not all of this work is as scientific as its generic title would suggest and some conclusions from the evidence appear more idealistic than objective. Nonetheless, it is supported by an impressive amount of research and is undoubtedly leading us towards a clearer understanding of how people work and react within organisations (Mullins, 2007).

We will explore each of these approaches and their application to the management of health and social care before concluding with a review of some key leadership theories.

Scientific management

The theory of scientific management, as developed by F.W. Taylor in the early 1900s (Taylor, 1911) contained two basic assumptions about people which probably represented the general view of management at the time and which have subsequently governed much of the use of incentives in organisations with both beneficial and damaging results. The first assumption was that mankind's incentive to work, his goal and purpose, was financial reward. In order to achieve this he apparently applied to his task some abstraction of sensory and muscular processes that the task demanded and either left at home or put into a state of suspended animation all other aspects of his personality – aims, aspirations, social needs, etc. The second implied assumption was that man was 'rational' in pursuit of this objective. Taylor believed that the deliberate restriction of output by workers, which deeply incensed him, resulted from inadequate management practices and from fear of unemployment. He was convinced that if standards of a 'fair day's work' and 'a fair day's pay' were systematically established and financial reward was associated with increased output, then workers would produce to the extent of their capabilities. Among theorists, the simple scientific management view of man has long been discredited; yet among practising managers, observation suggests it remains a widely held view (Mullins, 2007).

In professional practice in health and social care it is often suggested that we should be eclectic in our use of theory – we should make use of theory and perspectives to help us best understand a particular situation. The same applies to management – we perhaps need to build a repertoire of theoretical viewpoints we can draw on in helping us analyse and understand leadership and management problems (hence this chapter). Also, if later theorists have taken a different approach it does not mean that earlier work was invalid, rather it is still part of the domain of the discipline and it is better to perhaps see it as augmented or complimented rather than completely outdated or replaced.

- *Can you think of situations where Taylor's concern that managers should analyse tasks, determine the best ways of carrying them out and then ensure that workers follow their instructions is still valid?*

- *Can you think of situations where ensuring outputs are related to financial reward might be important?*

Elton Mayo and the Hawthorne experiments

The Hawthorne experiments, which refuted so dramatically many of the tacit assumptions held in organisations, were conducted between 1927 and 1932 at the Hawthorne works of the Western Electric Company in Chicago (Mayo, 1933). The National Academy of Sciences started the investigations to study the relationship between worker efficiency and workshop illumination and was conducted by means of a control group and an experimental group. The groups were involved in the assembly of telephone relays (a small, intricate mechanism comprising about 40 parts). At the outset, the lighting for the experimental group was improved, with the expected result that the output from the group increased. Unexpectedly, however, output from the control group also increased. The experimental group's lighting was then reduced and output again increased. It became apparent that some unknown factor, other than the quality of the illumination, was complicating an apparently straightforward investigation. Further changes were therefore introduced, relating to rest pauses, the length of the working day, free lunches, etc. Each was continued for a period of four to twelve weeks. The only change which did not occasion an increase in output was the introduction of six short rest pauses, which apparently upset the workers' rhythm. Finally, all improvements and alterations were removed and conditions were returned to what they had been at the outset of the experiment. Under these conditions output reached its highest level at any time in the experiment. Medical examinations showed no signs of cumulative fatigue and absenteeism had fallen by 80%. It also showed that each worker in the group had used their own working method and had varied it from time to time to avoid monotony.

Subsequently, the researchers at Hawthorne conducted further investigations into the operation of blank wiring (attaching wires to switches for parts of telephone equipment). This was an investigation into the operation of group pressures, conducted by an observer and an interviewer, and which did not involve the alteration of working conditions. This part of the investigation showed the power of an informal leader and the influence of the values and customs of the group. It was apparent that, to all but one of the group, adherence to group norms of production was a more powerful motivation than a financial incentive.

What had started out as a simple enquiry into the effects of illumination had developed into a demonstration of motives more complex and subtle than anyone had expected. A programme of interviews, introduced as part of the investigation, added to the information available. Some of the conclusions to be drawn from Mayo's (1933) work have been summarised as follows.

- Work is a group activity.

- The social world of the adult is primarily patterned about work activity.

- The need for recognition, security and sense of belonging is more important in determining workers' morale and productivity than the physical conditions under which they work.

- A complaint is not necessarily an objective recital of fact; it is commonly a symptom-manifesting disturbance of an individual's status position in the group.

- A worker's attitudes and effectiveness are conditioned by social demands both from inside and outside the workplace.

- Informal groups within the workplace exercise strong social control over the work habits and attitudes of the individual worker.

Put another way, there was more than enough evidence from these experiments to highlight the psychological naïvety of Taylor's theories. Emphasis had also been shifted from the individual to the group as the proper unit of study.

REFLECTION POINT 11.2

- *Do you agree with the conclusions of Mayo's work as above?*

- *How does this accord with the current emphasis on individual supervision? (See Chapters 4 and 5.)*

- *If informal groups are so important in determining people's behaviour how can you seek to influence them?*

The needs hierarchy

Another widely held view of motivation is that mankind is always directed towards the satisfaction of some need, and that these needs can be hierarchically arranged. As long as the lower ones are not met, they will act as motivators of behaviour but, once they have been satisfied, the individual will be motivated by the attempt to satisfy the next highest level of needs. These needs have been differently described and the number of levels is regarded by different authorities as anything from three to seven. The hierarchy described here is that propounded by A.H. Maslow (1943) and subsequently supported in largely the same form by a series of writers (e.g. Cooke *et al.*, 2005; Mook, 1987).

The first level is that of physiological needs – hunger, thirst, sexual desire, etc. (Figure 11.1). It is recognised that these needs cannot always be clearly isolated: a meal in company, for example, may meet social was well as physiological needs. *A person lacking food, safety, love, and esteem, would probably hunger for food more strongly than for anything else* (Maslow, 1943, p373). Man lives for bread alone when there is no bread, but when his stomach is filled, other and 'higher' level needs emerge and become the motivators of behaviour. And when these, in turn are satisfied, again new needs emerge, and so on. Thus *gratification becomes as important a concept as deprivation in motivation theory*, because it releases a person from one need and permits the emergence of another (Maslow, 1943, p375).

The second level of need is the need for safety. Needs for safety are seen at their most easily observable in children, who desire orderliness, consistency, stability; and in normal healthy adults in situations when their safety is, in fact, endangered. As is the case with physiological needs, the normal adult in our society is largely satisfied in his safety needs and frequently, therefore, they are not functioning as active motivators. 'Safety', of course, is used to imply more than just freedom from physical danger and the concept of 'security' may indicate better what is intended.

The third level of the needs hierarchy is love. These are quite simply the needs of love and affection and a sense of belonging.

The fourth level is the need for esteem. These can be classified in two types.

- The need for achievement, competence, adequacy, self-respect, etc.

- The need for recognition from others, reputation, prestige, appreciation, etc.

Satisfaction of these needs produces feelings of confidence, usefulness, worth; thwarting them gives rise to feelings of inferiority and helplessness.

The final level of need is the need for self-actualisation. Maslow describes this as the *desire to become more and more what one is; to become everything that one is capable of becoming* (Maslow 1943, p 382). This need will manifest itself in very different forms in different people according to aptitudes and capabilities. Generally, this need will not emerge clearly until the previous four are satisfied, i.e. one might expect the most creative behaviour from the most satisfied people.

The role in motivation of curiosity, learning and experimenting, etc. has not been discussed and it is suggested that the desire to know and understand can be seen as a need in itself (apart from the role that the cognitive processes play in the satisfaction of other needs). These, however, do not fit easily into the hierarchy and, indeed, interestingly appear to form themselves into a hierarchy, for instance, *the desire to know, to understand, to systematise, to organise, to analyse, to look for relations and meanings* (Maslow, 1943, p385).

The hierarchy of needs should not be seen as fixed and rigid in all cases. There are individual exceptions in whom, for example, self-esteem appears more important than love, or where self-actualisation appears to dominate everything. In certain cases, levels of aspiration may be permanently lowered by continuous deprivation. There may be apparent reversals of the hierarchical order simply because needs which have been satisfied for a long time become undervalued; we cease to be aware of their propensity until we are

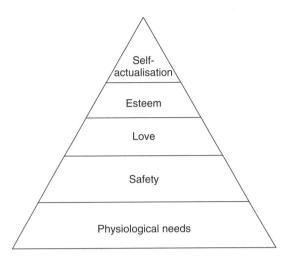

Figure 11.1 Maslow's (1943) hierarchy of needs

again deprived of satisfaction. It should also be noted that this hierarchy is not always manifested in behaviour. Behaviour has many other determinants.

It should not be assumed that the levels are so clear cut that each has to be 100% satisfied before the next emerges. Most people will be partially satisfied and partially unsatisfied in all their basic needs. The hierarachy of needs, as described by Maslow, McGregor and others is not specifically applicable to work situations but its relevance to organisations in a modern affluent society is not difficult to see. It is likely that the factors which motivate modern 'organisational' man are higher on this scale than much management practice has yet to realise.

REFLECTION POINT **11.3**

We suggested in Chapter 3 that your leadership needed to be needs-led. Maslow's (1943) hierarchy of need offers a different perspective on this.

- *Where are members of your team on Maslow's hierarchy?*
- *What do you do to respond to their needs and motivate them?*
- *What are your needs and how will these be met?*

Theory X and Theory Y

Douglas McGregor first put forward his concepts of Theory X and Theory Y in 1957 and subsequently developed them in his book *The Human Side of Enterprise* (1961). Theory X represents traditional assumptions made by management about people in organisations and is used in determining managerial behaviour towards people.

- The average human being has an inherent dislike of work and will avoid it if he can.
- Because of this human characteristic of dislike of work, most people must be coerced,

controlled, directed, and threatened with punishment to get them to put forth adequate effort toward the achievement of organisational objectives.

- The average human being prefers to be directed, wishes to avoid responsibility, has relatively little ambition and wants security above all (McGregor, 1961).

McGregor cites this as a view of people in organisations, which materially influences large areas of management activity. His claim, however, is that while this theory accounts for some organisational behaviour (otherwise it would not have persisted) there are many observed aspects of behaviour that are not consistent with this viewpoint. Therefore, he proposes Theory Y. It is not suggested that all employees are described by Theory Y or that none would be described by Theory X, but that Theory Y represents a more realistic description of workers in general. The assumptions of Theory Y are:

- the expenditure of physical and mental effort in work is as natural as play or rest;

- external control and the threat of punishment are not the only means for bringing about effort toward organisational objectives. Mankind will exercise self-direction and self-control in the service of objectives to which s/he is committed;

- commitment to objectives is a function of the rewards associated with their achievement;

- the average human being learns under proper conditions not only to accept but also to seek responsibility;

- the capacity to exercise a relatively high degree of imagination, ingenuity and creativity in the solution of organisational problems is widely, not narrowly, distributed in the population;

- under the conditions of modern organisational life, the intellectual potentialities of the average human being are only partly utilised.

(McGregor, 1961)

The trend of modern behavioural science research is to confirm Theory Y as a more competent set of assumptions about human nature than Theory X. Observation suggests, however, than many of the research findings of recent years have yet to be accepted by practising managers. There have been in many cases misunderstandings, sometimes leading to unduly extravagant claims and distortions by acolytes of their own particular master's message. It is difficult to conduct scientifically controlled research into any but the most peripheral areas of behaviour; consequently the way remains open for dissention. Behaviour is largely learned and the behaviour of people in organisations can illustrate what they have learned from their experience. In other words, management action based on given assumptions about people will tend to elicit a response, which is in line with those assumptions, thereby confirming initial beliefs. For example, it would be difficult to observe manifestations of Theory Y in an organisation whose management philosophy was based on a belief in Theory X.

McGregor also anticipates, in essence, Herzberg *et al.*'s (1959) 'motivation-hygiene' theory, emphasising the futility of providing ever-increasing means to satisfy lower level needs, when these have ceased to operate as predominant motivators, and the need for people to derive some satisfaction of their higher level needs from the work which they do. He claims that the major rewards provided by management yield satisfaction only when the individual is away from the job. Put another way, it is not surprising that many wage earners perceive work as a form of punishment – the price for various kinds of satisfaction away from the job. Herzberg *et al.* (1959) also found that the factors acting as positive motivators to work were always those connected directly with the job; while the 'hygiene' factors, the potential 'dissatisfiers' (matters which may demotivate but will never motivate) are those concerning the circumstances that surround the job.

Table 11.1 Man's attitude to work (adapted from McGregor, 1961)

Theory X	Theory Y
1. Man dislikes work and will avoid it if he can	1. Work is necessary to man's psychological growth
2. Man must be forced or bribed to put out the right effort	2. Man wants to be interested in his work and, under the right conditions, he can enjoy it
3. Man would rather be directed than accept responsibility, which he avoids	3. Man will direct himself towards accepted targets
4. Man is motivated mainly by money	4. Man will seek, and accept responsibility, under the right conditions
5. Man is motivated by anxiety about his security	5. The discipline a man imposes on himself is more effective, and can be more severe than any imposed on him
6. Most men have little creativity – except when getting round management rules!	6. Under the right conditions many are motivated by the desire to realise their own potential
	7. Creativity and ingenuity are widely distributed and grossly underused.

REFLECTION POINT **11.4**

McGregor's Theory X can be seen to be based on a Taylorist view of humanity and Theory Y on more humanistic perspectives such as Maslow's.

- *Is the management culture of your organisation based on Theory X or Theory Y?*
- *Is your team culture based on Theory X or Theory Y?*
- *If they are different what problems does this create for you and how do you manage them?*
- *What problems might there be in a Theory X organisation in providing a Theory Y-type service to people who use services?*

Herzberg

Herzberg (1966, 1987); *et al.* (1959) set out to understand what it was that gave people satisfaction at work, with the assumption that this would reveal what motivated them to work harder (Figure 11.2). He and others conducted many interviews of accountants and engineers – asking them to describe times when they were dissatisfied and times when they were highly satisfied. Analysis of these interviews showed that these two emotional states were caused by two different sets of conditions. The things that were largely responsible for dissatisfaction, if they were absent or inadequate, were:

- pay;
- relationship with peer, job security;
- status;
- company policy;
- working conditions;
- relationship with boss.

(Herzberg *et al.*, 1959)

They termed these hygiene factors. This rather odd term was taken from the analogy that just as clean water can help prevent disease, but not cure it, improving these factors would not satisfy people. Once we feel 'secure' in our jobs, making us 'more secure' will not result in improved motivation.

Herzberg *et al.* (1959) cite the extreme motivating psychological factors as:

- interesting work;
- significant achievement, personal growth;
- responsibility for worthwhile activities;
- advancement.

The key to meeting these needs was to give people additional responsibility, greater opportunity to use their talents, and more control over their jobs. These ideas were termed 'job enrichment'.

---

*REFLECTION POINT **11.5***

Look over Herzberg's 'hygiene' factors and the motivating factors in Figure 11.1 above.

- *Do you agree with the distinction between hygiene and motivating factors?*
- *What motivates you?*
- *What do you think motivates your team and what evidence have you got for this?*
- *What are the implications of what motivates you and your team for your leadership and management practice?*

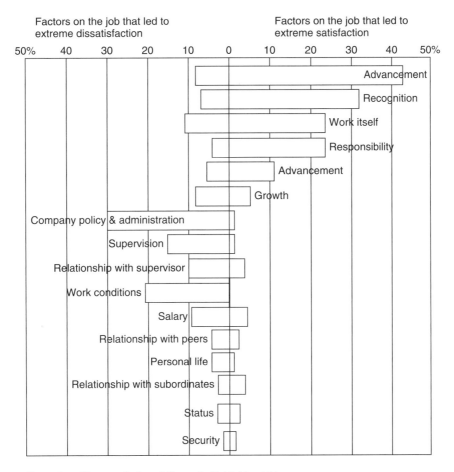

Reproduced by permission of Granada Publishing Ltd
from Frederick Herzberg's book *Work and the Nature of Man*

Figure 11.2 Job factors leading to satisfaction or dissatisfaction (based on Herzberg, 1966)

The impact of the group

Prior to the Hawthorne experiments the general tendency (though not universal) had been to concentrate on the individual as the unit of study in organisational psychology. Following Mayo's (1933) revelations there developed an awareness of the impact of the group on organisational behaviour and knowledge of group processes and group influences continues to be developed.

An important distinction is made between 'primary' and 'secondary' groups. The former are small groups of individuals in face-to-face relationships e.g. the family and workplace and the latter category comprises such groups as the company, the nation, etc., which include the primary groups within them, and which are too large for all members to have personal relationships with all other members. Primary and secondary groups should be seen as opposite ends of a continuum with a vague area in the middle. For the student of organisational behaviour, the important group is the primary group. Primary groups are crucial in determining an individual's personal attributes, their views, their values and their attitudes. They are one of the fundamental sources of discipline and self-control. It is fair to state that an individual's deepest feelings relate to primary groups; secondary groups are too remote.

A study of American flyers during the Second World War showed clearly that an individual's first loyalty was to his crew, then to his squadron, then a group of squadrons and finally to the particular Air Forces of which s/he was part. Feelings for the US Army were less strong, for the allied armies still less and so on. Loyalty to the people of the allied nations was barely measurable. The same pattern of diminishing strength of loyalty from the workplace to the organisation could be found in any large organisation, and its applications are clear. Essentially, it implies that an organisation will be at a disadvantage in trying to influence group workings in a way that is not compatible with their values.

Primary groups develop norms or standards or group values, and the nature of a group imposes powerful pressure on any individual to conform to the standards of the group. The mere fact that members of a group have similar attitudes does not necessarily mean that similarity is caused by group membership. People with similar attitudes tend to be attracted to one another. People receive their main social satisfaction from relationships with those who hold similar attitudes, and such people have the most influence on their subsequent attitudes. There is a complex interaction process at work. To refer to the hierarchy of needs, one could say that the need for love and esteem tends to be satisfied through membership of primary groups, whereas they tend not to be satisfied through secondary groups. The individual's need to retain his primary group membership, and the consequent pressure on him to conform to its values, is one of the most fundamental and important facts of organisational life. The primary groups within organisations are potent forces for either the furtherance or the obstruction of organisational objectives. One of the problems of high labour turnover is that it gives little opportunity for primary groupings to arise and makes problems of morale, discipline and control much more difficult.

REFLECTION POINT 11.6

- *Can you think of situations where the influence of primary working groups has undermined or come into conflict with the organisation and its objectives?*

- *What impact can belonging to different primary working groups have on the multidisciplinary team and service quality?*

- *Which primary groups most influence your leadership and management?*

Individuals within groups will occupy different 'roles' and have different status. They will, in other words, have a position in any group to which they belong and there will be an appropriate pattern of behaviour associated with that position. A person who belongs to several groups may have a quite different status in each. Status can originate from a variety of sources. The importance of status to the individual should not be underestimated – from the point of view of the social psychologist, the need of the individual for status and function is the most significant of his traits, and if this need remains unsatisfied, nothing else can compensate for its lack. Status is relative. It concerns the position of one person in relation to another, and raising the status of one necessarily reduces the status of the other. Its nature may be 'functional' or 'non-functional', which is to say that it can be based on skill, competence or hierarchical position. The former is likely to cause fewer difficulties for the group because it is less exclusive and once acquired is less easily lost. Status is not necessarily associated with promotion (recognition of craftsmanship or functional worth may serve the purpose fully) but the relationship between status and conformity to group values has important implications. Homans (1951) has postulated that the higher the rank of a person within a group, the more nearly his activities conform to the norms of the group and vice versa. The group, in fact, confers prestige on those who conform. The low ranking member has less to lose and therefore feels less pressure to conform.

Primary groups and secondary groups tend to make different 'role' demands on the individual. Secondary groups generally require more specific and predictable role behaviour, which the individual may find less natural and less easy to sustain. His ability to meet the demands of the role will vary according to his level of adjustment. Children, for example, will find it difficult to sustain secondary roles: i.e. to behave as they are expected to behave in a social setting outside the immediate family. Because of the personal nature of the relationships, status in primary groups is easily identified; it is less easily seen in secondary groups because of the greater complexity or the communications, hence the need for external signs or 'status symbols'.

Jennings (1960) has distinguished between what he calls the 'socio-group' and the 'psyche-group' and Moreno (1960) with his quaintly titled technique of 'sociometry' has studied the same aspects of group structure. The socio-group is an association which is formed for work or for the accomplishment of some objective; the psyche-group is formed purely for the member's satisfaction in the group activities, with no purpose external to itself. These two types should be regarded as opposite ends of a continuum: real groups will inevitably fall somewhere in between. As Homans (1951) puts it, any group will have an external system, which is task-centred, and an internal system, which is group-centred. An appreciation of these two structures within a group can facilitate the organisation of the group for maximum effectiveness. It should not, for example, be assumed that personal friendships and preferences (the psyche-group structure) is necessarily a good indicator of preferred working relationships (the socio-group structure).

The pattern of primary groups within organisations is commonly referred to as the 'informal' structure of organisations, contrasting with the 'formal' structure portrayed on the organisation chart. The importance of this structure, for anyone wishing to understand organisation behaviour, cannot be overestimated. Whether the formal and informal aspects of organisations should be seen as so sharply contrasted is another matter. That they are is perhaps an unhappy reflection on the way in which formal organisations have been designed.

Leadership theories

The following theories: group thinking; action-centred leadership; the decision-making continuum; situational leadership; and transformational leadership are also offered as significant leadership theories which have an impact on the leadership, management and supervision of staff in health and social care. The aim is to provide a very brief insight into these influential theories and for you to consider their impact in health and social care.

Group thinking

'How could we have been so stupid?' asked President John F. Kennedy, after he and a group of close advisors had blundered into the Bay of Pigs invasion. Stupidity was certainly not the explanation. The group who made the decision was one of the greatest collections of intellectual talent in the history of American government. Irving Janis describes the blunder as a result of 'group-think'.

Group-think occurs when too high a price is placed on the harmony and morale of the group, so that loyalty to the group's previous policies, or to the group consensus, overrides the conscience of each member. 'Concurrence-seeking' drives out the realistic appraisal of alternatives. No bickering or conflict is allowed to spoil the cosy 'we-feeling' of the group. Even the cleverest, most high-minded and well-intentioned of people, can have a blind spot. Janis (1972) identifies eight symptoms.

- Invulnerability – cohesive groups become over-optimistic and can take extraordinary risks without realising the dangers, mainly because there is no discordant warning voice.

- Rationale – cohesive groups are quick to find rationalisations to explain away evidence that does not fit their policies.

- Morality – there is a tendency to be blind to the moral or ethical implications of a policy. 'How could so many good men be wicked?' is the feeling.

- Stereotypes – victims of group-think quickly get into the habit of stereotyping their enemies or other people and do not notice discordant evidence.

- Pressure – if anyone starts to voice doubts the group exerts subtle pressures to keep him quiet; he is allowed to express doubts but not to press them.

- Self-censorship – members of the group are careful not to discuss their feelings or their doubts outside the group, in order not to disturb the group cosiness.

- Unanimity – unanimity is important so once a decision has been reached any divergent views are carefully screened out in people's minds.

- Mindguards – victims of group-think set themselves up as bodyguards to the decision. 'He needs all the support we can give him.' The doctrine of collective responsibility is invoked to stifle dissent outside the group.

REFLECTION POINT 11.7

- *Can you think of cases nationally where 'group-think' may have been a contributory factor in service breakdowns or problems?*

- *Can you think of team situations or care planning group scenarios from your own experience where 'group-think' might have led to unhelpful outcomes for people who use services?*

- *What can you and your team do to avoid 'group-think' undermining practice?*

Action-centred leadership

Professor John Adair (1979) used his research in both the armed forces and organisations to identify what successful leaders actually do. He then developed this functional model using the three circles concept (Figure 11.3).

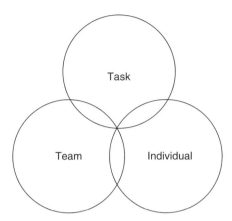

Figure 11.3 The three circles concept (Adair, 1979)

A leader is *a person who is appointed to achieve results with and through other people*. Whether or not these results are achieved and how much a leader needs to influence others in order to gain them, depends on varying factors. These include the nature of the task in question, the skills and needs (both technical and personal) of the individuals concerned, and the way they integrate as a team. Efficient leadership therefore requires flexibility and an awareness of these different requirements in order to strike an effective balance for the particular job in hand. This balancing act is shown by Adair's overlapping three circles.

TASK: Ensuring that the task is achieved

INDIVIDUAL: Satisfying the requirements of individuals within the team

TEAM: Nurturing and motivating the team as a whole.

Obviously these needs sometimes conflict with each other and one area will often require more attention than others. The trick is to achieve a long-term balance between all three and ensure that any imbalances are resolved comparatively quickly. In this way, if one individual demands a heavy input of time and energy for a while, the others will know that their requirements are also being looked after and will be met within the foreseeable future.

Adair's theory can be seen as integrating a number of key perspectives in leadership and management. For instance, in emphasising the management of the task it can be seen to be responding to Taylorist preoccupations, in emphasising the importance of the team it responds to the findings of the Hawthorne experiments and the importance of group life, in looking to the needs of the individual it could be seen to also embrace Maslow and self-actualisation. In noting the importance of leaders giving time to individuals and responding to individual needs it also accords very well with health and social care's culture that emphasises the importance of individual supervision. In fact, our supervisory practice can be held up as an exemplar of what Adair meant by the effective leadership of individuals. The challenge for health and social care leaders is perhaps ensuring this primacy of supervision is balanced by giving attention to team development and task management. The three dimensions of the model therefore offer us an important point of reference.

REFLECTION POINT *11.8*

- *Looking at your use of time, is it balanced across the three areas e.g. are you equally methodical and investing as much in unit and business planning, care planning and review and team building and development as in supervision? Do you have improvement plans for each of these areas of activity?*

- *Where are your strengths and weaknesses? In which of the three domains do you need to target your CPD as a manager and leader?*

Situational leadership

The theory of situational leadership (Hersey and Blanchard, 1988) suggests that the type of leadership adopted should ideally be dependent on a subordinate's 'maturity' – a term used to describe a team member's degree of competence and commitment in tackling a particular task or role. They identified four categories of leadership style, which could be applied (Figure 11.4):

Directing   the subordinate has little experience of the task in question but high enthusiasm and confidence. S/he needs showing/telling what to do but requires little support while carrying it out.

Coaching   the subordinate is more experienced but is also taking on more demanding tasks and so feels less confident. S/he needs showing/telling what to do but requires little support while carrying it out.

Supporting   the subordinate is well experienced at his/her job but for a variety of reasons (stale, unchallenged, stressed) lacks motivation. S/he needs high support from the leader while resolving the task/role in hand.

Delegating   the subordinate has all the technical and people skills required for the job, is experienced at it and highly motivated. S/he can be left to happily get on with it.

Because roles within a team are often dynamic, a subordinate's level of 'maturity' will fluctuate according to how assured s/he is at different tasks. Someone who is 'mature' in a long-standing job will be 'immature' when taking on new responsibility. Their leader can then offer technical or emotional support as appropriate until s/he grows in experience and confidence in that particular job. This type of leadership demands flexibility from a leader and an accurate assessment of their subordinates.

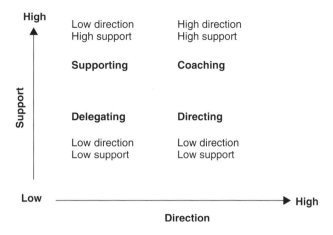

Figure 11.4 *Situational leadership (Hersey and Blanchard, 1988)*

REFLECTION POINT 11.9

We explored Hersey and Blanchard's approach in some detail in Chapter 3. Take time here to reflect on some of the other questions raised by their theory.

- *Have you got a clear picture of your team's individual abilities and performance or are there some you need to get to know better?*

- *Can you think of situations when a new responsibility change or service development meant a mature staff member needed more support and guidance?*

There may be more challenges to a leader in being 'flexible' than Hersey and Blanchard's theory might suggest. We proposed in Chapter 3 that Hersey and Blanchard's levels of maturity were very similar to Tuckman's (1965) stages of group development. This raises an interesting point, for part of Tuckman's schema involved a period of 'storming' when the power of a leader is challenged. As a team moves into storming, if it is to continue to mature, the leader must give them space to take some control and contribute, rather than reacting negatively and asserting their authority. Can you think of situations when your team has 'stormed'? Did your response allow them to contribute and take some control or did you respond by using your power to assert your authority and put them in their place?

The decision-making continuum

Leadership styles vary according to the characteristics of the leader concerned, the nature of the organisation s/he works in and the needs and expectations of their subordinates (Figure 11.5). Tannenbaum and Schmidt attempted to define different styles of leadership by looking at the level of participation subordinates have in the decision-making process. This varies according to their level of competence, training requirements and the nature of the task. The decision-making continuum is divided into seven categories that reflect the following:

- Tells   Makes decision and announces it.

- Sells   Element of persuasion in 'selling' decision.

- Explains Presents decision with the background that led to the decision, then invites discussion to build understanding.

- Tests   Presents tentative decision then invites alternative suggestions.

- Selects   Presents problem, invites suggestions then makes decision.

- Consults Defines limits, then reaches decision with subordinates.

- Joins   Defines limits, then abides by decision reached by subordinates.

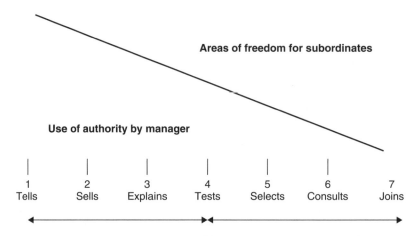

Figure 11.5 The decision-making continuum (Tannenbaum and Schmidt, 1973)

REFLECTION POINT **11.10**

This model is similar to and compliments Hersey and Blanchard's situational leadership theory. Even when theories are similar like this they are still useful as they can offer slightly different perspectives that can cast a new light on situations and help our thinking. For instance, Tannenbaum and Schmidt's continuum can pose some new questions for you.

- *Can you see in your practice that you use the range of approaches outlined in the continuum according to the needs of the staff member?*

- *The participation agenda suggests that we should 'join' with people who use services in making decisions (see Chapter 6). What will this demand from you and your team?*

Transformational leadership

A more recent leadership model is 'transformational leadership'. Transformational leadership is contrasted with 'transactional leadership' (Bass, 1985, Bass and Riggio, 2006). Transactional leadership is leadership by appointed managers using their legitimate authority, based on the contract of employment, to pursue organisational goals and motivating employees to achieve these goals using organisational reward systems. Transactional leadership is therefore closely associated with managerialism while, in contrast, transformational leadership focuses on changing and improving services and is not necessarily invested in appointed managers.

Transformational leadership can be seen as crucial to the achievement of the government's agenda to transform services (DH, 2008a). For instance, the Principles of Social Care Management (SfC/Topss, 2004) in Appendix 5 emphasises the importance of inspiring staff and the Leadership Qualities Framework (DH, 2009a) in Appendix 6 is a leadership model for all staff in the NHS, not just those in management positions.

So, transformational leadership inspires followers, challenges established processes in organisations and services and enables others to bring positive changes. As discussed in Chapter 2, transformational leadership is dependent on personal effectiveness. This is combined with a vision of how services could best be delivered or improved that is shared with colleagues and which inspires them (Kouzes and Posner, 2007). Transformational leadership is therefore not confined to appointed managers and is not dependent on authority, but rather engages teams in service development and improvement on a voluntary basis. It may also be founded upon and dependent on self-awareness (Hock, 2000).

REFLECTION POINT *11.11*

Look back to Chapter 2 to explore your personal effectiveness.

Do you think your personal effectiveness has improved through the different perspectives offered by this book and the developmental opportunities it has offered you? What aspects of your personal effectiveness will you try and improve in the future to enhance your leadership?

What is your vision of how services could best be delivered?

How will you encourage and support others to lead and develop services?

REFLECTION POINT *11.12*

Looking back over the theories and perspectives we have introduced you to in this chapter and the rest of the book, reflect on which ones you have found most useful and why. Accepting the need for us to develop a broad repertoire of theoretical perspectives, which theories or perspectives might be worth revisiting to see if you can make them more meaningful or better incorporate them into your thinking and practice?

Chapter summary

- The study of people in organisations has developed from the first naïve assumptions of scientific management to become a sophisticated and complex field.

- The importance of the group has been stressed in more than one study. The trend of current investigation and theory is undoubtedly away from 'rational economic' mankind, towards a concept of mankind to whom work is a natural, essential part of social life, seeking satisfaction of their 'higher' not 'lower' needs.

- There can be little doubt that we are working towards a more soundly based understanding of organisational behaviour but perhaps at times theorising could owe more to the writers' idealistic vision of human nature than to their scientific findings. Our health and social care value base will make some theories more attractive to us than others.

- Perhaps it is important that we should be able to accept, say, Theory Y as a generalisation while recognising that at times some people in organisations might be perfectly described by Theory X. As we are concerned with individuals in particular situations it is arguable that we need a repertoire of perspectives and our theoretical understanding of organisational behaviour should be the basis upon which as managers and leaders we fashion an understanding and approach for each separate situation.

FURTHER READING

Action-centred leadership offers a very useful model for health and social care managers because of the emphasis it places on supervision and team development as well as managing the task. Already very influential across the private sector, take a look at Adair's original work:

Adair, J. (1979) *Action Centred Leadership.* Aldershot: Gower.

Transformational leadership is a popular approach to leadership that focuses on leading change in turbulent times and the importance of vision in inspiring others. An important text is:

Kouzes, J.M. and Posner, B.Z. (2007) *The Leadership Challenge.* San Francisco: Jossey-Bass.

Appendix 1
Encouraging critical reflection

The following list of questions will help you to encourage a supervisee to reflect critically on their management of, and intervention in, a particular case. Obviously you will need to be selective and be careful that sessions don't turn into an interrogation!

Preparation

How appropriate was the referral?

How helpful was the referral information?

How well did you prepare? (Checking background information, anticipating users'/carers' likely reactions, risk analysis, objectives and plan for the intervention, research, seeking advice.)

What did you expect to find/would happen?

What were your objectives and what was your plan?

What explanation/theory did you hold to explain the problem/situation before you met them?

Participation

Did you begin to build a relationship with the users/carers, did they engage with you?

How are they contributing to/influencing the intervention?

What are their expectations of the intervention?

Did everyone get a chance to contribute? Was anyone excluded?

What are their strengths that you can build on?

What family and community resources do they/could they use?

How did you empower the users/carers?

What are the family's strengths and resources?

Feelings and emotions

What did you feel?

What do you think they felt?

How might they be manipulating you?

What would they like you to think or do?

What are they frightened might happen?

What explanations are there for your emotional reactions?

Managing the intervention

What did you not understand?

What information do you need to get?

Did the intervention go to plan?

What were the key events/pivotal moments?

What were the key outcomes?

What are the risks in the situation and how would you evaluate them?

What have other services/providers done and how effective was it?

What are you doing to support other service providers?

What organisational actions supported/hampered you in the intervention?

Were you personally safe throughout, what are the risks to you?

What other courses of action were open to you? What other methods could you have used?

Evaluation

Did you meet legal requirements?

Did you follow national and local policy?

Did you meet performance and quality standards?

Is there a clear needs analysis, care plan and timeline?

Is the plan on schedule? To what extent is it meeting their needs?

To what extent are you building an effective working relationship?

Are you meeting/working with all the key people or is someone missing or not expressing their views?

What would you do differently if you could?

Are you managing the risks effectively?

How effective has the network of service providers been in meeting the users'/carers' needs?

What other services would help?

Have you kept a clear up-to-date record?

How could organisational practices improve?

How has your emotional response influenced the intervention?

What would you say have been the strengths and weaknesses of your practice?

What is the best/worst case scenario?

Future plan of action

Are there urgent actions you must take?

What will you do next time?

What is your long-term plan?

What resources will you need and how will you get them?

What must you research?

What must you explore further?

How will you improve the co-ordination and delivery of the network of provision?

How can you be better supported?

Learning

What have you learnt from the intervention?

How will it affect your future practice?

Can you share it with colleagues?

What have the users/carers learnt?

What can the network of providers learn? How can you help them to do so?

What can the organisation learn? How can you help it to do so?

What learning needs has the intervention helped you to identify?

How will you meet your future learning needs and further develop your practice?

Appendix 2

Personal reflection on a supervision session – some key questions

The full Effective Supervision Unit provides the basis for reflection on supervision practice. However, some useful quick questions to consider after a session are:

Reflecting on the management of the task

Did you get the information you needed to prepare?

Had your staff member prepared?

Did you check progress on actions from the previous session?

Did you agree an agenda and cover it?

Did each item get the time it needed according to its priority?

Are you both clear on actions, i.e. who, what and when?

Are there any other issues that the session didn't cover or information that you need? What will you do about this?

Is the range of supervision needs (see Figure 4.1) being met by your supervision sessions in the long term or are dimensions getting insufficient attention?

Are all cases getting the attention they need?

Reflecting on the relationship

(Based on the National Occupational Standards for Counselling CLG2.1, ENTO, 2007)

Were there any areas of conflict? Have they been resolved? How were they resolved?

Did you leave sufficient space for your staff member's agenda and allow your staff member to contribute?

What feeling did you experience during the sessions and what generated them?

How do you feel at the end of the session? What might be generating those feelings?

Are you in any ways stuck or struggling to work with this staff member? What might be causing this? What can you do?

Did your staff member show any signs of discomfort during the session? What might have caused this?

When did they seem engaged and positive? What might have caused this?

What do you think your staff member might be feeling at the end of the session? What might have caused this?

Are you developing and improving your practice as a supervisor?

ENTO (2007) *National Occupational Standards for Counselling CLG2.1*. Leicester: ENTO.

Available at:

www.ento.co.uk/standards/counselling/Counselling%20NOS%20FULL%20Suite%20-%20Approved%20Sept%2007%20_post%20unit%20t.pdf

Appendix 3
A supported decision tool

Taken from DH (2007b) *Independence, Choice and Risk: A Guide to Best Practice in Supported Decision Making pp 49–51*

Annex A

A supported decision tool

This tool is designed to guide and record the discussion when a person's choices involve an element of risk. It will be particularly helpful to a person with complex needs or if someone wants to undertake activities that appear particularly risky. It can be amended to suit different user groups.

It can be completed by the practitioner with the person or by the person themselves with any necessary support. It is important that, in discussing any risk issues, the person has as much information as possible (in an appropriate form) and fully appreciates and genuinely understands any consequences, to enable them to make their best decisions.

The tool could be adapted for use within existing needs assessment and care planning processes. It also has potential application for any organisation or individual providing advice and support services to people who are self-funders and ineligible for support from their local councils.

Using the tool

Practitioners need to:

- ensure that the person has the right support to express their wishes and aspirations;
- assume capacity unless otherwise proven;
- consider the physical and mental health of the person and any specialist services they need or are already receiving.

Issues for the practitioner to consider

When using the tool with the individual, consider carefully the following aspects of the person's life and wishes:

- dignity;

- diversity, race and culture, gender, sexual orientation, age;

- religious and spiritual needs;

- personal strengths;

- ability/willingness to be supported to self care;

- opportunities to learn new skills;

- support networks;

- environment – can it be improved by means of specialist equipment or assistive technology?

- information needs;

- communication needs – tool can be adapted (braille, photographs, simplified language);

- ability to identify own risks;

- ability to find solutions;

- least restrictive options;

- social isolation, inclusion, exclusion;

- quality of life outcomes and the risk to independence of 'not supporting choice'.

Supported decision tool

1. What is important to you in your life?

2. What is working well?

3. What isn't working so well?

4. What could make it better?

5. What things are difficult for you?

6. Describe how they affect you living your life.

7. What would make things better for you?

8. What is stopping you from doing what you want to do?

9. Do you think there are any risks?

10. Could things be done in a different way, which might reduce the risks?

11. Would you do things differently?

12. Is the risk present wherever you live?

13. What do you need to do?

14. What do staff/organisation need to change?

15. What could family/carers do?

16. Who is important to you?

17. What do people important to you think?

18. Are there any differences of opinion between you and the people you said are important to you?

19. What would help to resolve this?

20. Who might be able to help?

21. What could we do (practitioner) to support you?

Agreed next steps – who will do what.

How would you like your care plan to be changed to meet your outcomes?

Record of any disagreements between people involved.

Date agreed to review how you are managing.

Signature

Signature

Appendix 4

National Occupational Standards for first line managers

For the detailed management standards and guidance go to: **www.management-standards.org.uk/**

Unit Number	National Occupational Standard
A2	Manage your own resources and professional development
B6	Provide leadership in your area of responsibility
B11	Promote equality of opportunity and diversity in your area of responsibility
C2	Encourage innovation in your area of responsibility
C5	Plan change
C6	Implement change
D1	Develop productive working relationships with colleagues
D3	Recruit, select and keep colleagues
D6	Allocate and monitor the progress and quality of work in your area of responsibility
D7	Provide learning opportunities for colleagues
E1	Manage a budget
E5	Ensure your own actions reduce risks to health and safety
E6	Ensure health and safety requirements are met in your area of responsibility
F1	Manage a project
F6	Monitor and solve customer service problems
F8	Work with others to improve customer service
SfC and CWDC unit	Effective supervision

Appendix 5
The ten principles of social care management

Skills for Care has identified a number of distinctive things that social care managers do. Good social care managers:

- inspire staff;

- promote and meet service aims, objectives and goals;

- develop joint working/partnerships that are purposeful;

- ensure equality for staff and service users driven from the top down;

- challenge discrimination and harassment in employment practice and service delivery;

- empower staff and service users to develop services people want;

- value people, recognise and actively develop potential;

- develop and maintain awareness and keep in touch with service users and staff;

- provide an environment and time in which to develop reflective practice, professional skills and the ability to make judgements in complex situations; and

- take responsibility for the continuing professional development of self and others.

(SfC/Topss (2008) *Leadership and Management Strategy Update 2008*)

These ten principles of social care management need to lie at the heart of any programme of education and training for social work leaders and managers approved by the GSCC.

Appendix 6

The Leadership Qualities Framework (LQF)

A brief overview of the 15 qualities is given below.

Cluster one: Personal qualities

1. **Self belief** – The inner confidence that you will succeed and can overcome obstacles to achieve the best outcomes for service improvement.

2. **Self awareness** – Knowing your own strengths and limitations and understanding your own emotions and the impact of your behaviour on others in diverse situations.

3. **Self management** – Being able to manage your own emotions and be resilient in a range of complex and demanding situations.

4. **Drive for improvement** – A deep motivation to improve performance in the health service and thereby to make a real difference to others' health and quality of life.

5. **Personal integrity** – A strongly held sense of commitment to openness, honesty, inclusiveness and high standards in undertaking the leadership role.

Cluster two: Setting direction

1. **Seizing the future** – Being prepared to take action now and implement a vision for the future development of services.

2. **Intellectual flexibility** – The facility to embrace and cut through ambiguity and complexity and to be open to creativity in leading and developing services.

3. **Broad scanning** – Taking the time to gather information from a wide range of sources.

4. **Political astuteness** – Showing commitment and ability to understand diverse groups and power bases within organisations and the wider community, and the dynamic between them, so as to lead health services more effectively.

5. **Drive for results** – A strong commitment to making service performance improvements and a determination to achieve positive service outcomes for users.

Cluster three: Delivering the service

1. **Leading change through people** – Communicating the vision and rationale for change and modernisation, and engaging and facilitating others to work collaboratively to achieve real change.

2. **Holding to account** – The strength of resolve to hold others to account for agreed targets and to be held accountable for delivering a high level of service.

3. **Empowering others** – Striving to facilitate others' contribution and to share leadership, nurturing capability and long-term development of others.

4. **Effective and strategic influencing** – Being able and prepared to adopt a number of ways to gain support and influence diverse parties with the aim of securing health improvements.

5. **Collaborative working** – Being committed to working and engaging constructively with internal and external stakeholders.

The aim of the LQF is to provide a single model of leadership relevant to NHS staff working in a wide variety of clinical and non-clinical roles. As this Good Practice Guide will demonstrate, the LQF is a very flexible model. It can be used in a variety of ways to enhance leadership skills and behaviours across the service and to foster a shared understanding of what leadership means in modernising the NHS. For further information about the LQF and to download a copy of the Framework, see: **www.nhsleadershipqualities.nhs.uk**

References and bibliography

Adair, J. (1979) *Action Centred Leadership.* Aldershot: Gower.

Adair, J. (2005) *How to Grow Leaders.* London: Kogan Page.

Adair, J. (2006) *Effective Leadership Development.* London: Chartered Institute of Personnel and Development.

Adams J.D., Hayes, J. and Hopson, B. (1976) *Transition – Understanding and Managing Personal Change.* London: Martin Robertson.

Adams, R., Dominelli, L. and Payne, M. (2002) *Critical Practice in Social Work.* Basingstoke: Palgrave Macmillan.

Argyris, C. (1960) *Understanding Organisational Behaviour.* Homewood, IL: Dorsey Press.

Argyris, C. and Schon, D. (1978) *Organizational Learning: A Theory of Action Perspective.* Reading, MA: Addison Wesley.

Armstrong, M. (1995) *Human Resource Management Strategy and Action.* London: Kogan Page.

Audit Commission (2004) *Overview of Seven Years of Joint Reviews.* London: Audit Commission.

Banks, S. (2002) Professional Values and Accountabilities, in Adams, R., Dominelli, L. and Payne, M. *Critical Practice in Social Work.* Basingstoke: Palgrave Macmillan.

Barham, K., Fraser, J. and Heath, L. (1998) *Management for the Future.* Berkhamsted and London: Ashridge College.

Barnes, C., Mercer, G. and Din, I. (2003) *Research Review on User Involvement in Promoting Change and Enhancing the Quality of Social Care Services for Disabled People, Final Report for SCIE.*

Bass, B.M. (1985) *Leadership and Performance Beyond Expectations.* New York: Free Press.

Bass, B.M. and Riggio, R.E. (2006) *Transformational Leadership.* London: Lawrence Erlbaum.

Bean, J. and Hussey, L. (1996) *Managing the Devolved Budget.* London: HB Publications.

Belbin, M.R. (1993) *Team Roles at Work.* Oxford: Butterworth Heinemann.

Beresford, P. (2003) *It's Our Lives: A Short Theory of Knowledge, Distance and Experience.* London: Citizen Press.

Beresford, P. and Croft, S. (2002) Involving Service Users in Management: Citizenship, Access and Support, in Reynolds, J. *et al. The Managing Care Reader.* London: Routledge.

Blanchard, K., Onken, W. and Burrows, H. (1994) *One Minute Manager Meets the Monkeys.* London: Harper Collins Business.

Bovaird, T. and Nutley, S. (1989) Financial Management in the Public Sector, in Taylor, I. and Popham, G. (eds) *An Introduction to Public Sector Management.* London: Unwin Hyman.

Brookfield, S. (1995) *Becoming a Critically Reflective Teacher.* San Francisco: Jossey-Bass.

Brookfield, S. (1998) *Training Educators of Adults.* New York: Routledge.

Brown, K. and Gray, I. (2007) *Scoping and Development of a Regional PQ Leadership and Management Pathway.* Bristol: Skills for Care South West.

Brown, K., Keen, S. and Rutter, L. (2006) *Partnerships, CPD and APL.* Birmingham: Learn to Care.

Brown, K., Keen, S. and Young, N. (2005) *Making It Work.* Birmingham: Learn to Care.

Burgoyne, J. (1988) Management Development for the Individual and the Organisation. *Personnel Management,* Vol. 20, June, pp40–44.

Cameron, K. (2003) Social Work Practice and Accountability, in *Social Work and the Law in Scotland.* Part 1, chap. 5, pp54–62. Palgrave Macmillan/The Open University. Available on: **http://openlearn.open.ac.uk/file.php/3758/K207_2_Reader_Ch5.pdf**

Carr, S. (2004) *Has Service User Participation Made a Difference to Social Care Provision?* SCIE Position Paper 3. Bristol: Policy Press.

Carr, S. (2008) *Personalisation: A Rough Guide.* London: SCIE. Available on: **www.scie.org.uk/publications/reports/report20.pdf**

Cass E., Robbins, D. and Richardson, A. (2009) *Dignity in Care.* London: SCIE. Available on: **www.scie.org.uk/publications/guides/guide15/whistleblowing/index.asp**

CCETSW (1995) *Rules and Requirements for the Diploma in Social Work.* London: CCETSW.

Centre for Post-Qualifying Social Work (2007) *Statistics – Highest Qualification on Entry (South West) 2004.*

Chislett, V. and Chapman, A. (2005) *Multiple Intelligence Test Based on Gardner's Multiple Intelligences Model.* Available on: **www.businessballs.com**

Cleaver, H., Wattam, C. and Cawson, P. (1998a) *Assessing Risk in Child Protection – Summary of Research Findings.* London: NSPCCInform. Available on: **www.nspcc.org.uk/Inform/publications/Downloads/assessingriskinchildprotection_wdf48173.pdf**

Cleaver, H., Wattam, C., Cawson, P. and Gordon, R. (1998b) *Children Living at Home. The Initial Child Protection Enquiry: Ten Pitfalls and How to Avoid Them.* London: NSPCCInform. Available on: **www.nspcc.org.uk/Inform/publications/Downloads/tenpitfalls_wdf48122.pdf**

Cooke, B., Mills, A.J., Kelley, E.S. (2005) Situating Maslow in Cold War America: A Recontextualization of Management Theory. *Group and Organization Management,* Vol. 30, No. 2, pp129–50.

Corley, A. and Thorne, A. (2006) Action Learning: Avoiding Conflict or Enabling Action. *Action Learning: Research and Practice,* Vol. 3, No.1, April 2006, pp31–44.

Coulshed, V., Mullender, A., Jones, D.N. and Thompson, N. (2006) *Management in Social Work.* Basingstoke: Macmillan.

Cranton, P. (1996) *Professional Development as Transformative Learning: New Perspectives for Teachers of Adults.* San Francisco: Jossey Bass.

Crawford, M., Rutter, D. and Thelwall, S. (2003) *User Involvement in Change Management: A Review of the Literature, Report to NHS Service Delivery and Organisation Research and Development Programme.* NHS SDO.

Csikszentmihalyi, M. (1988) The Flow Experience and its Significance for Human Psychology, in Csikszentmihalyi, M., Csikszentmihalyi, I.S (eds) *Optimal Experience: Psychological Studies of Flow in Consciousness.* Cambridge: Cambridge University Press.

Csikszentmihalyi, M. (1990) *Flow: The Psychology of Optimal Experience.* New York: Harper & Row.

Csikszentmihalyi, M. (2008) *What Makes a Life Worth Living.* Retrieved from YouTube **http://uk.youtube.com/watch?v=fXIeFJCqsPs**

CWDC (Children's Workforce Development Council) (2008) *The National Occupational Standards for Commissioning, Procurement & Contracting for the Social Care and Children and Young Peoples' Workforces (level 5).* Available on: **www.cwdcouncil.org.uk/assets/0000/2431/Unit_and_element_titles_L5.doc**

CWDC/Skills for Care (2007) *Effective Supervision.* Available on: **www.skillsforcare.org.uk/files/Effective%20Supervision%20unit.pdf**

CWDC/Skills for Care (2007) *Providing Effective Supervision.* **www.skillsforcare.org.uk/developing_skills/leadership_and_management/providing_effective_supervision.aspx**

C4EO The Centre for Excellence and Outcomes in Children and Young People's Services. Available on: **www.c4eo.org.uk/default.aspx**

Danso, C., Greaves, H., Howell, S., Ryan, M., Sinclair, R. and Tunnard, J. (2003) *The Involvement of Children and Young People in Promoting Change and Enhancing the Quality of Services: A Research Report for SCIE from the National Children's Bureau.*

DCSF (2008) *Every Child Matters Outcomes Framework.* London: HMSO. Available on: **http://publications.everychildmatters.gov.uk/eOrderingDownload/DCSF-00331-2008.pdf**

DCSF (2009) *The Protection of Children in England Action Plan – The Government Response to Lord Laming.* London: Stationery Office. Available on: **http://publications.dcsf.gov.uk/eOrdering Download/DCSF-Laming.pdf**

Demos **www.demos.co.uk**

Derby City Council (2007) *Adult Services and Health Commission Report of the Director of Corporate and Adult Services.* Available on: **http://cmis.derby.gov.uk/CMISWebPublic/Binary.ashx?Document=9372**

Dewey, J. (1897) *My Pedagogic Creed.* Retrieved from **www.infed.org/archives/e-texts/e-dew-pc.htm**

DfES (2004) *Every Child Matters – Change for Children.* London: HMSO. Available on: **http://publications.everychildmatters.gov.uk/eOrderingDownload/DfES10812004.pdf**

DfES/DH (Department of Health) (2006) *Options for Excellence. Building the Social Care Workforce of the Future.* London: DfES/DH. Available on: **www.dh.gov.uk/en/SocialCare/workforce/DH_4131862**

DH (Department of Health) (1993) *A Vision for the Future: Report of the Chief Nursing Officer.* London: HMSO.

DH (Department of Health) (2000) *A Quality Strategy for Social Care.* London: DH.

DH (Department of Health) (2004) *The NHS Knowledge and Skills Framework (NHS KSF) and the Development Review Process (October 2004).* Available on: **www.dh.gov.uk/en/Publicationsandstatistics/Publications/PublicationsPolicyAndGuidance/DH_4090843**

DH (Department of Health) (2006) *Our Health, Our Care, Our Say* (White Paper). Available on: **www.dh.gov.uk/en/Healthcare/Ourhealthourcareoursay/index.htmPublicationsPolicyAndGuidance/DH_074217**

DH (Department of Health) (2007a) *Putting People First: A Shared Vision and Commitment to the Transformation of Adult Social Care.* London: DH. Available on: **www.dh.gov.uk/en/Publicationsandstatistics/Publications/PublicationsPolicyAndGuidance/DH_081118**

DH (Department of Health) (2007b) *Independence, Choice and Risk: A Guide to Best Practice in Supported Decision Making.* London: DH. Available on: **www.dh.gov.uk/en/Publicationsandstatistics/Publications/PublicationsPolicyAndGuidance/DH_074773**

DH (Department of Health) (2007c) *World Class Commissioning Competencies.* London: DH. Available on: **www.dh.gov.uk/en/Managingyourorganisation/Commissioning/Worldclasscommissioning/Competencies/index.htm**

DH (Department of Health) (2008a) *Transforming Social Care* (DH Local Authority Circular). Available on: **www.dh.gov.uk/en/Publicationsandstatistics/Lettersandcirculars/LocalAuthorityCirculars/DH_081934**

DH (Department of Health) (2008b) *Putting People First – Working to Make It Happen: Adult Social Care Workforce Strategy – Interim Statement.* London: DH. Available on: **www.dh.gov.uk/en/Publicationsandstatistics/Publications/PublicationsPolicyAndGuidance/DH_085642**

DH (Department of Health) (2008c) *The NHS in England: The Operating Framework for 2009/10.* London: DH. Available on: **www.dh.gov.uk/en/Publicationsandstatistics/Publications/PublicationsPolicyAndGuidance/DH_091445**

DH (Department of Health) (2008d) *High Quality Care For All: NHS Next Stage Review Final Report.* London: DH.

DH (Department of Health) (2008e) *Department of Health Personalisation Web Pages. Introduction to Personalisation.* Available on: **www.dh.gov.uk/en/SocialCare/Socialcarereform/Personalisation/DH_080573**

DH (Department of Health) (2009a) *The Leadership Qualities Framework.* London: DH. Available on: **http://www.nhsleadershipqualities.nhs.uk/** [Accessed 17 February 2009]

DH (Department of Health) (2009b) *Inspiring Leaders: Leadership for Quality.* London: DH. Available on: **www.dh.gov.uk/en/Publicationsandstatistics/Publications/PublicationsPolicyandGuidance/DH_093395**

Dictionary.com (2009) LLC. Available on: **http://dictionary.reference.com/browse/effectiveness**

Doel, M., Carroll, C., Chambers, E., Cooke, J., Hollows, A., Laurie, L., Nancarrow, S. (2007) *Developing Measures for Service User and Carer Participation in Social Care* (SCIE).

Egan, G. (1998) *The Skilled Helper – A Problem Management Approach to Helping.* 6th edition. California: Brooks Cole.

ENTO (2007) *National Occupational Standards for Counselling.* Available on: **www.ento.co.uk/standards/counselling/Counselling%20NOS%20FULL%20Suite%20%20Approved%20Sept%2007%20_post%20unit%20t.pdf**

Everitt, A. and Hardiker, P. (1996) *Evaluating for Good Practice.* Basingstoke: Macmillan.

Fayol, H. (1916) *General and Industrial Management.* London: Pitman.

Field, R. (2007) *Managing with Plans and Budgets in Health and Social Care.* Exeter: Learning Matters.

Fisher, R. and Ury, W. (1992) *Getting to Yes.* London: Random House Business Books.

Flynn, N. (2002) *Public Sector Management.* Harlow: Prentice Hall.

Frank, E. (1991) The UK's Management Charter Initiative: The First Three Years. *Journal of European Industrial Training,* Vol. 17, No.1, pp9–11.

Freire, P. (2000) *Pedagogy of the Oppressed.* New York: Continuum.

Gill, A., Hutchinson, R. and Jones, L. (2009) *OBA Toolkit.* Available on: **www.c4eo.org.uk/ obatoolkit/needtologin.aspx**

Glendinning, C., Clarke, S., Hare, P., Inna Kotchetkova, I., Maddison, J. and Newbronner, L. (2006) *Outcomes-Focused Services for Older People. SCIE Adults' Services Knowledge Review 13.* Bristol: SCIE. Available on: **www.scie.org.uk/publications/knowledgereviews/kr13.pdf**

Goleman, D. (1998) *Working with Emotional Intelligence.* London: Bloomsbury.

Goleman, D., Boyatzis, R.E. and McKee, A. (2002) *The New Leaders: Transforming the Art of Leadership into the Science of Results.* Lancaster: Time Warner.

GSCC (General Social Care Council) (2002) *Guidance on the Assessment of Practice in the Workplace.* London: GSCC.

GSCC (General Social Care Council) (2004) *Code of Practice for Social Care Workers and Code of Practice for Employers of Social Care Workers.* London: GSCC.

GSCC (General Social Care Council) (2005a) *Post-Qualifying Framework for Social Work Education and Training.* London: GSCC.

GSCC (General Social Care Council) (2005b) *Specialist Standards and Requirements for Post-Qualifying Social Work Education and Training. Leadership and Management.* London: GSCC.

GSCC (General Social Care Council) (2005c) *Post Registration Training and Learning (PRTL) Requirements for Registered Social Workers. Advice and Guidance on Good Practice.* London: GSCC.

GSCC (General Social Care Council) (2008) *Social Work At Its Best: A Statement of Social Work Roles and Tasks for the 21st Century.* London: GSCC.

GSCC (General Social Care Council) (2009)/Social Work Connections (2009) *Newsletter of the General Social Care Council.* Sept 2009, Issue 6. London: Ten Alps Publishing.

Guest, D.E. and Conway, N. (2002) *Pressure at Work and the Psychological Contract.* London: CIPD.

Habermas, J. (1989) *The Structural Transformation of the Public Sphere.* Cambridge: Polity Press.

Hafford-Letchfield, T. (2006) *Management and Organisations in Social Work.* Exeter: Learning Matters.

Hafford-Letchfield, T., Leonard, K., Begum, N. and Chick, N.F. (2008) *Leadership and Management in Social Care.* London: Sage.

Hamm, R. M . (1988) Clinical Intuition and Clinical Analysis: Expertise and the Cognitive Continuum, in Dowie, J. A. and Elstein, A. S. (eds) *Professional Judgement: A Reader in Clinical Decision Making.* Cambridge: Cambridge University Press.

Handy, C. (1985) *Understanding Organisations.* London: Penguin Business.

Harkness, D. (1995) The Art of Helping in Supervised Practice: Skills, Relationships and Outcomes. *The Clinical Supervisor,* 13(1), pp63–76.

Harkness, D. and Hensley, H. (1991) Changing the Focus of Social Work Supervision: Effects on Client Satisfaction and Generalised Contentment. *Social Work,* 37, pp506–512.

Harkness, D. and Poertner, J. (1989) Research and Social Work Supervision. A Conceptual Review. *Social Work,* 34(2), pp115–118.

Harrison, K. and Ruch, G. (2007) Social Work and the Use of Self: On Becoming a Social Worker, in Lymbery, M. and Postle, K. (eds) S*ocial Work. A Companion to Learning.* London: Sage.

Hartle, F., Snook, P., Apsey, H. and Browton, R. (2008) *The Training and Development of Middle Managers in the Children's Workforce – Hay Group Report to the Children's Workforce Development Council.* London: Hay Group. Available on: **www.cwdcouncil.org.uk/assets/0000/2362/Training_ and_development_of_middle_managers_in_the_children_s_workforce.pdf**

Haughey, D. (2009) *Pareto Analysis Step by Step.* Project Smart UK. Available on: **www.projectsmart.co.uk/pareto-analysis-step-by-step.html**

Hawkins, P. and Shohet, R. (2000) *Supervision in the Helping Professions.* Buckingham: Open University.

Hawthorne, L. (1975) Games Supervisors Play. *Social Work,* 20, pp179–183.

Healy, K. (2000) *Social Work Practices: Contemporary Perspectives on Change.* London: Sage.

Henwood, M. and Grove, B. (2006) *Here to Stay? Self-directed Support: Aspiration and Implementation – A Review for the Department of Health.* Towcester: Melanie Henwood Associates.

Hersey, P. and Blanchard, K.H. (1974). So You Want to Know Your Leadership Style? *Training and Development Journal,* February 1974, pp1–15.

Hersey, P. and Blanchard, K. H. (1988) *Management of Organisational Behaviour: Utilising Human Resources.* New Jersey: Prentice Hall.

Hersey, P. and Blanchard, K.H. (1993) *Management of Organisational Behaviour: Utilising Human Resources.* 6th edition. London: Prentice Hall.

Herzberg, F. (1966) *The Work and the Nature of Man.* Cleveland, OH: The World Publishing Company.

Herzberg, F. (1987) One More Time: How Do You Motivate Employees? *Harvard Business Review,* 65(5), pp109–120.

Herzberg, F., Mausner, B. and Snyderman, B. B. (1959) *The Motivation to Work.* New York: John Wiley & Sons.

Hinshelwood, R.D. and Manning, N. (1979). *Therapeutic Communities.* London: Kogan Page.

Hock, D. (2000) The Art of Chaotic Leadership. *Leader to Leader,* 15 (Winter 2000) pp20–26. Available on: **www.leadertoleader.org/knowledgecenter/journal.aspx?ArticleID=62**

Holmes, T.H and Rahe, R.H. (1967) The Social Re-adjustment Rating Scale. *Journal of Psychosomatic Research,* 11, pp213–218.

Homans, C.G. (1951) *The Human Group.* London: Routledge & Kegan Paul.

HSE (Health and Safety Executive) (2005) *Working Alone in Safety – Controlling the Risks of Solitary Workers.* Sudbury: Health and Safety Executive. Available on: **www.hse.gov.uk/pubns/indg73.pdf**

IiP (Investors in People) (2007) *Auditing Organisational Development Diagnostic Tool. Training Need Analysis Form.* Available on: **http://diagnostic.iipuk.co.uk/**

IiP (Investors in People) (2009) website. *Investors in People – Improving Business Performance.* Available on: **www.investorsinpeople.co.uk/Pages/Home.aspx**

Induction (c.a. 2005) SfC (Skills for Care/England) website. Retrieved 10th May 2007 from: **http://www.topssengland.net/view.asp?id=58**

Institute for Innovation and Improvement (NHS) (2010) *Project Management Guide.* **www.institute.nhs.uk/quality_and_service_improvement_tools/quality_and_service_improvement_ tools/project_management_guide.html**

Ishikawa, K. (1985) *What is Total Quality Control? The Japanese Way.* Englewood Cliffs, NJ: Irwin.

Janis, I. (1971) Groupthink Among Policy Makers, in Nevitt Sanford and Craig Comstock (eds) *Sanctions for Evil.* San Francisco: Jossey-Bass. Available on: **www.er.uqam.ca/nobel/d101000/ JanisGroupthinkPolicyMakers.pdf**

Janis, I. (1972) *Victims of Groupthink: A Psychological Study of Foreign Policy Decisions and Fiascoes.* Boston, MA: Houghton Mifflin.

Jennings, E.E. (1960) *An Anatomy of Leadership: Princes, Heroes and Supermen.* New York: Harper.

Johnson, B. (1996) *Polarity Management.* Amherst, MA: HRD Press.

Johnson, G., Scholes, K. and Whittington, R. (2008) *Exploring Corporate Strategy.* 8th Edition. Harlow: Prentice Hall.

Joy-Mathews, J., Megginson, D. and Surtees, M. (2004) *Human Resource Development.* London: Kogan Page.

Kadushin, A. (1979) Games People Play in Supervision, in Munson, C.E. (ed) *Social Work Supervision: Classic Statements and Critical Issues.* New York: Free Press.

Kadushin, A. and Harkness, D. (2002) *Supervision in Social Work.* New York: Columbia University Press.

Keen, S., Gray, I., Parker, J., Galpin, D. and Brown, K. (eds) (2009) *Newly Qualified Social Workers: A Handbook for Practice.* Exeter: Learning Matters.

Keirsey, D. and Bates, M. (1984) *Please Understand Me.* 5th Edition. California: Prometheus Nemesis.

Knight, S. (2002) *NLP at Work.* 2nd Edition. London: Nicholas Brealey Publishing.

Kotter, J.P. and Cohen, D.S. (2002) *The Heart of Change.* Harvard: Business School Press.

Kotter, J.P. and Schlesinger, L.A. (1979) Choosing Strategies for Change. *Harvard Business Review*, March/April, pp106–114.

Kouzes, J.M. and Posner, B.Z. (2007) *The Leadership Challenge.* San Francisco: Jossey-Bass.

Learning Organisation Audit (ca. 2006) Retrieved from the SCIE (Social Care Institute for Excellence) website: **www.scie.org.uk/publications/learningorgs/files/key_characteristics_2.pdf**)

Levin, E. (2004) *Involving Service Users and Carers in Social Work Education.* Retrieved from: **www.scie.org.uk/publications/resourceguides/rg02.pdf**

Lord Laming (2009) *The Protection of Children in England: A Progress Report.* London: HMSO. Available on: **http://publications.everychildmatters.gov.uk/eOrderingDownload/HC-330.pdf**

Lowes, L. and Hulatt, I. (eds) (2005) *Service Users' Involvement in Health and Social Care Research.* London: Routledge.

Machiavelli, N. (1992) *The Prince.* Translator N. H. Thomson. New York: Dover.

Maslow, A.N. (1943) A Theory of Human Motivation. *Psychological Review* 50(4), pp370–396.

Mayhew, N. (2006) *Board Level Development – Beyond Change Management.* Available on: **www.executive.modern.nhs.uk/inview/inviewarticle.aspx?id=58**

Mayo, G. E. (1933) *The Human Problem of an Industrialized Civilization.* London: Macmillan.

MBTI (2007) *Step 1 Report Booklet 2007.* CPP Incorporated.

McGregor, D. (1961) *The Human Side of Enterprise.* NY: McGraw Hill.

McSherry, R., Kell, J. and Pearce, P. (2002) Clinical Supervision and Clinical Governance. *Nursing Times,* 4 June, 2002, Vol. 98, Issue 23, p30.

McSherry, R., Pearce, P. and Tingle, J. (2002) *Clinical Governance: A Guide to Implementation for Healthcare Professionals.* Oxford: Blackwell.

Megginson, D. (1994) Planned and Emergent Learning: A Framework and Method. *Executive Development,* 7(6), pp29–32.

Mehra, A., Smith, B.R., Dixon, A.L. and Robertson, B. (2006) Distributed Leadership in Teams – The Network of Leadership Perceptions and Team Performance. *The Leadership Quarterly,* Vol 17, pp232–245.

MESOL (Management Education Scheme by Open Learning) (1999) *The Health and Social Services Manager.* Open Business School, Milton Keynes: Open University Press. Available on: **www.mesol.org.uk/**

Mind tools (2009) *How Understanding Team Roles Can Improve Team Performance.* Available on: **www.mindtools.com/pages/article/newLDR_83.htm**

Mook, D.G. (1987) *Motivation: The Organization of Action.* New York: Norton.

Moreno, J.L. (1960) *The Sociometry Reader.* Glencoe, NY: Free Press.

MSC (Management Standards Centre) (2008) *The National Occupational Standards for Management and Leadership – the Full List of the National Occupational Standards.* London: MSC. Available on: **www.management-standards.org/content_1.aspx?id=10:5406&id=10:1917**

Mullins, I. (2007) *Management and Organisational Behaviour.* 8th edition. Harlow: Prentice Hall.

Net MBA Business Knowledge Centre (2009) *Gantt Chart.* Available on: **www.netmba.com/operations/project/gantt/**

Oakland, J. (1996) *Total Quality Management.* Oxford: Butterworth Heinemann.

O'Connor, J. and Seymour, J. (2003) *Introducing NLP.* London: Thorsons.

Ofsted (2008) Haringey Children's Services Authority Area Review. London: Ofsted. Available on: **www.ofsted.gov.uk/oxcare_providers/la_download/(id)/4657/(as)/JAR/jar_2008_309_fr.pdf**

O'Leary, D. and Lownsbrough, H. (2007) *The Leadership Imperative*. Available on: **www.demos. co.uk/publications/leadershipimperative**

Peters, T. and Austin, N. (1985) *A Passion for Excellence*. New York: Random House.

Phillipson, J. (2002). Supervision and Being Supervised, in Adams, R., Dominelli, L. and Payne, M. *Critical Practice in Social Work*. Basingstoke: Palgrave Macmillan.

Platt, D. (2007) *The Status of Social Care – A Review 2007*. Available on: **www.dh.gov.uk/en/ Publicationsandstatistics/Publications/**

Qureshi, H. (2001) Summarising Intended Outcomes for Older People at Assessment, in Qureshi, H. (ed) *Outcomes in Social Care Practice, Report 7*. York: Social Policy Research Unit, University of York.

RCN (Royal College of Nursing) (2003a) *Clinical Supervision in the Workplace – Guidance for Occupational Health Nurses*. London: RCN. Available on: **www.rcn.org.uk/__data/assets/ pdf_file/0007/78523/001549.pdf**

RCN (Royal College of Nursing) (2003b) *Clinical Governance – an RCN Resource Guide*. London: RCN.

Reinhold, R. (2010) *Personality Pathways: Exploring Personality Type and its Applications*. Available on: **www.personalitypathways.com**

Reynolds, J., Henderson, J., Seden, J., Charlesworth, J. and Bullman, A. (eds) (2002) *The Managing Care Reader*. London: Routledge.

Robinson, J. (2005) Improving Practice Through a System of Clinical Supervision. *Nursing Times*, 101, 23, pp30–32.

Rogers, C. and Freiberg, H. J. (1993) *Freedom to Learn*. 3rd edition. New York: Merrill.

Rolfe, G., Freshwater, D. and Jasper, M. (2001) *Critical Reflection for Nursing and the Helping Professions*. Basingstoke: Palgrave.

Schein, E. H. (1965) *Organizational Psychology*. New Jersey: Englewood Cliffs.

Schlossberg, N.K. (1981) A Model for Analyzing Human Adaptation to Transition. *Counseling Psychologist*, 9(2), pp2–18.

SCIE (Social Care Institute for Excellence) (2003) *SCIE Guide 1: Managing Practice. Managing Work – Workload Management*. Available on: **www.scie.org.uk/publications/guides/guide01/section3/ workload.asp**

SCIE (Social Care Institute for Excellence) (2004) *Learning Organisations – A Self Assessment Resource Pack*. Bristol: SCIE.

SCIE (Social Care Institute for Excellence)/Diggins, M. (2004) *SCIE Guide 5: Teaching and Learning Communication Skills in Social Work Education Appendix B: The SCIE Practice Review: Teaching and Learning in Social Work – Communication (full text)*. Available on: **www.scie.org.uk/ publications/guides/guide05/appendixb.asp**

SCIE (Social Care Institute for Excellence) (2006) *Learning Organisation Audit*. Available on: **www.scie.org.uk/publications/learningorgs/files/key_characteristics_2.pdf**

SCIE/Butt, J. (2006) *Stakeholder Participation Race Equality Discussion Paper 3: Are We There Yet? Identifying the Characteristics of Social Care Organisations that Successfully Promote Diversity.* Bristol: SCIE. Available on: **www.scie.org.uk/publications/raceequalitydiscussionpapers/redp03.pdf**

SCIE (Social Care Institute for Excellence) (2007) *People Management Website.* Available on: **www.scie-peoplemanagement.org.uk**

SCIE/Doel, M., Carroll, C., Chambers, E., Cooke, J., Hollows, A., Laurie, L., Maskrey, L. and Nancarrow, S. (2007) *SCIE Guide 20: Participation – Finding Out What Difference It Makes.* Bristol: SCIE.

Senge, P.M. (1990) *The Fifth Discipline. The Art and Practice of the Learning Organisation.* London: Random House.

SfC South West (2000) *We're Here to Help You Improve Your Workforce – the Value of Learning and Creating a Learning Environment.* Bristol: SfC South West.

SfC (Skills for Care England)/Topss (2004) *Leadership and Management – a Strategy for the Social Care Workforce.* Leeds: SfC.

SfC (Skills for Care England) (ca. 2005) *Continuing Professional Development.* Leeds: SfC. Available on: **www.topssengland.net/view.asp?id=693**

SfC (Skills for Care England) (2005) Leadership & Management Strategy, product 7. 2nd edition. *A Guide to the Evaluation of Leadership and Development.* Available on: **www.skillsforcare.org.uk/ developing_skills/leadership_and_management/leadership_and_management_strategy.aspx**

SfC (Skills for Care England) (2006a) Leadership & Management Strategy, product 3. 2nd edition. *Mapping of Leadership and Management Standards.* Leeds: SfC

SfC (Skills for Care England) (2006b) A *Manager's Guide to Developing Strategic Uses for National Occupational Standards.* Leeds: SfC. Available on: **www.skillsforcare.org.uk/developing_skills/ National_Occupational_Standards/National_Occupational_Standards_(NOS)_introduction.aspx**

SfC (Skills for Care England) (2007) *Effective Supervision.* Leeds: SfC. Available on: **www.skillsforcare.org.uk/files/Effective%20Supervision%20unit.pdf**

SfC (Skills for Care) (2008) *The Skills for Care Leadership and Management Strategy Update 2008.* Leeds: SfC. Available on: **www.skillsforcare.org.uk/developing_skills/leadership_and_management/ leadership_and_management_strategy.aspx**

SfC (Skills for Care England) (2009) *Toolkit to Help People Employ Their Own Personal Assistants.* Leeds: SfC. Available on: **www.skillsforcare.org.uk/entry_to_social_care/recruitment/PAtoolkit.aspx**

SfC/CWDC (2006a) *Continuing Professional Development for the Social Care Workforce – Strategy.* Leeds: SfC. Available on: **www.skillsforcare.org.uk/developing_skills/Continuing_Professional_ Development/Continuing_Professional_Development_(CPD)_strategy.aspx**

SfC/CWDC (2006b) *Continuing Professional Development for the Social Care Workforce – the Framework.* Leeds: SfC. Available on: **www.skillsforcare.org.uk/developing_skills/Continuing_ Professional_Development/Continuing_Professional_Development_(CPD)_strategy.aspx**

SfC/SfH (2008) *Common Core Principles to Support Self Care.* Available on: **www.skillsforcare**.

Shulman, L. (1993) *Interactional Supervision.* Washington DC: NASW Press.

Social Work Connections (2009) *Newsletter of the General Social Care Council.* Sept 2009, Issue 6. London: Ten Alps Publishing.

Stein, D. (2009) *Teaching Critical Reflection.* Available on: **www.inspiredliving.com/business/ reflection.htm**

Steiner, R. (2004) *Human Values in Education.* Herndon: Steiner Books.

Storey, J. (1995) HRM Still Marching On or Marching Out? In Storey, J. (ed) *Human Resource Management – A Critical Text.* London: Routledge.

Tannenbaum, R. and Schmidt, W.H. (1973) How to Choose a Leadership Pattern. *Harvard Business Review,* 51(3), pp162–180.

Taylor, F.W. (1911) *Principles of Scientific Management.* New York & London: Harper & Brothers.

Taylor, I. and Popham, G. (eds) (1989) *An Introduction to Public Sector Management.* London: Unwin Hyman.

Topss England (2000) *Modernising the Social Care Workforce – the First National Training Strategy for England.* Leeds: Topss.

Topss England, Care Council for Wales, Northern Ireland Social Services Council (2002) *National Occupational Standards for Social Work: Values and Ethics. Statement of Expectations from Individuals, Families, Carers, Groups and Communities Who Use Services and Those Who Care for Them.* Leeds: Topss.

Torrington, D. and Hall, L. (1998) *Human Resource Management.* London: Prentice Hall.

Tsui, M.S. (2001) *Towards a Culturally Sensitive Model of Social Work Supervision in Hong Kong.* Unpublished doctoral dissertation. Faculty of Social Work, University of Toronto.

Tsui, M.S. (2005) *Social Work Supervision – Contexts and Concepts.* London: Sage.

Tuckman, B.W. (1965) Developmental Sequence in Small Groups. *Psychological Bulletin,* 63, pp384–99.

Walker, C. (2004) *Getting Through Your Probationary Period.* The SGH Solicitors website. Retrieved from: **www.sghlaw.com/employmentlaw/articles/probationary-period.htm**

Waskett, C. (2009) An Integrated Approach to Introducing and Maintaining Supervision: the 4S Model. *Nursing Times,* 105, p17. Available on: **www.nursingtimes.net/nursing-practice-clinical-research/ acute-care/an-integrated-approach-to-introducing-and-maintaining-supervision-the-4s- model/5000899.article**

Watson, T.J. (2002) *Organising and Managing Work. Organisational, Managerial and Strategic Behaviour in Theory and Practice.* Harlow: Pearson Education.

Wenger, E. (1998) *Communities of Practice. Learning, Meaning and Identity.* Cambridge: Cambridge University Press.

Wenger, E. (2006) *Communities of Practice: A Brief Introduction.* Available on: **www.ewenger.com/theory/index.htm**

Willis, P. (1999) Looking for What It's Really Like: Phenomenology in Reflective Practice. *Studies in Continuing Education,* 21, No. 1, pp91–112.

Williams, S. and Rutter, L. (2007) *Enabling and Assessing Work-based Learning for Social Work – Supporting the Development of Professional Practice.* Birmingham: Learn to Care.

Yukl, G. (1998) *Leadership in Organisations.* Harlow: Prentice Hall.

Index

221